R PROGRAMMING
FOR BEGINNERS

R Programming for Beginners

Sandhya Arora

Professor, Department of Computer Engineering
MKSSS's Cummins College of Engineering for Women
Pune, Maharashtra

Latesh Malik

Associate Professor and Head, Department of Computer Science & Engineering
Government College of Engineering
Nagpur, Maharashtra

Universities Press

R PROGRAMMING FOR BEGINNERS

UNIVERSITIES PRESS (INDIA) PRIVATE LIMITED

Registered Office
3-6-747/1/A & 3-6-754/1, Himayatnagar, Hyderabad 500 029, Telangana, India
info@universitiespress.com; www.universitiespress.com

Distributed by
Orient Blackswan Private Limited

Registered Office
3-6-752 Himayatnagar, Hyderabad 500 029 Telangana, India

Other Offices
Bengaluru / Chennai / Guwahati / Hyderabad
Kolkata / Mumbai / New Delhi / Noida / Patna

First published 2020
Reprinted 2026

Cover and book design:

502340

ISBN 978-93-89211-56-6

Typeset in Adobe Garamond Pro 10.5 points *by*
Cameo Corporate Services Limited, Coimbatore

Printed in India by
Kensington Printing & Packaging, Noida 201 301

Published by
Universities Press (India) Private Limited
3-6-747/1/A & 3-6-754/1, Himayatnagar, Hyderabad 500 029, Telangana, India

Preface

Today, the buzzwords Data Science and Machine Learning are gaining importance as they help solve many business problems. Underlying these two areas are statistical techniques and the software programs to implement them.

The R language is very useful in the field of statistical computation and data science because of its versatility. It offers various techniques such as clustering, classification techniques, text mining, non-linear/linear modelling and classical statistical tests along with basic programming and very strong built-in functions. In addition, the R language is free, open-source, very adaptable, extensible and a perfect fit for Big Data solutions. It also supports many graphical techniques to visualise and present data effectively.

One of the biggest surprises of this book is that we cover basic programming concepts in R, along with some concepts to teach you – the student – about data science and machine learning skills. If you master both, you will be a powerful computer-augmented data scientist.

The chapters of the book are arranged in this sequence: the fundamentals of R are presented in chapters 1–16, while advanced concepts and functions are dealt with in chapters 17–24. All the chapters include discussions of case studies and their programming in R.

Chapter 1 provides an overview of the R programming language, its features, basic data types and functions, and the advantages and disadvantages of using R. It also explains the steps in setting up the R environment in Linux/Fedora and Windows. Debugging is very important for any programming language and it has been observed that R programmers do not use its debugging features. To remedy this, this chapter also explains the debugging functions in R.

Chapter 2 deals with data definitions and categorisation. It provides an overview of data in the statistical context and lists the different sources of data, the main companies involved and the tools used to categorise data. It also explains the scales of measurement, defines the data cube and explains its operations.

Chapter 3 defines operators in R – arithmetic, relational, logical and miscellaneous. It also explains operator precedence and associativity in R. **Chapter 4** deals with control statements and functions in R – `if`, `if-else` and nested `if` statements; `ifelse()` function; the `repeat`, `next`, `switch` and `break` statements; `for` and `while` loops and the different forms of `return`.

Chapter 5 explains R code interfacing with C code, using the `.C()` and `.Call()` functions, and with Python code, using the `rPython`, `reticulate` and `rpy2` packages. **Chapter 6** deals with defining and creating a vector, assigning a name to the elements of a vector, and creating and using integer, logical and character vector indexes. Various arithmetic operations on vectors, recycling rule for vector elements, value coercion, deletion of vectors and sorting of vector elements is also discussed.

Chapter 7 explains matrix creation, coercion and subsetting, and arithmetic operations on matrices and arrays. It also describes the special matrices in R and the calculation of eigenvalues and eigenvectors of matrices. **Chapter 8** details the creation of lists and the operations, access and manipulation of list elements, merge and apply functions, recursive lists and sorting and searching lists.

Chapter 9 discusses data frames – definition, creation, extraction of data, expansion using the `cbind()` and `rbind()` functions, merge and sort and how to use the `lapply()` and `sapply()` functions. **Chapter 10** is about data factors and tables. It explains how to create factors and use the `summary()`, `labels()`, `levels()` and `table()` functions. It also deals with creating and visualising table data, the `prop.table()` and `margin.table()` functions and how to perform cross-tabulation of data.

Chapter 11 describes how to create regular expressions, use regular expression commands and string manipulation functions and explains the categories of regular expressions. **Chapter 12** defines classes and objects in R using S3 and S4. It also clarifies the concept of generic and user-defined functions and how to use methods from S3 and S4.

Chapter13 explains with examples the processing of input and output in R – how to read data from the keyboard and from a file, how to write output to the monitor and to files, how to create different types of files and modify them using file functions, and how to create and set up directories.

R is very rich in quality plots, that is, data representation and visualisation using well-defined built-in functions**.** **Chapter 14** deals with how to define and create graphs in R and explains the functions used to create histograms, kernel density plots, dot plots, bar charts, line charts, pie charts, box plots, scatter plots and three-dimensional plots.

Chapter 15 describes the `apply()` family of functions in R used to manipulate groups or slices of data, comprising `lapply()`, `sapply()`, `tapply()`, `mapply()` and `vapply()`. The R profiler helps to optimise code in terms of its execution time. **Chapter 16** provides a detailed discussion of the R profiler – one of the unique features of this book.

Up to this point, the book elucidates basic and advanced programming concepts. The remaining chapters deal with concepts relating to statistics, data science and machine learning.

Chapter 17 discusses descriptive statistics concepts. The built-in statistical functions in R used to measure central value, dispersion and shape, as well as the five-number summary, are explained. **Chapters 18** and **19** distinguish between probability and statistics and sampling distributions. They discuss discrete and continuous probability distributions such as normal, binomial, multimodal, Poisson, chi-squared, student's t and the F test.

Chapter 20 details the correlation coefficient and its computation in R. It also deals with regression analysis, its types and the steps to build simple, multiple and logistic regression models in R. **Chapter 21** elaborates on statistical inference, one- and two-tailed tests, how to define the null and alternative hypotheses and errors in hypothesis testing. This chapter also discusses implementation of t-tests and the chi-squared test in R.

Chapter 22 explains the purpose of ANOVA, its types and how to implement it in R. **Chapter 23** discusses Machine Learning (ML) concepts in R – the basics, some learning and classification algorithms and R codes. It includes the naive Bayes classifier, decision tree classifier, k-Nearest Neighbour method, K-means clustering and association rule mining. **Chapter 24** elaborates on text mining, that is, sentiment analysis in R, as well as text preprocessing and the N-grams model.

Mastering all the concepts presented here will greatly improve and enhance your competence as a data scientist, as this book teaches not only the basic concepts, constructs and functions of R but also the underlying statistical techniques, machine learning and visualisation concepts of this language.

Sandhya Arora
Latesh Malik

Acknowledgments

This book is the outcome of queries from students, our lecture notes and lab material. We have been associated with this subject matter for more than five years through lectures, workshops and seminars.

Many professionals have helped us write this book. The Universities Press team initiated, designed, edited and indexed the book. We offer them our heartfelt thanks for their editorial and production support. We would like to thank all the reviewers of this book, who with their critical comments and creative suggestions helped us to improve the text.

Many of the ideas in this book come from Statistics and related courses such as Data Science and Machine Learning. We would like to thank all our professors, who helped and taught us the basic concepts of these subjects. Thanks is also due to R and RStudio software, as well as the IDE development team.

We would like to take this opportunity to thank our mentors, teachers and friends for motivating us throughout this journey. We also thank all our college colleagues and principal, who have given immense support in moulding this work. Thanks also, to our students, as without their queries and curiosity, the idea of writing this book would never have taken form.

Finally, we would like to thank our family members for their support, good wishes, encouragement and understanding while we wrote this book.

Sandhya Arora
Latesh Malik

Contents

To Our Beloved
Father, the late Sh. B.D. Bhagat
and
Mother, Smt. Kaushalya Bhagat

CHAPTER

1 Introduction to R Programming

Objectives

At the end of this chapter, you will be able to

- Provide an overview of the R programming language
- List the features of the R language
- State the advantages and disadvantages of using R
- Explain the steps for setting up the R environment in Linux/Fedora and Windows
- Describe the basic data types and functions of R
- Explain the debugging functions in R

1.1 | OVERVIEW OF R

R is a programming language and environment used for statistical computing and representation. It was originally developed by Ross Ihaka and Robert Gentleman and is currently managed by the R Development Core Team. It first came to prominence in 1993 at the Department of Statistics of the University of Auckland, New Zealand. It is considered as an open-source implementation of the S language, which was developed by John Chambers at Bell Laboratories during the early 1980s. Today, Google, Facebook, Microsoft, Bank of America and many other companies use R.

R is an open-source, interpreted computer language that contains more than 8000 packages, which are used for statistical analysis, data manipulation, data visualisation, machine learning and more. It is one of the most powerful solutions for Big Data analysis.

As with every programming language, R too has its pros and cons. The main advantages of using R (as shown in Fig. 1.1) are as follows:

- It is open source, and hence, free.
- It has excellent functionality for effective graphical representation of data.
- It is easy to use.

The following are the important features of, or reasons to learn and use, R:

- R has well-defined conditional loops, rich built-in functions, facility for user-defined recursive functions and effective input/output facilities.
- R allows the user to import data from a wide variety of resources, such as from text files, statistical packages and different data stores.
- R provides a vast set of operators to work on different data types, such as arrays, lists, factors, frames, vectors and matrices.

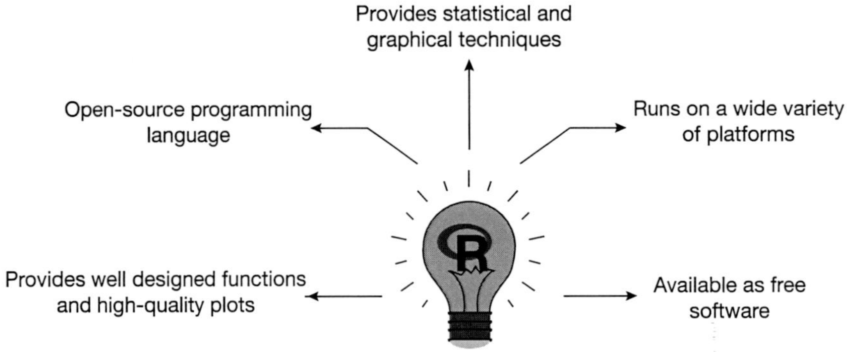

Fig. 1.1: Advantages and features of the R programming language

- R contains comprehensive statistical routines for performing all kinds of data analytics.
- R provides state-of-the art graphics facilities for visualisation of complex data.
- R has the facility to integrate R programs with that of other languages, such as C/C++, JAVA and Python.
- R can compete with other commercially available statistical packages, such as Statistical Package for the Social Sciences (SPSS) and Statistical Analysis System (SAS).
- Support from the R user community is easy to obtain. Tutorials, data sets and discussion forums about R can be accessed online.

However, there are also some disadvantages. R may appear to be relatively easy to learn at the beginning, but it is hard to master. The R language is command based, which may make it inconvenient for statisticians and other users who are not computer professionals to use it. This steep learning curve sometimes results in poorly written R code that is hard to read and maintain. Such code may also slow down the process if users are working with large data sets. To take full advantage of the R language, users must have a strong theoretical background in statistics.

1.2 | INSTALLATION OF R

R is one of the world's most widely used open-source programming tools and it provides a software environment for graphical representation, information reporting and statistical analysis. R is licensed under the GNU General Public License (GPL) and is freely available for research and development purposes. Binary pre-compiled versions of R are available for commonly used operating systems such as Windows, Linux, Fedora and Red Hat. The RStudio integrated development environment (IDE) can be downloaded, installed and configured from www.r-project.org. R can also be installed from the Comprehensive R Archive Network (CRAN) mirror sites.

The steps in the installation of R for Windows and Linux/Fedora are discussed below.

Windows

1. Go to the RStudio website (https://www.rstudio.com/products/rstudio/download or https://cran.r-project.org/bin/windows) and download the files. There are two versions of the R executable: 32-bit and 64-bit. Download the appropriate version for your system.
2. Install the R package (filename: R-3.6.0-win.exe) and then RStudio (filename: 1.0.136.exe).
3. Launch R by clicking the R icon. The RGui window will open, showing the R Console (Fig. 1.2).

   Clear the R Console by pressing <Ctrl> + L. The Icon bar contains icons that can be used to open a script, load a workspace and save the current workspace. The Menu can also be used to access these features. Short commands can be executed at the R prompt, >.

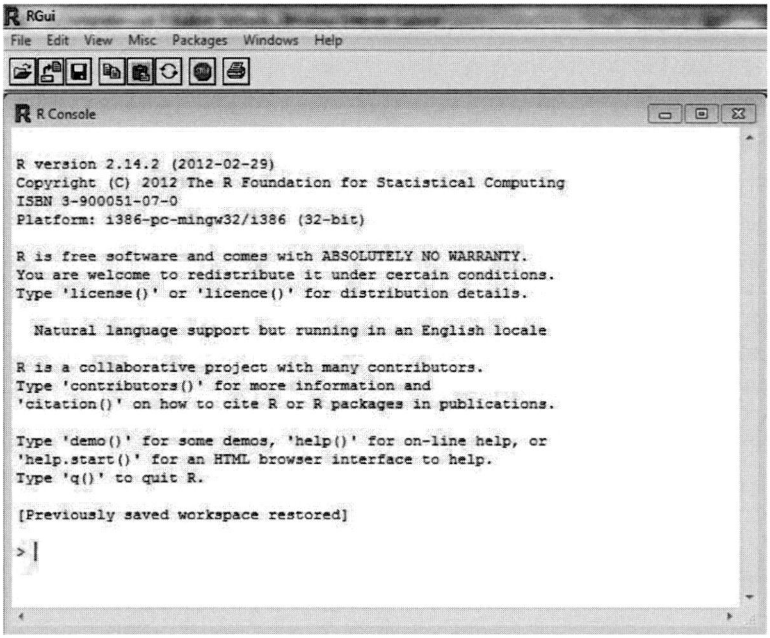

Fig. 1.2: The RGui window showing the R Console

4. Select File-> New Script to open a separate window (Fig. 1.3) to type a set of commands and then save them in a file for future execution. A set of commands can also be executed by selecting the code and pressing <Ctrl> + R.

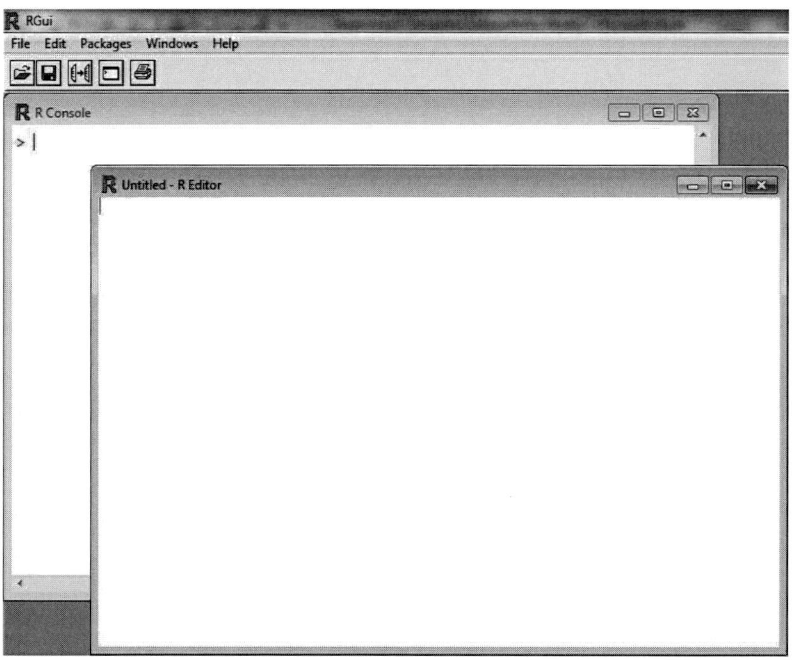

Fig. 1.3: The RGui window with a new R Editor window open

Linux

The R binary for many Linux versions is available at cran-r-project.org. However, you can use the `yum` command to install R as follows:

```
$yum install R    # To install the R environment and its standard packages
```

1. Launch the R prompt by typing R in the terminal window: `$ R`
2. You will see a prompt, >, which allows you to type R commands for execution. Typing the `q()` function at the R prompt will enable you to quit the R session. R includes extensive help facilities. Use `help.start()` to open a browser window displaying the help manuals.

Download and install RStudio from https://www.rstudio.com/products/rstudio/download. Alternatively, you can install it using the command:

```
>sudo dnf install $(curl -s https://www.rstudio.com/products/rstudio/
download/ | grep -o "\"[^ \"]*x86_64.rpm\"" | sed "s/\"//g")
```

1.3 | INSTALLATION AND LOADING OF R PACKAGES

In R, you can install the required package using the `install.packages()` function. For example, to install the `ggplot2` package, which helps users to plot charts and graphs, you can use the following command at the R prompt:

```
>install.packages("ggplot2")
```

The package can be installed from the R command line or from the shell.

At the R command line, type:

```
> install.packages()
```

At the shell prompt, type:

```
$ R CMD INSTALL
```

To use a specific package, you must first load it in R by using the `library()` function.

To load the `ggplot2` package, type:

```
> library(ggplot2)
```

1.4 | R – BASIC SYNTAX

We can enter the code for a program either at the R command prompt or in an R script file. Let us examine these two methods.

R command prompt

```
$R
>tempString <- "Hello, R World!"
>print (tempString)
[1] "Hello, R World!"
```

Here, the first statement assigns a string, `"Hello, R World!"`, to the string variable, `tempString`. The `print()` function on the next line prints the value stored in `tempString`. It must be remembered that R is a case-sensitive language.

Rscript file: Usually, while writing a program, we type all the statements in a file, called the Rscript. We can execute these scripts at the command prompt with an R interpreter. Given below is a sample code that can be saved in a file called test.R:

```
tempString <- "Hello, R World!"
print (tempString)
```

Rscript can be executed at the command prompt:

```
> Rscript test.R
```

When we run this program, we obtain the following output:

```
[1] "Hello, R World!"
```

The `source("filename")` function submits a script file to the current session of R. You can then run your Rscript, which contains a set of R statements:

```
>source("test.R")
```

When you run the above program using the `source()` function, the following output is produced:

```
[1] "Hello, R World!"
```

1.5 | DATA TYPES AND OBJECTS

Data types play a vital role in the development of any application. In the R programming language, data types need not be declared explicitly, unlike in C or JAVA. Every variable in R is assigned an R object and the data type of the R object becomes the data type of the variable. R objects are data structures that have some attributes and methods.

Some of the data types used in R are given below:

- List
- Vector
- Matrix
- Array
- Factor
- Data frame

These data types are discussed in detail in subsequent chapters.

The atomic data types (representing the lowest level of detail) of R are listed in Table 1.1.

Table 1.1 Atomic data types of R

Data type	Example	Verify
Logical	TRUE, FALSE	> temp <- TRUE >print(class(temp)) Output will be – [1] "logical"
Numeric	32.3, 35, 222	>temp <- 123.5 >print(class(temp)) Output will be – [1] "numeric"
Integer	22L, 314L, 0L	>temp <- 12L >print(class(temp)) Output will be – [1] "integer"
Complex	43 + 12i	>temp <- 12+52i >print(class(temp)) Output will be – [1] "complex"
Character	'ab', "bad", "FALSE", '223.4'	>temp <- "TRUE" >print(class(temp)) Output will be – [1] "character"
Raw	"JAVA" is stored as 4a 41 56 41	>temp <- charToRaw("Hello") >print(class(temp)) Output will be – [1] "raw"

A comment in R is denoted by the # symbol.

R has many functions that help programmers to perform basic operations on these data types. We will now discuss some of the basic functions of R.

```
>is.numeric(2)    # Checks whether the given input is numeric
TRUE
>is.integer(2)    # Checks whether the given input is an integer
FALSE
>is.integer(2L)    # Checks whether the given input is an integer
TRUE

>class("welcome to R")  # Displays the class of the input
[1] "character"
>class(42)
[1] "numeric"
>class(41L)
[1] "integer"

>as.numeric(TRUE)  # Displays the input as numeric
[1]  1
>as.numeric(FALSE)
[1] 0
>as.character(6)  # Displays the input as character
[1] "6"
```

1.6 | VARIABLES

Variables are used to store any type of data whose value can be changed. An identifier is a unique name given to a variable. The rules for creating identifiers are given below:

- Identifiers can be a combination of letters, digits, period (.) and underscore (_).
- They must start with a letter or a period.
- Reserved words cannot be used.
- They cannot start with a digit.

  Examples of valid identifiers: I, sum, fine_interest, m5

  Examples of invalid identifiers: cost@3, 7yen, _paise, TRUE, .three

1.7 | CONSTANTS

In contrast to variables, constants are entities whose value cannot be changed during the execution of the program. Constants are of two types: numeric and character.

1.7.1 Numeric Constants

Numeric constants can take any numeric value of the type integer, double or complex. The type of the constant can be verified using the `typeof()` function.

If you wish to assign an integer value to a constant, it should be followed by `L`; and if you wish to assign a complex type to a constant, it should be followed by `i`. The default data type is double.

```
> typeof(8)
[1] "double"
> typeof(8L)
[1] "integer"
> typeof(8i)
[1] "complex"
```

By default, numeric constants are decimal numbers. If you wish to use hexadecimal numbers, it must be preceded by `0x` or `0X`, as given below:

```
> 0xff
[1] 255
> 0XF + 1
[1] 16
```

1.7.2 Character Constants

Character constants can be represented using single quotes (') or double quotes (") as delimiters.

```
> 'pinnacle'
[1] "pinnacle"

> typeof ("6")
[1] "character"
```

1.7.3 Built-in Constants

Some built-in constants have been defined in R, along with their values, such as the names of the months, the letters of the alphabet, and so on.

```
> LETTERS  # Set of all capital alphabets

[1] "A" "B" "C" "D" "E" "F" "G" "H" "I" "J" "K" "L" "M" "N" "O" "P" "Q"
"R" "S"
[20] "T" "U" "V" "W" "X" "Y" "Z"

> letters # Set of all small alphabets

[1] "a" "b" "c" "d" "e" "f" "g" "h" "i" "j" "k" "l" "m" "n" "o" "p" "q"
"r" "s"
[20] "t" "u" "v" "w" "x" "y" "z"

> pi
[1] 3.141593

> month.name
[1] "January"   "February"  "March"     "April"     "May"       "June"
[7] "July"      "August"    "September" "October"   "November"  "December"
```

If we assign a value to a built-in constant, it will override the predefined value.

```
> pi <- 9.8
> pi
[1] 9.8
```

1.8 | COMMENTS

Comments are used to make the code descriptive and easy to understand. They are not compiled but form part of the source code and are used to make it understandable. Commented lines should begin with # and one space followed by the text to describe the code.

We can even place short comments after some code, preceded by two spaces, #, one space, then the text. For example

```
# Is 8 greater than 6?
> isTRUE(8>6)
[1] TRUE

> x <- 5
> (x < 10) && (x > 2)  # && means AND
[1] TRUE
```

1.9 | DEBUGGING IN R

When a program has no syntax error but the output is incorrect due to a logical error, we need to find the error or bug in the program. The procedure to identify and fix program bugs is called debugging.

There are a number of functions that help in debugging programs:

- `traceback()`
- `debug()`
- `browser()`

Apart from these, the `trace()` and `recover()` functions are also used. Calling `trace()` on a function allows the user to insert bits of code into a function, while `recover()` allows us to check the variables in the upper-level functions of the function calling hierarchy.

1.9.1 traceback()

When a function in R fails and we want to know in which function the error occurred, we can use the `traceback()` function, immediately after the error. This function prints a list of the functions that were called before the error occurred. The functions are printed in reverse order.

For example:

```
> f<-function(x) {
+  r<-x+10*g(x)
+  r
+   }
> g<-function(y) {
+  r<-(y+100)* h(y)
+   r
+  }
> f(-1)
Error in if (r < 10) r^2 else r^3 : missing value where TRUE/FALSE needed
In addition: Warning message:
In log(z) : NaNs produced
> traceback()
3: h(y) at #2
2: g(x) at #2
1: f(-1)
```

1.9.2 debug()

The `traceback()` function does not tell us where in the function the error occurred. In order to know which line caused the error, we may want to step through the function using `debug()`. While debugging, we can simply type "c" to continue to the end of the current section of code.

For example, for the above program:

```
> debug(f)
> f(-1)
debugging in: f(-1)
debug at #1: {
    r <- x + 10 * g(x)
    r
}

Browse[2]> print(x)
[1] -1
Browse[2]>
```

At the `Browse` prompt, the following commands can be used:

- `Q`: Quits debugging
- `where`: Tells you where you are currently
- `n`: Executes the current line and prints the next line
- `ls()`: Lists all the objects in the local environment
- `print(x)`: Displays the value of x at the current execution point

1.9.3 browser()

Sometimes, we may not want to step through all the code, line by line, but begin debugging only after a certain point. The `browser()` function helps us pause at certain points.

For example:

```
> f<-function(x) {
+  browser()
+  r<-x+10*g(x)
+  r
+   }
> g<-function(y) {
+  r<-(y+100)* h(y)
+   r
+  }
> f(-1)
Called from: f(-1)
Browse[1]> Called from: h(y)
Browse[1]> ls()
[1] "x"
Browse[1]> z
Browse[1]> n
debug at #3: r <- x + 10 * g(x)
Browse[2]> c
Error in if (r < 10) r^2 else r^3 : missing value where TRUE/FALSE needed
In addition: Warning message:
In log(z) : NaNs produced
```

EXERCISES

Concept-based Questions

1. Select the logical values of R from the following:
   a. TRUE b. "hello"
   c. 2L d. NA
2. The R language is:
   a. Interpreted
   b. Compiled
   c. Both of the above
   d. None of the above
3. A comment in R is denoted by which of the following symbols?
   a. * b. #
   c. / d. $
4. Pick out the advantage of using the R language:
   a. Point and click program
   b. R packages
   c. Publication-quality visualisation
   d. Reproducibility
5. An R script is used for:
   a. Reproducibility
   b. Automating work
   c. Point and click program
   d. Auto-complete function
6. The R programming language is a dialect of:
   a. B b. C
   c. S d. K
7. R was created by Ross Ihaka and Robert Gentleman in 1991 at the Department of Statistics in the University of ________:
   a. John Hopkins b. California
   c. Harvard d. Auckland
8. In which year was R version 1.0.0 released to the public?
   a. 2000 b. 2005
   c. 2010 d. 2012
9. Which of the following is the most accurate about the R language?
   a. Free
   b. Paid
   c. Available for free trial only
   d. None of the above
10. The primary source code copyright for R is held by which foundation?
    a. A b. S
    c. C d. R
11. Which of the following is used for statistical analysis in the R language?
    a. RStudio
    b. Studio
    c. Heck
    d. None of the above
12. Which of the following will start an R program?
    a. `$ R` b. `> R`
    c. `* R` d. All of the above
13. Which one of the following is not an atomic data type in R?
    a. Integer b. Logical
    c. Data frame d. Character
14. If you execute the operation `>temp<-14` in the R prompt, what is the class of object that is determined after executing `>class(temp)` at the R prompt?
    a. Numeric b. Integer
    c. Complex d. Real
15. If a command is not complete at the end of a line, which prompt does R display at the command line by default?
    a. * b. –
    c. + d. All of the above
16. Command lines typed at the console are limited to how many bytes?
    a. 3000
    b. 4095
    c. 5000
    d. None of the above
17. Which of the following statements is an alternative to "?solve"?
    a. `help(solve)` b. `man(solve)`
    c. `hel(solve)` d. All of the above

Answers

1. a	**2.** a	**3.** b	**4.** b	**5.** a	**6.** c	**7.** d	**8.** a	**9.** a	**10.** d
11. a	**12.** a	**13.** c	**14.** a	**15.** c	**16.** b	**17.** a			

Programming Questions

1. Write the R commands to differentiate between raw vectors and other vectors.
2. Write the R commands to create a data type and check its class.
3. Write the R commands to convert input data to character and numeric types.
4. Write the R script to create variables for the height and width of a rectangle and to display its area.
5. Write the R script to perform and display basic arithmetic on variables.
6. A horse is grazing in a square field of width 20 cm. It is tethered with a rope half as long as the width of the field. What is the area of the field that the horse is unable to graze? Write the R script for this.
7. Perform the following using R commands/scripts:
   a. Assign 52 to a variable named `my_apples`.
   b. Initialise a variable `my_oranges` to "Fifty two".
   c. Set a variable `my_logical` to FALSE.
   d. To the variable `my_fruit`, assign the addition of a numeric and a character variable, that is, `my_apples` and `my_oranges`.
   e. Display the `my_fruit` variable value.
8. Write an R code to perform the task of record maintenance, where the following information is recorded:
   a. Each day's total gain or loss is stored in the variable `total_daily`
   b. Overall profit or loss per day of the week
   c. Total money lost over the week
9. Perform the following in R:
   a. Initialise four character variables: `name`, `age`, `employed` and `salary`.
   b. Transform `age` to numeric type and store in the variable `age_clean`.
   c. Initialise `employed_clean` with the result obtained by converting `employed` to the logical type.
   d. Convert the respondent's salary to numeric and store it in the variable `salary_clean`.
10. Write the R code for displaying a student mark sheet and the result (pass/fail).

CHAPTER 2

Data Definitions and Categorisation

Objectives

At the end of this chapter, you will be able to

- Provide an overview of data in the statistical context
- List the different sources of data
- Define Big Data, list the main companies involved and the tools used
- Categorise data and explain the scales of measurement
- Define a data cube and explain its operations

2.1 | OVERVIEW OF DATA

All data-based systems involve the collection and interpretation of data, conversion of data into useful information and numerical and statistical analysis. In business and industry, statistical information is required for decision making. In our daily life too, we require information to make informed decisions. For example, before making a purchase, you may want to compare the same product from different manufacturers based on parameters such as customer reviews, cost, size, and so on. Thus, relevant information should be made available to the decision makers.

2.1.1 Data vs Information

Data can be collected from various input sources and devices, but sometimes this data cannot be used directly. It must be processed, interpreted, organised and structured so as to make it meaningful. Processed data is called information. Given below are examples of data and information:

- Temperature readings taken over the past 10 years is data. If this data is analysed to find global warming patterns, then it is information.
- Traffic to a website is data. If the traffic is analysed for certain types of virus attacks, it is information.

2.1.2 Growth of Data

According to the International Data Corporation (IDC) Digital Universe Study of May 2010, the Digital Universe will grow by a factor of 44 from 2009 to 2020. IBM estimated (in 2016) that data is growing at an annual compound rate of 64%. Terabytes of data is the average measure of size that is used today, which is expected to increase to petabytes, exabytes and zettabytes.

2.2 | SOURCES OF DATA

The amount of data generated and collected is growing exponentially. About 90% of data is generated from the sources discussed below.

Internet: The Internet is the main source of data. Online search, internet banking and e-commerce all generate enormous volumes of data. Also, the number of people with access to the Internet is increasing and automation of systems is also contributing to the growth in data.

Social media: The use of social media such as Facebook, Snapchat, Twitter, WhatsApp, Instagram, LinkedIn, and so on, has fuelled data creation. This data includes text, photos, audio and video, which require the storage of huge amounts of data with fast retrieval. For more information about the data collected from social media, please see the Data Never Sleeps 5.0 report.

Communication: Digital data for communication between machines, from machines to humans and between humans is increasing day by day. We send data through various means such as email, voice SMS, Facebook Messenger, Skype or WhatsApp calls. This data can be text, pictures or videos. Thus, communication systems are a big source of data.

Digital photos: Today, most mobiles phones are equipped with high-resolution cameras. Anyone can upload data from photo albums over the Internet. Trillions of photos are stored on servers and retrieved at speed. These photos are also shared on multiple social media networks, generating even more data.

Services: Most people and businesses use services such as Google Maps, internet banking, online trading, and so on. Repositories of information like Wikipedia also allow people to update its pages. Increased use of such services generates a tremendous amount of data.

Internet of things (IOT): Smart devices that interact with each other generate a lot of data. Home automation, e-farming and robotics require devices to interact with each other through the Internet. This information, when stored on a cloud or streamed online, becomes a big source of data over time.

Every source of data requires certain related tools and needs to be processed in different ways.

2.3 | BIG DATA

Big Data refers to large and complex data sets that can be structured, semi-structured or unstructured and which will typically not fit into the memory available to be processed. Such data may need to be processed in-place, which means that computation must be performed wherever the data resides. It is not possible for such systems to process a vast amount of data within the timeframe mandated by the business.

Big Data comprises the 5Vs: velocity, volume, value, variety and veracity.

- **Volume**: This refers to the size of the data set. It may be in KB, MB, GB, TB or PB, based on the type of the application that generates or receives the data.
- **Variety**: This refers to the types of data that can exist, such as text, audio, video and photos. It refers to heterogeneous sources of data, both structured and unstructured. Data presented in the form of emails, photos, videos, monitoring devices, PDFs, audio, and so on, are also heterogeneous data that need to be handled by a single application.
- **Velocity**: This refers to the speed at which data flows into business processes, application logs, networks and social media sites, sensors, devices, and so on. The speed of retrieval of data should remain the same irrespective of the size of the data. Thus, velocity refers to the low-latency, real-time speed at which the analytics need to be applied. A typical example of this would be to perform analytics on a continuous stream of data originating from a social networking site or aggregation of disparate sources of data.

- **Value:** This refers to insight of data. Every data extracted might not be meaningful. As cost is involved in collecting and analysing data, the value of the data is important.
- **Veracity:** It refers to the trustworthiness of the data. An example of this is GPS data. The reliability and accuracy of this data is very important. Satellite signals are sometimes lost in urban areas because of buildings and other structures. So, in this case, data must be fused with other data sources such as road data or data from accelerometers.

2.3.1 Big Data vs Small Data

Big data and small data can be differentiated based on the data source, volume, velocity and variety (Table 2.1).

Table 2.1 Differences between Big Data and small data based on data source, volume, velocity and variety

Property	Big data	Small data
Data source	Non-structured data generated from sources such as: - Social media - IOT - Twitter - Blogs - Devices - Video, images, etc. - Logs generated by the system	Structured data generated from sources such as: - Relational data in tabular form - Transaction data
Volume	In TB, PB, EB or ZB	GB or TB
Velocity	High velocity and real-time data	Low velocity or batch data Can wait for response
Variety	Structured/Unstructured or multistructured data	Structured data

2.3.2 Major Players in Big Data

- Google
- Apache Hadoop
- MapReduce
- Apache Mahout
- Apache HBase
- Apache Cassandra

These are the major players in Big Data and providing data handling tools to store and compute the data. Google provides cloud and Big Data processing tools. Apache Hadoop can handle multiple computers to solve a problem. MapReduce allows you to process and generate big data sets with a parallel, distributed algorithm on a cluster. Apache HBase handles the storage of big data at multiple locations.

2.3.3 Big Data Tools

Table 2.2 lists the main Big Data tools in use.

Table 2.2 Types of Big Data tools and their examples

Type of tool	Example
NoSQL databases	CouchDB , MongoDB, Redis, Cassandra, HBase, Hypertable, Voldemort, ZooKeeper, BigTable, Riak
MapReduce	Acunu, Hive, Hadoop, Pig, Cascading, Caffeine, S4, MapR, Flume, Kafka, Oozie, Greenplum, Cascalog
Storage	S3, HDFS, GDFS
Servers	AWS Elastic Beanstalk, Amazon EC2, Elastic, Heroku, Google App Engine
Processing	BigSheets, R language, Mechanical Turk, Solr/Lucene, Datameer, Tinkerpop

2.4 | DATA CATEGORISATION

Data can be categorised according to the scale of measurement. Data has its own property and can be continuous or discrete. Qualitative and quantitative data may be required to represent the system based on the properties of the data.

2.4.1 Entity and Attributes

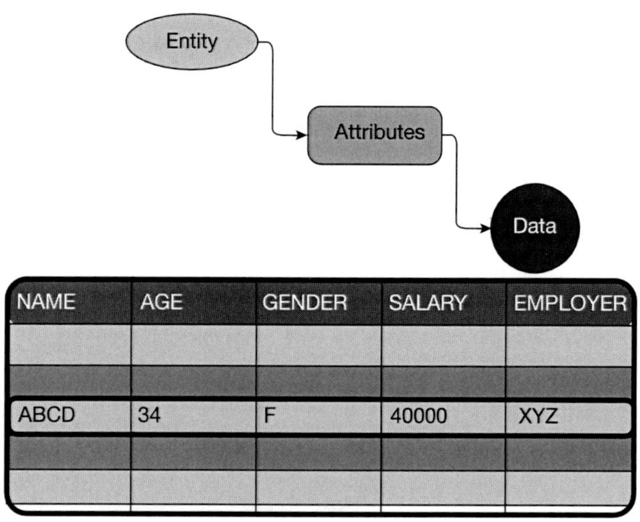

Fig. 2.1: Entity, attributes and data

- **Entity:** A particular thing is called an entity or object. An entity can be a single thing, person, place or object. Data can be stored about such entities.
- **Attribute:** An attribute is a measurable or observable property of an entity.
- **Data:** A measure of an attribute of an entity is called data.

2.4.2 Scales of Measurement

Scales of measurement describe the nature of the information assigned to a variable. They specify the way in which variables can be defined or categorised.

The four scales of measurement are nominal, ordinal, interval and ratio. The nominal and ordinal scales are considered under qualitative data, while the interval and ratio scales come under quantitative data.

Qualitative data comprises measures of values and is expressed as numbers or categories. It is descriptive and conceptual. Quantative data is measured using numbers and values. It is concise and close ended. Quantative data can be further classified as continuous or discrete.

Qualitative data

Nominal scale: Here, data categories are given names so as to provide a label. There is no hierarchical relationship (order) between the categories. One category is not the parent of or superior to another category. Examples: Gender (Male / Female), Blood Groups (A / B / O / AB), Religion (Hindu / Muslim / Christian / Buddhist).

Ordinal scale: Here, the categories can be placed logically in a meaningful order but the difference between the categories is not known. Examples: (a) Rank (First / Second / Third): The ranks can be placed logically in ascending or descending order but the difference in marks between the ranks is not known, nor can it be predicted from the ranks. (b) Rating (Excellent / Very Good / Good): A rating of Excellent or Good is meaningful but the difference between the ratings is not known.

Quantitative data

Interval scale: Here, the values can be ordered, they are meaningful and the difference between the values can be quantified. Values appear in the form of numbers or numerical values and are meaningful but cannot be multiplied, divided, added or subtracted. Doubling the value has no meaning due to the absence of absolute zero. Examples: (a) Trend analysis: In market analysis, it is useful to know the trends over various time intervals. Trend analysis on interval data can be performed by taking surveys in multiple iterations, using the same question. (b) SWOC analysis: This is performed to analyse the strength, weakness, opportunity and challenge for an organisation from interval data. (c) Temperature measurement: Measuring temperature over an interval in Fahrenheit and Celsius.

Ratio scale: This is similar to interval-scale data but, in addition, it allows users to compare the intervals or differences. The values can be ordered and are meaningful. Difference and addition is possible, as is doubling, due to the presence of absolute zero. Examples: (a) Temperature measurement: Measurement of temperature on the Kelvin scale is ratio-scale data because 100 K is twice as hot as 50 K. The difference in temperature values is also meaningful and can be ordered. (b) Measurement of height in inches. (c) Measurement of weight in kilograms.

Quantitative data may be classified as discrete or continuous, as described below. Fractions are not meaningful here.

Discrete: Values that can be specified as whole numbers and which cannot be further divided. For example, the number of classes, number of children, number of votes, PAN card number.

Continuous: Any numerical value (including fractions) that is meaningful and which can be broken down further. For example, weight: 1 kg, 1.1 kg, 1.5 kg can be measured in fractions and is meaningful; height: 5 feet, 5.1 feet, and so on; capacity of a tank: 1 litre, 1.5 litres, and so on. These numerical values are continuous.

2.5 | DATA CUBE

A data cube is a multidimensional data model that views data in the form of a cube. It is characterised by two parameters: dimension, which is the perspective or entity with respect to which an organisation wants to maintain a record, and fact, which comprises the actual values in the record. For example, the rainfall data of the Meteorological Department can consist of two parameters: Time (Year, Season, Month, Week, Day, etc.) and Location (Country, Region, State, etc.). In the two-dimensional representation shown in Fig. 2.2, the rainfall data for the North-East region is displayed with respect to different months for a period of years.

Region: North-East

Month

Year	Jan	Feb	Mar	Apr	May	Jun	Jul	Aug	Sep	Oct	Nov	Dec
2005												
2006												
2007												
2008												
2009												
2010												

Fig. 2.2: Two-dimensional view of rainfall data for the North-East region over different months for several years

Suppose we want to represent data according to Time (Year, Month) as well as the East, West and North-East regions of a country. The two-dimensional view for this data is shown in Fig. 2.3.

East

Month

Year	Jan	Feb	Mar	Apr	May	Jun	Jul	Aug	Sep	Oct	Nov	Dec
2005												
2006												
2007												
2008												
2009												
2010												

Fig. 2.3 (a): Two-dimensional view of rainfall data for the East over different months for several years

West

Month

Year	Jan	Feb	Mar	Apr	May	Jun	Jul	Aug	Sep	Oct	Nov	Dec
2005												
2006												
2007												
2008												
2009												
2010												

Fig. 2.3 (b): Two-dimensional view of rainfall data for the West over different months for several years

North-East

Month

Year	Jan	Feb	Mar	Apr	May	Jun	Jul	Aug	Sep	Oct	Nov	Dec
2005												
2006												
2007												
2008												
2009												
2010												

Fig. 2.3 (c): Two-dimensional view of rainfall data for the North-East over different months for several years

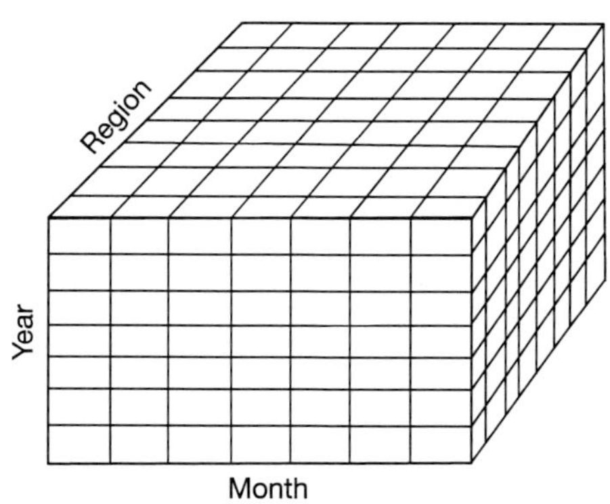

Fig. 2.4: Three-dimensional data cube of rainfall data for the East, West and North-East regions over different months for several years

The data cube shown in Fig. 2.4 gives us a three-dimensional view of this rainfall data.

2.5.1 Data Cube Operations

To demonstrate the operations explained in this section, we use employee data: Employee (department name, gender, salary).

The following data processing operations can be performed on data cubes:

- Roll-up
- Drill-down
- Slice and dice
- Pivot

Roll-up This operation calculates the aggregation on a data cube based on rows or columns or hierarchy or whole data. It accomplishes this in one of the following ways – by grouping based on a concept hierarchy or by reducing a dimension.

Roll up is an operation that converts data from finer granularity to coarser granularity with the help of aggregation. For example, employees work in a department and we can calculate the department-wise salary using the group-by clause. However, if you want to display the grand total of all the salaries or the gender-wise salary in each department, we need to roll up the data using the group-by clause, ROLLUP (department, gender).

Table 2.3 Salary data based on Department and Gender

Department	Gender	Salary_sum
Computer Sc	Male	80000
Computer Sc	Female	85000
Computer Sc	All genders	165000
Electrical	Male	76000
Electrical	Female	120000
Electrical	All genders	196000
All departments	All genders	361000

Drill-down This is the reverse of the roll-up operation. Here, group data is expanded into its subparts. It can performed by stepping down (expanding) a concept hierarchy for a dimension or by introducing a new dimension.

Here, the conversion is from coarser to finer granularity. For example, country-wise aggregation is converted to city-wise data. In this operation, one or more new dimensions may be added. It navigates through the data from less detailed to highly detailed. For the example given in the roll-up operation, drill-down would take place when we are interested in the employee data in every department.

Slice In a slice operation, cross-tabulation is carried out for specific values other than for a fixed third dimension. This operation selects one or more specific dimensions from a given cube based on selection criteria and creates a new sub-cube. It reduces the dimensionality of a cube. In other words, it extracts a slice from a data cube for a particular quarter. We may not be interested in the entire data cube but only in a subpart. For example, displaying employee data from the Computer Science department.

Dice This operation defines a sub-cube by performing a selection on two or more dimensions. For example, displaying the salary of female employees in the Computer Science department.

	foo	bar	baz	zoo
0	one	A	1	x
1	one	B	2	y
2	one	C	3	z
3	two	A	4	q
4	two	B	5	w
5	two	C	6	t

→

bar	A	B	C
foo			
baz	1	2	3
zoo	4	5	6

Fig. 2.5: The pivot technique

Pivot This is a technique of changing from one dimensional orientation to another. It is also called rotation (Fig. 2.5).

EXERCISES

Multiple Choice Questions

1. Point out the correct statement:
   a. Raw data is an original source of data
   b. Preprocessed data is an original source of data
   c. Raw data is the data obtained after processing
   d. None of the above
2. Which of the following is performed by a data scientist?
   a. Define the question
   b. Create reproducible code
   c. Challenge results
   d. All of the above
3. Which of the following is the most important language for Data Science?
   a. Javab. Ruby
   c. R
   d. None of the above
4. Which of the following terms is appropriate for the figure?

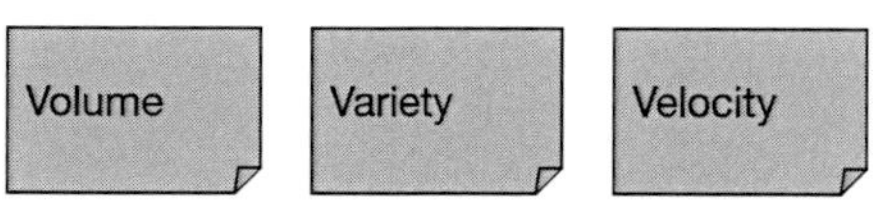

   a. Large Data b. Big Data
   c. Dark Data d. None of the above
5. Which of the following characteristics of Big Data is relatively more concerned with Data Science?
   a. Velocity b. Variety
   c. Volume d. None of the above
6. Data that can be modelled as dimension attributes and measure attributes is called _______ data.
   a. Multi-dimensional
   b. Single-dimensional
   c. Measured
   d. Dimensional
7. The process of viewing the cross-tab (single dimensional) with a fixed value of one attribute is:
   a. Slicing
   b. Dicing
   c. Pivoting
   d. Both slicing and dicing
8. The operation of moving from finer granularity to coarser granularity (by means of aggregation) is called ________.
   a. Roll-up b. Drill-down
   c. Dicing d. Pivoting

Answers

1. a	2. d	3. c	4. b	5. b	6. a	7. a	8. a

Concept-based Questions

1. What is the smallest and largest unit used to measure the size of data?
2. How big is a quintillion measure?
3. Give examples of the smallest and largest entities of data.
4. Give FIVE parameters with which data can be categorised as (i) Simple, (ii) Moderately Complex and (iii) Complex.
5. What types of data are involved in the following applications?
   a. Weather forecasting
   b. Mobile usage of all customers of a service provider
   c. Anomaly (fraud) detection in a bank
   d. Person categorisation, that is, identifying a human
   e. Air traffic control in an airport
   f. Streaming data from all flying aircrafts of Boeing
6. Consider an image as an entity.
   a. What are the attributes necessary to represent an image?
   b. Categorise each attribute according to data categorisation.
   c. Suppose two images are given. Give an idea to check if two images are identical or not.
7. How you can convert a data of interval type to ordinal type? Give an example. What are the problems with such a transformation? Is the reverse possible? Justify your answer.
8. What are the different properties used to categorise data according to the NOIR data categorisation?
9. Given an entity "STUDENT" with the following attributes, identify the NOIR category to which each of them belongs.

Scholarship Amount	Name	Roll No	Date of Birth	Aadhar No.	Gender	Mobile No.	Email Id

10. Explain the concept of data cube to represent hyper-dimensional data. Also explain with suitable diagrams the following:
    a. Roll-up
    b. Drill-down
    c. Slice
11. Using the concept of data cube, show how YouTube can archive videos of all types.
12. Give FOUR differences between data of scale types interval and ratio.

CHAPTER

3 Operators

Objectives

At the end of this chapter, you will be able to

- Define operators in R and list their types
- List and describe the arithmetic operators
- List and describe the relational operators
- List and describe the logical operators
- List and describe the miscellaneous operators
- Explain operator precedence and associativity in R

3.1 | INTRODUCTION TO OPERATORS

An operator (symbol) is an indication to the compiler to perform a specific mathematical – arithmetic, bitwise or logical – manipulation on data. The following operators are available in the R language (Fig. 3.1):

- Arithmetic
- Relational
- Logical
- Miscellaneous

<table>
<tr><td>Arithmetic operators</td><td>+</td><td>–</td><td>*</td><td>/</td><td>%%</td><td>%/%</td><td>^</td></tr>
<tr><td>Relational operators</td><td><</td><td>></td><td>==</td><td><=</td><td>>=</td><td>!=</td><td></td></tr>
<tr><td>Logical operators</td><td>&</td><td>|</td><td>!</td><td>&&</td><td>||</td><td></td><td></td></tr>
<tr><td>Assignment operators</td><td>=</td><td><-</td><td>-></td><td><<-</td><td>->></td><td></td><td></td></tr>
<tr><td>Miscellaneous operators</td><td>:</td><td>%in%</td><td>%*%</td><td></td><td></td><td></td><td></td></tr>
</table>

Fig. 3.1: Operators in R

3.2 | ARITHMETIC OPERATORS

The arithmetic operators supported by R are + (addition), – (subtraction), * (multiplication), / (division), ^ (exponent), %% (modulus remainder from division) and %/% (integer division). These operators are used to carry out mathematical operations on data.

For example:

```
> t <- 15

> d <- 46

> t+d
[1] 61

>  t-d
[1] -31

> t*d
[1] 690

> d/t
[1] 3.066667

> d%/%t
[1] 3

> d%%t
[1] 1

> d^t
[1] 8.737103e+24
```

Arithmetic operators on vectors:

```
> t1 <- c( 6, 7.6, 8)
> t2 <- c(6,3,1)
> t1+t2
[1] 12.0 10.6  9.0
> t1-t2
[1] 0.0 4.6 7.0
> t1*t2
[1] 36.0 22.8  8.0
> t1/t2
[1] 1.000000 2.533333 8.000000
> t1%%t2
[1] 0.0 1.6 0.0
> t1%/%t2
[1] 1 2 8
> t1^t2
[1] 46656.000   438.976     8.000
```

3.3 | RELATIONAL OPERATORS

Relational operators compare the given data values and return TRUE or FALSE. In other words, they perform a logical comparison. TRUE and FALSE are reserved words used to denote logical constants. For example, to check whether two objects are equal, the double equal to operator can be used to check if the logical value TRUE equals the logical value TRUE (TRUE == TRUE) and the result of this query is a logical value – in this case, TRUE; the check on TRUE == FALSE will return FALSE.

Logical variables can also be used to check equality or perform comparisons of other data types such as string, numeric or logical. The opposite of the equality operator is the inequality operator, !=. For example, the output of "hello != goodbye" will be TRUE.

To check if one object is greater than or equal to/less than or equal to another object, the greater than or equal to operator (>=)/the less than or equal to (<=) can be used. For example 5>=3 and 3>=3 will evaluate as TRUE. Table 3.1 lists the relational operators in R.

Table 3.1 Relational operators and their description

Operator	Description
<	Less than
>	Greater than
<=	Less than or equal to
>=	Greater than or equal to
==	Equal to
!=	Not equal to

For example:

```
> t1 <- 15
>  t2<- 16
> t1<t2
[1] TRUE
> t1>t2
[1] FALSE
> t1<=15
[1] TRUE
> t2>=22
[1] FALSE
> t2 == 16
[1] TRUE
> t1 != 15
[1] FALSE
```

Relational operators on vectors:

```
>v <- c(2,5.5,6,9)
>t <- c(8,2.5,14,9)
>print(v>t)
 [1] FALSE  TRUE FALSE FALSE
>print(v < t)
 [1]  TRUE FALSE  TRUE FALSE
>print(v == t)
 [1] FALSE FALSE FALSE  TRUE
>print(v<=t)
 [1]  TRUE FALSE  TRUE  TRUE
>print(v>=t)
 [1] FALSE  TRUE FALSE  TRUE
>print(v!=t)
 [1]  TRUE  TRUE  TRUE FALSE
```

3.4 | LOGICAL OPERATORS

To perform Boolean operations on data, logical operators are used (Table 3.2).

Table 3.2 Boolean operations and their execution

Operator	Execution
&, &&	AND
|, ||	OR
xor()	EXCLUSIVE OR
!	Logical NOT
isTRUE(x)	Tests if x is TRUE
TRUE	True (non-zero values)
FALSE	False (zero values)

There are two versions of the AND and OR operators. The shorter form (& and |) perform element-wise comparisons. The result will have the length of the longer operand.

However, the longer form (&& and ||) evaluates from left to right, examining only the first element of each vector. Evaluation proceeds only until the result is determined, thus giving a single-length logical vector. This longer form is preferred in conditional statements.

For example:

```
> x <- c(1,2,0,TRUE)

> y <- c(FALSE,TRUE,FALSE,TRUE)

> x&y
[1] FALSE  TRUE FALSE  TRUE

> x&&y
[1] FALSE
> !x
[1] FALSE FALSE  TRUE FALSE

> x|y
[1]  TRUE  TRUE FALSE  TRUE

> x||y
[1] TRUE


> 8 > 7
[1] TRUE

> 7 < 5
[1] FALSE

Is 8 less than 6?
> isTRUE(8<6)
[1] FALSE

Is 8 greater than 6?
> isTRUE(8>6)
[1] TRUE

> t1 <- 5
> (t1 < 10) && (t1 > 2)  # && means AND
[1] TRUE

> t1 <- 5
> (t1 < 20) || (t1 > 5) # || means OR
[1] TRUE
> (t1 > 20) || (t1 > 5)
[1] FALSE

> x = 10
> y = 20
Is x equal to 10 and is y equal to 20?
> (x == 10) & (y == 20) # == means exactly equal to
[1] TRUE
```

```
Is x equal to 10 and is y equal to 2?
> (x == 10) & (y == 2)
[1] FALSE

x = 11:16
> x
[1] 11 12 13 14 15 16
> (x>12)|(x<15)    # Checks if value is greater than 12 or less than 15
[1] TRUE TRUE TRUE TRUE TRUE TRUE
> (x>14)|(x<16)    # Checks if value is greater than 14 or less than 16
[1] TRUE TRUE TRUE TRUE TRUE TRUE
>x[(x>12)|(x<15)]   # Finds which values are greater than 12 or smaller
than 15
[1] 11 12 13 14 15 16

> x = 11:16 # Generates x = 11,12,13,14,15,16
> (x > 12) && (x < 15)     # Checks only for the first element of x, that
is, x[1]
[1] FALSE
is equivalent to:
> (x[1] > 12) & (x[1] < 15)
[1] FALSE
```

3.5 | MISCELLANEOUS OPERATORS

R also has operators that are used for specific purposes and special computations, as shown in Table 3.3.

Table 3.3 Miscellaneous operators in R

Operator	Description
:	Colon operator, used to create a sequence of numbers for a vector
%in%	Used to identify if an element belongs to a vector
%*%	Used to multiply matrices

The example given below explains the use of these operators:

```
>v <- 2:8
> v
 [1] 2 3 4 5 6 7 8
>v1 <- 18
>v2 <- 22
>t <- 1:20
>print(v1 %in% t)  # Checks if 18 exists in values from 1 to 20
>print(v2 %in% t)  # Checks if 22 exists in values from 1 to 20
 [1] TRUE
[1] FALSE
>Mat = matrix( c(3,6,5,1,7,4), nrow = 2,ncol = 3,byrow = TRUE)
>tm = Mat %*% t(Mat)        # Matrix multiplication
>print(tm)
      [,1] [,2]
[1,]   70   65
[2,]   65   66
```

3.6 | PRECEDENCE AND ASSOCIATIVITY OF OPERATORS

Table 3.4 shows operator precedence, from the highest to the lowest, and associativity in the R programming language.

Table 3.4 Operator precedence and associativity

Operator	Description	Associativity
^	Exponent	Right to left
-x, +x	Unary minus, Unary plus	Left to right
%%	Modulus	Left to right
*, /	Multiplication, Division	Left to right
+, –	Addition, Subtraction	Left to right
<, >, <=, >=, ==, !=	Comparisons	Left to right
!	Logical NOT	Left to right
&, &&	Logical AND	Left to right
|, ||	Logical OR	Left to right
->, ->>	Rightward assignment	Left to right
<-, <<-	Leftward assignment	Right to left
=	Leftward assignment	Right to left

```
>2+5*6      # Associativity is left to right
[1] 32
>(2+5)*6  # We can change associativity by using parathensis
[1] 42
> (1 > 2 + 3 && 4)
[1] FALSE
```

The above expression is equivalent to `((1>(2+3))&&4)`, that is, `(2+3)` is evaluated first and results in 5. Then `(1>5)` evaluates as `FALSE(0)` and `(0&&4)` executes, resulting in `FALSE(0)`.

EXERCISES

Multiple Choice Questions

1. Which one of the following is the correct outcome of the command `(x < 15) || (x > 12) & (x < 15) && (x > 12)||(x == 17)`, when `x = 13` and when `x = -13`?
   a. `FALSE` and `FALSE`
   b. `TRUE` and `TRUE`
   c. `FALSE` and `TRUE`
   d. `TRUE` and `TRUE`

2. Suppose `x = 3:18`, which one of the following correctly specifies the outcome of the statement: `x[(x > 4) & (x < 17)]` and `x[(x > 5) || (x < 18)]`?
   a. `13 14 15 16` and `5 6 7 8`
   b. `5 6 7 8 9 10 11 12 13 14 15 16` and `3 4 5 6 7 8 9 10 11 12 13 14 15 16 17 18`

c. `5 6 7 8` and `13 14 15 16.`
d. Both are `5 6 7 8`

3. Suppose `x = 10:50`, which one of the following is the correct command to find out which of the values in x are greater than 30 and less than 40?
a. `x[(x > 30) & (x < 40)]`
b. (x > 40) & (x < 50)
c. `x[(x >= 40) & (x >= 40)]`
d. `x[(x <= 40) & (x <= 40)]`

4. Suppose `x = 45:80`, which one of the following is the correct outcome of `(x > 80) && (x < 70) and (x > 80) || (x < 70)`?
a. `TRUE` and `FALSE`
b. `FALSE` and `FALSE`
c. `TRUE` and `TRUE`
d. `FALSE` and `TRUE`

5. Suppose `x = 13:17`, which one of the following is the correct outcome of `x[(x > 12) || (x < 15)]`?
a. `TRUE`
b. `FALSE`
c. `13 14 15 16 17`
d. `17 16 15 14 13`

6. Which one of the following is the correct outcome of the command `>x[(x^2 + 6*x < 500)]`, where `>x <- c(20, 65, 27, 55, 38, 37, 18, 52, 160, 237, 170, 61, 88, 52, 49, 12, 4, 24, 18, 22)`?
a. `[1] 20 65 27 55 38 37 52 160 237 170 61 88 52 49 24 22`
b. `[1] 20, 65, 27, 55, 38, 37, 18, 52, 160, 237, 170, 61, 88, 52, 49, 12, 4, 24, 18, 22`
c. `[1] 18 12 4 18`
d. `[1] NULL`

Answers

1. d	**2.** b	**3.** a	**4.** d	**5.** c	**6.** c

Programming/Concept-based Questions

1. Generate a sequence of values 210 to 222 and write the R commands to find values greater than 211 and less than 215.
2. Create a vector of flowers and use R commands to find a given flower in the vector.
3. Create two vectors using user input, and using R commands perform addition, multiplication, division and subtraction of vector elements.
4. Create a vector of random values and check if it contains any value less than 45.
5. Create a student mark sheet and print the total grades of student for pass/fail.

CHAPTER 4

Control Statements and Functions

Objectives

At the end of this chapter, you will be able to

- Define control statements in R
- Explain the `if`, `if-else` and nested `if` statements in R
- Discuss the `ifelse()` function
- Explain the `repeat`, `next`, `switch` and `break` statements
- Explain the `for` and `while` loops
- Discuss the different forms of `return`

4.1 | INTRODUCTION

Control statements enable you to control the flow of execution inside a function. In most problems, iterative statements are necessary. The commonly used control statements are `if`, `else`, `for`, `while`, `repeat`, `break`, `next` and `return`. Here, we discuss each of these in detail with examples.

4.2 | THE `if` STATEMENT

The syntax of the `if` statement contains a condition – if the condition evaluates as TRUE, the R code associated with the `if` statement is executed.

```
if (condition) {
    # Do something
}
```

In the case of an `if-else` statement, the code associated with the `else` statement is executed whenever the condition of the `if` statement is not satisfied. Control flow in `if` statements is shown in Fig. 4.1.

```
if (condition) {
    # Do something
} else {
    # Do something else
}
```

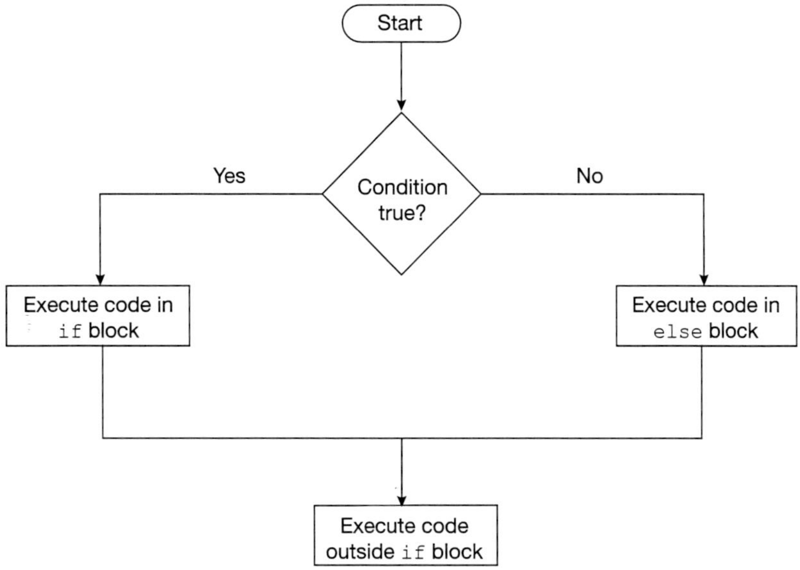

Fig. 4.1: Control flow in `if` statements

You can place one or more `if` statements inside another `if` statement, to add even more control.

```
if (condition1) {
   if(condition2) {
      # Code if both if statements pass
} else {
         # Code if condition1 passes and condition2 fails
   }
} else {
   # Code if condition1 fails
}
```

There are many cases where programs are customised even further; for example, the `if-else, if-else` statement. The general rules of using the `if` and `else` statements are applicable in R, but you should be careful while using the `if-else, if-else` statement. An `if` can be associated with zero or one `else`, and the `else` must appear last.

```
if (condition1) {
    # Do something1
} else  if(condition2){
    # Do something2
}
else{ expression3
}
```

For example:

```
>a <- 6
>if (a <= 60) {
    print("a is less than 60")
} else {
    print("a is greater than 60")
}
```

Output:

```
[1] "a is less than 60"
```

If we change the a as a<-120 and then run the same if statement, the output will be

```
[1] "a is greater than 60"
```

The `ifelse()` function in R: The syntax of the ifelse() function is given as:

```
ifelse(test_expression, tx, ty)
```

Here, the parameters test_expression, tx and ty are of the logical vector type. The return value is a vector of the same length as test_expression. This returned vector will take values from tx if test_expression evaluates as TRUE for that position vector value and from ty if test_expression is FALSE for that position vector value. The vectors tx and ty are recycled according to the rule, whenever necessary.

For example, the code given below checks whether vector numbers are even or odd, and it prints "even No" or "odd No" as required:

```
a=c(2,1,4,5,6)
> ifelse((a%%2)==0,"even No","odd No")
[1] "even No" "odd No"  "even No" "odd No"  "even No"
```

4.3 | THE for STATEMENT

The for, while and do-while statements are used to iterate through the written code. Here, there are two different kinds of loops: entry controlled and exit controlled. In entry-controlled loops, the test condition is checked first and if it is false, the loop body will not be executed at all. In the case of exit-controlled loops, the loop body will be executed once even if the test condition is false. The for and while loops come under the entry-controlled loop category. The do-while loop is an example of an exit-controlled loop.

The syntax of the for loop consists of a variable that can be used inside the loop for iterating over the list of elements in a vector or a list. It also consists of the start, end and successive values till the end of the sequence.

The basic syntax of the for loop statement in R is given below:

```
for (variable  in start:end) {
   statements
}
```

For example:

```
for (t in 1:5) {
    print(t)
}

> x <- c("Marks1=98", "Marks2=67",
"marks3=78", "Marks4=56")
>for (i in x) {
    print(x[i])
}
```

Output:

```
[1] NA
[1] NA
[1] NA
[1] NA
```

```
> for (i in x) {
   print(i)
  }
```

Output:

```
[1] "Marks1=98"
[1] "Marks2=67"
[1] "marks3=78"
[1] "Marks4=56"
```

```
>for (i in 1:4) {
    print(x[i])
}
```

Output:

```
[1] "Marks1=98"
[1] "Marks2=67"
[1] "marks3=78"
[1] "Marks4=56"
```

```
>for (i in seq(x)) {
    print(x[i])
}
```

Output:

```
[1] "Marks1=98"
[1] "Marks2=67"
[1] "marks3=78"
[1] "Marks4=56"
```

Nested loops can be used to print matrix values, as given below.

```
>mt <- matrix(1:10, 2)
>for (t1 in seq(nrow(mt))) {
    for (t2 in seq(ncol(mt))) {
        print(mt[t1, t2])
    }
}
```

Output:

```
[1] 1
[1] 3
[1] 5
[1] 7
[1] 9
[1] 2
[1] 4
[1] 6
[1] 8
[1] 10
```

While iterating through the list and data frame types, the `names()` function is used, as shown below. Another way of displaying the contents of a data frame using the `for` loop is by using [[ ]] (two square brackets) to access the elements of the data frame. The difference between the two methods is that in the latter, the name of the column in the data frame is not displayed.

```
> studentname<-c("sandhya","Urmila","latesh")
> age <-c(21,22,23)
> diabetes <-c("type1","type2","type2")
> studentdata <-data.frame(studentname,age,diabetes)
> for (i in names(studentdata)){
      print(studentdata[i])
}
```

Output:

```
  studentname
1 sandhya
2 Urmila
3 latesh
  age
1 21
2 22
3 23
  diabetes
1 type1
2 type2
3 type2
```

We can print the above data frame using the command

```
>for (i in names(studentdata)){
  print(studentdata[[i]])
}
```

Output:

```
[1] sandhya Urmila  latesh
Levels: latesh sandhya Urmila
[1] 21 22 23
[1] type1 type2 type2
Levels: type1 type2
```

4.4 | THE while LOOP

The syntax of the `while` loop is as follows:

```
while (test-expression) {
   statement
}
```

Here, `test-expression` evaluates to a Boolean value. Statements inside the `while` loop will be executed only if `test-expression` evaluates to TRUE. When you use the `while` loop, ensure that there is a way to exit the loop. Figure 4.2 shows the control flow of `while` loops.

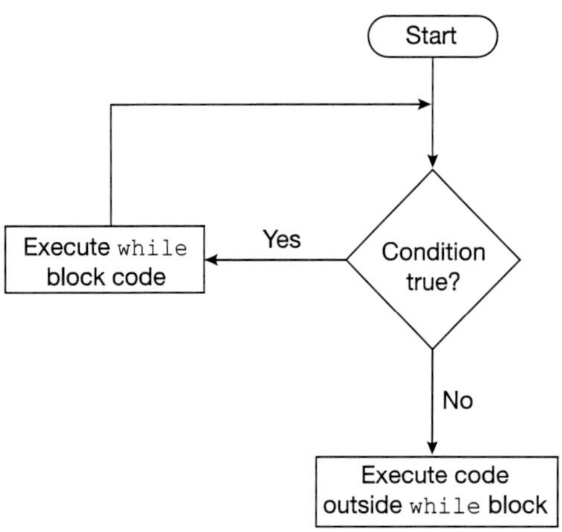

Fig. 4.2: Control flow of `while` loops in R

For example:

```
>temp <- 1
>while (temp < 6) {
    print(temp)
    temp <- temp + 1
}
```

Output:

```
[1] 1
[1] 2
[1] 3
[1] 4
[1] 5
```

4.5 | THE `repeat` AND `break` STATEMENTS

The `repeat` statement executes the specified statements repeatedly till the terminating condition evaluates to TRUE, after which execution breaks. The syntax of `repeat` and `break` is given below:

```
>repeat {
    statements
    if (test-expression) {
        break
    }
}
```

For example:

```
>xt <- 11
>repeat {
print(xt)
xt = xt+1
if (xt <= 16){
break
}
}
```

Output:

```
[1] 11
[1] 12
[1] 13
[1] 14
[1] 15
```

4.6 | THE `next` STATEMENT

There may be situations where we want to skip the current iteration of a loop without terminating it. The `next` statement in R programming helps us achieve this. On encountering `next`, the R parser skips execution of the statements for evaluation in the current iteration and instead starts the next iteration of the loop, from the beginning.

For example:

```
>for (t in 1:20) {
    if (t%%2 == 1) {
        next
    } else {
        print(t)
    }
}
```

Output:

```
[1] 2
[1] 4
[1] 6
[1] 8
[1] 10
[1] 12
[1] 14
[1] 16
[1] 18
[1] 20
```

This loop checks for even/odd number and prints only even numbers up to 20. It skips over the odd numbers using the `next` statement.

4.7 | THE `switch` STATEMENT

The syntax of the `switch` statement in R is as follows:

```
switch(expression-variable, case1,case2,case3,...)
```

Here, the programmer can check `expression-variable` against a list of values specified as case1, case2, as so on. The parameter `expression-variable` is an integer value. Multiple `case` statements can be contained within a `switch` statement. No default argument is specified in the `switch` case. If `expression-variable` is a string, it is matched to the names of elements. If no match occurs in any case specified, an unnamed element value is returned.

For example:

```
x <- switch( 2,"one","two","three")
> x
```

Output:

```
[1] "two"
```

4.8 | FUNCTIONS

R functions are very similar to the functions of C, JAVA, and so on. However, they have a functional programming flavour, as R functions are like R objects; that is, you can perform everything with functions that you would with R objects. The syntax for writing a function in R is as follows:

```
function-name < - function(argument)
{   function body......}
```

4.8.1 The `return()` Function

The `return()` function returns the result of the processing performed by a function. The syntax of the `return()` function is:

```
return(expression)
```

Any valid object can returned from the `return` statement.

The example given below returns a statement about whether a given number is positive, negative or zero.

```
>checknumber <- function(x) {
if ((x %% 2)== 0) {
result <- "Even Number"
}
else if ((x%%2)!= 0) {
result <- "Odd Number"
}
else {
result <- "Zero"
}
return(result)
}
```

Here are some sample runs:

```
> checknumber(12)
[1] "Even Number"
> checknumber(-20)
[1] "Even Number"
> checknumber(1)
[1] "Odd Number"
```

The value of the last evaluated expression is returned automatically in the case of missing returns from a function. For example, the above function can be rewritten as

```
>checknumber <- function(x) {
if ((x %% 2)== 0) {
result <- "Even Number"
}
else if ((x%%2)!= 0) {
result <- "Odd Number"
}
else {
result <- "Zero"
}
result
}
```

The `return` statement should be the last statement of the function; if not, the function will end prematurely and control will reside at the place from which the function was called.

```
>checknumber <- function(x) {
if ((x %% 2)== 0) {
return("Even Number")
}
else if ((x%%2)!= 0)  {
return("Odd Number")
}
else {
return("Zero")
}
}
```

In the above example, if `x%%2 == 0`, the function immediately returns "Even Number" without executing the rest of the function body.

You can return multiple values from a function. We can use list or some other object inside a function and return it from that function for this purpose.

For example:

```
>multi_return <- function() {
my_list <- list("name" = "sandy", "rollno" = 20, "result" = "pass")
return(my_list)
}
```

Here, we create a list `my_list` containing multiple elements and we return this single list; that is, we return all the elements of the list.

```
> a <- multi_return()
>a
$name
[1] "sandy"

$rollno
[1] 20

$result
[1] "pass"
```

4.9 | SOME SOLVED EXAMPLES

Example 4.1: Obtain input from the user

Code:

```
>stud.name <- readline(prompt="Enter name: ")
>stud.age <- readline(prompt="Enter age: ")
>stud.age <- as.integer(stud.age)
>print(paste("Hi,", stud.name, "next year you will be", stud.age+1, "years
old."))
```

Output:

```
Enter name: sandy
Enter age: 15
[1] "Hi, sandy next year you will be 16 years old."
```

Example 4.2: Multiplication table

Code:

```
# Convert input from the user to
integer
>num_t = as.integer(readline(prompt
= "Enter a number: "))
>for(i in 1:10) {
print(paste(num_t,'x', i, '=',
num_t*i))
}
```

Output:

```
Enter a number: 7
[1] "7 x 1 = 7"
[1] "7 x 2 = 14"
[1] "7 x 3 = 21"
[1] "7 x 4 = 28"
[1] "7 x 5 = 35"
[1] "7 x 6 = 42"
[1] "7 x 7 = 49"
[1] "7 x 8 = 56"
[1] "7 x 9 = 63"
[1] "7 x 10 = 70"
```

Example 4.3: Find the factorial of a number

Code:

```
>num-f = as.integer(readline(prompt="Enter a number for factotial: "))
>fact = 1
>if(num-f < 0) {
print("Invalid number input for factorial calculation")
} else if (num-f == 0) {
print("The factorial of 0 is equal to 1")
} else {
>for(i in 1:num-f) {
fact = fact * i
}
>print(paste("The factorial of", num-f ,"is calculated as",fact))
}
```

Output:

```
Enter a number for factorial: 8
[1] "The factorial of 8 is calculated as 40320"
```

Example 4.4: Simple calculator in R

Code:

```
# A menu-driven simple calculator to perform addition, subtraction,
multiplication and division using functions
>addnum <- function(a, t) {
return(a + t)
}
>subtractnum <- function(a, t) {
return(a - t)
}
>multiplynum <- function(a, t) {
return(a * t)
}
>dividenum <- function(a, t) {
return(a / t)
}
# Obtain input from the user
>print("Select operation.")
>print("option1.Add")
>print("option2.Subtract")
>print("option3.Multiply")
>print("option4.Divide")
>choice = as.integer(readline(prompt="Enter choice[1/2/3/4]: "))
>t1 = as.integer(readline(prompt="Enter the first number: "))
>t2 = as.integer(readline(prompt="Enter the second number: "))
>operator <- switch(choice,"+","-","*","/")
>resultofoperation <- switch(choice, addnum(t1, t2), subtractnum(t1, t2),
multiplynum(t1,t2), dividenum(t1, t2))
>print(paste(t1, operator,t2, "=", resultofoperation))
```

Output:

```
[1] "Select operation."
[1] "option1.Add"
[1] "option2.Subtract"
[1] "option3.Multiply"
[1] "option4.Divide"
Enter choice[1/2/3/4]: 4
Enter the first number: 20
Enter the second number: 4
   [1] "20 / 4 = 5"
```

Example 4.5: Write an R program to print the Fibonacci series

Code:

```
>len<-12
>fibval <-numeric(len)
>fibval[1]<-0
>fibval[2]<-1
>for (i in 3:len) {
  fibval[i]<-fibval[i-1]+fibval[i-2]
}
>cat("Fibonacci numbers are ",fibval)
```

Output:

```
Fibonacci numbers are 0 1 1 2
3 5 8 13 21 34 55 89
```

Example 4.6: Count of odd numbers in arguments

Code:

```
> oddcount <- function(x) {
t <- 0 # Assign 0 to t
for (a in x) {
if ((a %% 2) == 1) t <- t+1
}
return(t)
}
```

Output:

```
> t<-c(1,2,3,4,5,7,9)
> oddcount(t)
[1] 5
```

Example 4.7: Write a program that prints the sum of the numbers from 1 to *n*, where *n* is input

Code:

```
> n=as.integer(readline(prompt="Enter number: "))
t<-0
for (i in 1:n) {
  t <-t+i
}
print(paste("sum is",t))
```

Output:

```
[1]Enter number: 5
   sum is 15
```

Example 4.8: Write a program that prints a multiplication table for numbers up to *n*

Code:

```
> #  Input from the user
num = as.integer(readline(prompt = "Enter a number: "))
for(j in 1:num){
  print(paste("Table of",j, "is as below"))
for(i in 1:10) {
  print(paste(j,'x', i, '=', j*i))
}
}
```

Output:

```
[1] Enter a number: 3
[1] "Table of 1 is as below"
[1] "1 x 1 = 1"
[1] "1 x 2 = 2"
[1] "1 x 3 = 3"
[1] "1 x 4 = 4"
[1] "1 x 5 = 5"
[1] "1 x 6 = 6"
[1] "1 x 7 = 7"
[1] "1 x 8 = 8"
[1] "1 x 9 = 9"
[1] "1 x 10 = 10"
[1] "Table of 2 is as below"
[1] "2 x 1 = 2"
[1] "2 x 2 = 4"
[1] "2 x 3 = 6"
[1] "2 x 4 = 8"
[1] "2 x 5 = 10"
[1] "2 x 6 = 12"
[1] "2 x 7 = 14"
[1] "2 x 8 = 16"
[1] "2 x 9 = 18"
[1] "2 x 10 = 20"
[1] "Table of 3 is as below"
[1] "3 x 1 = 3"
[1] "3 x 2 = 6"
[1] "3 x 3 = 9"
[1] "3 x 4 = 12"
[1] "3 x 5 = 15"
[1] "3 x 6 = 18"
[1] "3 x 7 = 21"
[1] "3 x 8 = 24"
[1] "3 x 9 = 27"
[1] "3 x 10 = 30"
```

EXERCISES

Multiple Choice Questions

1. If `x = 23`, which one of the following is the correct outcome of `y`, where
`> y=if ( x==23 ) { x <- x^3+3 } else { x <- x^2-3 }`?

a. `12164` b. `12170`
c. `526` d. `123`

2. Suppose `x = c(12,4,16,8,20,5,14)`, which one of the following is the correct output of
`ifelse(x < 10, 2+x, 2*x)`?

a. `[1] 14 8 18 16 22 10 16`
b. `[1] 14 6 18 10 22 7 16`

c. `[1] 24 8 32 16 40 10 28`
d. `[1] 24 6 32 10 40 7 28`

3. Which one of the following is the correct outcome of the following `while` loop?

```
>x <- 20
>while(x < 35) {x <- x^2+10;
if (x == 30) break; print(x);
}
```

a. `[1] 410`
b. `[1] 20`
c. `[1] 410`
`[1] 410`
d. `[1] 20`
`[1] 20`
`[1] 35`
`[1] 35`

4. Which one of the following is the correct outcome of the command
`rep(c("CL1", " CL2", " CL3"), each=3)?`

a. `[1] "CL1" "CL1" "CL1" " CL2" " CL2" " CL2" " CL3" " CL3" " CL3"`
b. `[1] "CL1" "CL2" "CL3" " CL1" " CL2" " CL3" " CL1" " CL2" " CL3"`
c. `[1] CL 1 2 3 CL 1 2 3`
d. `[1] CL 1 1 CL 2 2 CL 3 3`

5. Which one of the following is the correct outcome of
`>for(i in 12:14) {print(1 - 2i + i^2)}?`

a. `[1] 121`
`[1] 144`
`[1] 169`
b. `[1] -23 + i2`
`[1] -25 + i2`
`[1] -27 + i2`
c. `[1] 145 - 2i`
`[1] 170 - 2i`
`[1] 197 - 2i`
d. `[1] 169`
`[1] 144`
`[1] 121`

6. Which one of the following is the correct outcome of
`for(i in 10:14) {print(i + 2*i + 3*i**3)}?`

a. `[1] i + 2*i + 3*i**3`
`[1] i + 2*i + 3*i**3`
`[1] i + 2*i + 3*i**3`
`[1] i + 2*i + 3*i**3`
b. `[1] 3030`
`[1] 4026`
`[1] 5220`
`[1] 6630`
`[1] 8274`
c. `[1] 120`
`[1] 132`
`[1] 144`
`[1] 156`
`[1] 168`
d. `Error...`

Answers

1. b	**2.** d	**3.** a	**4.** a	**5.** c	**6.** b

Programming/Concept-based Questions

1. Create a matrix and print it in matrix form using the iterative `for` and `while` loops.
2. Write an R program to create three vectors, namely `patientid`, `age` and `diabetes`. Print these values using a `for` loop.
3. Create an R function to print the first 150 prime numbers.
4. Write an R program to check if the given input is odd or even.
5. Write an R program to print the sum of even numbers that lie between 100 and 200.
6. Create a function to calculate the GCD and LCM of two numbers.

CHAPTER

5 Interfacing with R

Objectives

At the end of this chapter, you will be able to

- Explain R code interfacing with C code, using the `.C()` and `.Call()` functions
- Explain R code interfacing with Python code, using the `rPython`, `reticulate` and `rpy2` packages

5.1 | INTRODUCTION TO EXTENDING R

The R programming language can be easily extended using R code. We can write R scripts, R functions or R packages for this purpose. Here, we will examine how we can interface R with C, C++ and Python.

5.2 | INTERFACING R WITH C/C++

In this section, we will discuss how to call C/C++ functions from the R environment.

5.2.1 Prerequisites

The first step in interfacing R with C or C++ is to ensure that the appropriate compiler (cc or gcc) is installed on the system. For Linux/Ubuntu, there are no additional requirements. However, for Windows, we need to download Rtools from the CRAN mirror site and change the PATH variable. This variable should include the executable directory of Rtools as well as that of the C compiler. Rebooting Windows will ensure that these changes are incorporated.

5.2.2 Interfacing C Code with `.C()` and `.Call()`

The functions `.C()` and `.Call()` can be used in R to call C functions. The `.C()` call is a very basic way of calling C functions in R, where the arguments and return value of the function must be primitive. The `.Call()` function is more complex as it accepts and returns complex data types such as list/matrix/other data structures.

5.2.3 Writing and Calling C Code

To interface C code with the R environment, functions written in C should have `void` as the return type and the arguments should be passed by reference. Files containing C code must have the `#include <R.h>` line at the top. Any special function used in C requires the inclusion of that particular header file. We can use R to compile the C code, rather than calling the C compiler directly. For example, to compile code written in the file hello.c, the following command can be used:

```
>R CMD SHLIB hello.c
```

This command creates a file called hello.so in Linux and hello.dll in Windows. It is a dynamic link library and can be dynamically loaded into R. This .dll file name can be changed as follows:

```
>R CMD SHLIB -o newhelloname.so hello.c
```

After compiling the C code, launch R and load the library. Then, load the external C code from the .dll or .so file using the `dyn.load()` function.

```
> dyn.load('hello.so'')    for Unix
> dyn.load('hello.dll'')   for Windows
```

Now all of the functions written in the file hello.c will be available for R to use and call.

5.2.4 Running the Program

The first program discussed here is the "Hello, world!" program. This will print the string "Hello, world!", *n* number of times on the screen.

```
helloworld1 <- function(tmp) {
for(t in 1: tmp) {
cat("Hello, world!\n")
}
}
```

Now, if we want to modify this by including the functionality of loops, we can write the appropriate C code and call it from R code using the `.C()` function. First, we create a file called test.c with a function that takes parameters by reference and the `void` return type (as mentioned earlier).

```
#include <R.h>
void test(int *m)
{
int tmp;
for(tmp=0; tmp < *m; tmp++) {
Rprintf("Hi, C and R!\n");
}
}
```

The main() function is not required here as we are simply writing a C function and not a C program. Instead of the print() function, we use the Rprintf() function as we need the output to be sent to the R console. The R program is as follows:

```
helloworld2 <- function(n) {
.C("test", as.integer(n))
}
```

The first parameter to the .C() function is the name of the C function to be called (in quotes); in our case, the name of the function is "test". Other parameters comprise the arguments of the C function. In this case, the C function has only one argument, n, the number of times "Hi, C and R!" must be printed on the screen. Here, the parameter value is typecast to integer.

5.2.5 C Data Structures

R objects are stored in S-expressions, that is, in SEXP in the C program. Therefore, all functions created in C return SEXP and take SEXP as argument input. A SEXP is a variant type, with subtypes for all R data structures. The most important types are given below:

- REALSXP: numeric vector
- INTSXP: integer vector
- LGLSXP: logical vector
- STRSXP: character vector
- VECSXP: list
- CLOSXP: function (closure)
- ENVSXP: environment

The library pryr needs to be installed as it includes the sexp_type() function, which is used to access these names:

```
>library(pryr)
>sexp_type(101L)
## [1] "INTSXP"
>sexp_type("ba")
## [1] "STRSXP"
>sexp_type(F)
## [1] "LGLSXP"
>sexp_type(list(ab = 1))
## [1] "VECSXP"
>sexp_type(pairlist(ab = 1))
## [1] "LISTSXP"
```

5.3 | INTERFACING R WITH PYTHON

There are two ways to interface R with Python. One is by calling Python functions from R and the other is by calling R functions from Python. To call Python functions from R, we can use the rstudio/reticulate/rPython package. To call R functions from Python, the rpy2 package can be used.

5.3.1 The rPython Package

We can use the code given below to install the `rPython` package and use it:

```
>install.packages("rPython")
>require("rPython")
>python.exec("def f(x) return sum(range(x))")
>python.call("f", 10)
```

Output is 55.

5.3.2 The reticulate Package

This package is used for interoperability of Python with R. It has many features that help us work between R frames and Python pandas data frames, R matrices and Python numpy arrays, embedding R sessions and Python sessions, and so on.

The `reticulate` package can be downloaded from CRAN and installed as follows:

```
>install.packages("reticulate")
```

Importing Python modules This enables us to import Python modules and use it from the R environment. For example, in the code given below, the Python module os is imported and the `listdir()` function is used:

```
>library(reticulate)
>ost <- import("os")
>ost$listdir(".")
 [1]
 [5]
 [9] "DESCRIPTION"      "docs"             "external"          "index.html"
[13] "index.Rmd"        "inst"             "issues"            "LICENSE"
[17] "man"              "NAMESPACE"        "NEWS.md"           "pkgdown"
[21] "R"                "README.md"        "reticulate.Rproj"  "src"
[25] "tests"            "vignettes"
```

Sourcing scripts We can also write scripts in Python and use it in the R environment. The `source_python()` function creates an object that can be used in R.

For example, for a Python script saved as test.py:

```
def addnum(a,b):
   return a+b


>library(reticulate)
>source_python('test.py')
>addnum(15, 3)
   [1] 18
```

5.3.3 The `rpy2` Package

The `rpy2` package is used to call R from Python by importing it into Python. This is explained below:

```
import rpy2
import rpy2.robjects as robjects
rt = robjects.r # Gets R object through which we interact with an R
instance

rt["pi"]        # Gets the pi

robjects.globalenv[] is used to create a variable:
r["mtvar"] = 3       # Failed, TypeError
robjects.globalenv[ "mtvar"] = 3       # OK, fine
```

Interact with numpy:

```
from rpy2.robjects import numpy2ri
numpy2ri.activate()
r.sum(np.arange(20))
```

We can add a function with a string:

```
robjects.reval("f<-function (a,b) a+b")
r.f(13,14)      #   Returns 27
```

We can also load packages:

```
from rpy2.robjects.packages import importr
utils = importr("utils")
base = importr("base")
```

EXERCISES

Multiple Choice Questions

1. The package used for interfacing R code with Python is:
   a. `reticulate` b. `rpy2`
   c. None of the above d. Both (a) and (b)
2. C/C++/Java codes can be interfaced with R code:
   a. True
   b. False

Answers

1. d **2.** a

Programming/Concept-based Questions

1. Write the R code to interface a C function of *n* even-number summations.
2. Write the Python code to create a graphical presentation of any built-in data set and interface it with R code.

CHAPTER

6 Vectors

Objectives

At the end of this chapter, you will be able to

- Define a vector and explain how to create vectors or a sequence of elements
- Assign a name to the elements of a vector
- Create and use integer, logical and character vector indexes
- Explain the arithmetic operations that can be performed on vectors
- State the R recycling rule for vector elements
- Explain value coercion
- Describe vector deletion
- Sort the vector elements in ascending or descending order using the `sort()` function

6.1 | OVERVIEW OF VECTORS

R has a comprehensive set of built-in mathematical functions and is rich in different data types. This makes it an effective programming language to use as a supercharged scientific calculator. One of R's greatest strengths is its ability to evaluate functions over an entire vector – this eliminates the need to write that functionality in a loop and use subscripts.

In R, the most basic data object is the vector. A vector is a sequence of elements of the same data type. In other words, vectors are homogeneous. There are six types of atomic vectors: logical, integer, double, complex, character and raw. The elements of a vector are called its components. You can create character, numeric and logical vectors, as shown in Fig. 6.1. However, if you try to mix data types, you will find that R forces the data into one mode.

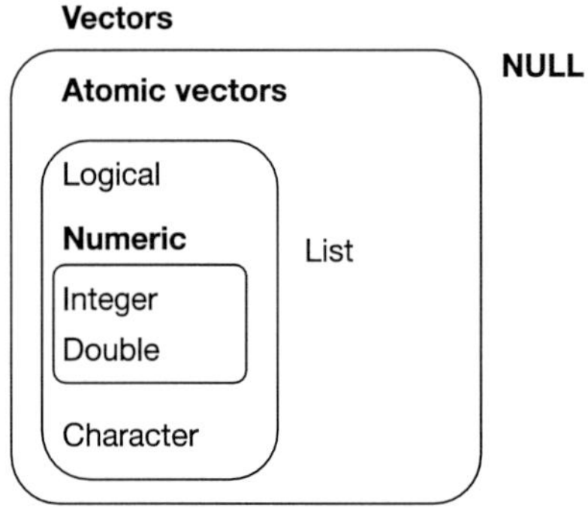

Fig. 6.1: Types of vectors

6.2 | CREATING A VECTOR

Vectors can be created in different ways. They are most commonly created using the combine function, which allows users to combine values into a vector.

(a) The combine function `c()` can be used to form a vector.

```
> apple <- c("red","pink","green")          # Create a vector
> print(apple)
> print(class(apple))                        # Obtain and display the class of
the vector
```

When we execute the above code, we obtain the following output:

```
[1] "red"    "pink" "green"
[1] "character"
```

(b) The : operator can also be used to create a vector of consecutive numbers.

```
> x <- 11:17; x
[1] 11 12 13 14 15 16 17
> y <- 2:-4; y
[1]  2  1  0 -1 -2 -3 -4
```

(c) More complex sequences, such as defining the number of points in an interval or the step size, can be created using the `seq()` function.

```
>vec=seq(1, 13, by=2)             # Specify step size
>vec
1]  1  3  5  7  9 11 13

> vec=seq(1, 15, length.out=5)    # Specify the length of the vector
>vec
[1]  1.0  4.5  8.0 11.5 15.0

> vec <- c(11, 25, 34, 99, 00, 67)
> typeof(vec)
[1] "double"
> length(vec)   # Displays the length of the vector
[1] 6
>str(vec) # Displays the complete structure of the R object with details
of variables and its data types
num [1:6] 11 25 34 99 00 67

> vec <- c(11, 15.4, TRUE, "java")
> vec
[1] "11"      "15.4"    "TRUE"   "java"
> typeof(vec)
[1] "character"
```

When you add elements, you are reassigning the vector. For example, we can append the numbers 11:15 to our vector:

```
> x <- c([1:10])
> x
[1] 1 2 3 4 5 6 7 8 9 10
```

Now, let us reassign x by adding the numbers 11 through 15 to it. We are taking x and then appending (concatenating) the sequence 11, 12, 13, 14, 15 to the 10-element vector to produce a 15-element vector we have stored as x.

```
> x <- c(x, 11:15)
> x
[1] 1 2 3 4 5 6 7 8 9 10 11 12 13 14 15
```

R allows programmers to name the data elements of a vector. Naming in R is just a way of attaching labels to the vector elements to avoid ambiguity and to make the program more readable. R uses the `names()` function to name the vector elements.

```
> remain <- c(11,14,10,15)
> shapes <- c("spades", "hearts", "diamonds", "clubs")
>names(remain)<-shapes
>remain
spades    hearts diamonds    clubs
      11        14        10              15
```

The `min()`, `max()`, `which.max()` and `which.min()` functions are used to find the maximum and minimum values of a vector and their position in the vector.

```
> vec<-c(34,2,1,33)
> vec
[1] 34  2  1 33
> min(vec)
[1] 1
> max(vec)
[1] 34
> which.max(vec)    # Position of maximum value in vector
[1] 1
> which.min(vec)    # Position of minimum value in vector
[1] 3
```

6.3 | ACCESSING THE ELEMENTS OF A VECTOR

Often, we may want to access only some of the vector elements or perhaps an individual element of a vector. This can be accomplished by using square brackets [ ] with vectors and is called indexing a vector. R offers flexibility in indexing a vector. You can use a logical, integer or character vector for indexing. The position of the vector elements starts with 1 (and not 0, as in some other languages).

- Passing a vector of positive numbers as indexing elements returns the vector containing the elements at those locations.

- Passing a vector of negative numbers as indexing elements returns the vector containing the elements everywhere except at those locations.
- Passing a logical vector as indexing elements returns the vector containing elements where the index is TRUE.
- For named vectors, passing a character vector of names as indexing elements returns the slice of the vector containing the elements with those names only.

These options are explained below with examples.

6.3.1 Integer Vector Index

As mentioned earlier, unlike in most programming languages, the vector index in R starts from 1. To access a specific vector element, positive/negative indexing can be used. A vector of integers can also be used as an index to access specific elements. Negative integers used for indexing a vector will return all the elements except those at the specified locations. While specifying indexes, we cannot mix positive and negative integer values. Real numbers used for indexing are truncated to integers.

```
> tmp=c(0 , 12 , 42 , 63 , 84 ,90)
> tmp
[1]  0  12  42  63  84  90
> tmp[4]              # Access the fourth element
[1] 63
> tmp[c(2, 5)]        # Access the second and fifth elements
[1] 12  84
> tmp[-1]             # Access all but the first element
[1]  12  42  63  84  90
> tmp[c(2, -4)]       # It is an error as you cannot mix positive and
negative integers
Error in x[c(2, -4)] : only 0s may be mixed with negative subscripts
> tmp[c(2.4, 3.54)]      # Real numbers are truncated to integers, so it
accesses the second and third elements
[1] 12  42
```

6.3.2 Logical Vector Index

Specifying logical values as index values for accessing vector elements helps us filter through a vector. Vector elements at positions where the logical vector specified as indexing is TRUE are returned.

```
> temp=c(-1 ,- 2 , 4 , 6 )
> temp[c(TRUE, FALSE, TRUE, FALSE)]
[1] -1  4

> temp[temp < 0]
[1] -1 -2
> temp[temp > 0]
[1] 4 6
```

In the above example, the expression `temp>0` will result in a logical vector (`FALSE`, `FALSE`, `TRUE`, `TRUE`), which is then used for indexing the `temp` vector.

6.3.3 Character Vector Index

Each element of a vector can be named to create an index. When dealing with named vectors, this type of indexing is useful.

```
> tmp <- c("first"=3, "second"=0, "third"=9)
> names(tmp)
[1] "first"  "second" "third"
> tmp["second"]
second
0

> tmp[c("first", "third")]
first third
3     9
```

You can assign names to vector values in the following way:

```
>v=c("sandhya","latesh")
>v
[1]"sandhya" "latesh"
```

We now name the first member as `First`, and the second member as `Last`.

```
>names(v)=c("First", "Last")
>v
First     Last
"sandhya""latesh"
>v["First"]
[1]"sandhya"
>v[c("Last", "First")]
Last   First
"latesh" "sandhya"
```

6.3.4 Out-of-Range Vector Index

If an index is out of range, NA will be reported for the missing value.

```
>s[10]
[1]NA
```

6.3.5 Duplicate Index

Using duplicate values while indexing in a vector is allowed in R. This results in the retrieval of a member multiple times in the vector. The following code retrieves a vector element twice in a single operation.

```
>tmp<-c("aa","bb","cc")
> tmp[c(2, 3, 3)]
[1] "bb" "cc" "cc"
```

6.4 | VECTOR MANIPULATION AND VECTOR ARITHMETIC

A vector can be modified using the assignment operator. Reassignments can be used to truncate the elements of a vector.

```
> x
[1] 1 5 4 9 0
> x[2] <- 6; x          # Modify the second element
[1] 1 6 4 9 0
> x[x<5] <- 15
> x
[1] 15  5 15  9  15  # Modify elements less than 5
> x <- x[1:3]; x        # Truncate x to the four elements
[1] 1 5 4
```

6.4.1 Vector Arithmetic

Vector arithmetic operations are performed member by member. In the following code, two vectors, a and b, are used to explain vector arithmetic.

```
>a=c(1, 3, 5, 7)
>b=c(1,2,4,8)
```

Vector a multiplied by 5, that is, 5*a, will result in the multiplication of all elements of vector a by 5.

```
> 5* a
[1] 5 15 25 35
```

Adding a to b, that is, a + b, will result in a vector whose members are the sum of the corresponding members of a and b.

Other mathematical operations are explained below:

```
> a + b
[1] 2 5 9 15
> a-b
[1] 0 1 1 -1

> a * b
[1] 1 6 20 56

> a / b
[1] 1.000 1.500 1.250 0.875
```

```
>prod(a)      # Multiplication of all elements of a vector
[1] 105

>sum(a)    # Sum of all elements of a vector
[1] 16

>length(a)   # Length of a vector
[1] 4
```

6.4.2 Vector Element Recycling

We can perform arithmetic operations on vectors of unequal length as well. When two vectors of unequal length are used for operations, the shorter one will be recycled. In other words, the values of the shorter vector will be repeated to match the length of the longer vector. In the example given below, vectors `tmp1` and `tmp2` are of different lengths, so their sum is computed by recycling the values of the shorter vector.

```
> tmp1=c(1 , 2 , 4 , 6 )
> tmp2=c(3, 5)
> tmp1+tmp2
[1]  4  7  7 11
```

In R programming, vectors have a function `rep()` that enables the user to create a vector with repeating elements as specified in its parameter.

```
>rep(11:15,3)
[1] 11 12 13 14 15 11 12 13 14 15 11 12 13 14 15
>rep(11:15,each=3)
[1] 11 11 11 12  12 12 13 13 13 14 14 14 15 15 15
>rep(1:5, length.out=7)
[1] 1 2 3 4 5 1 2
```

6.4.3 Combining Vectors

The `c()` function can be used to combine the given vectors. For example, the two vectors `tmp1` and `tmp2` are combined into a new vector, which contains elements from both the vectors.

```
>tmp1 =c(12, 23, 25)
>tmp2=c("aaa","abb","acc","add","aee")
>c(tmp1, tmp2)
[1]"12" "23" "25" "aaa" "abb" "acc" "add" "aee"
```

6.4.4 Value Coercion

A vector in R can only hold elements of the same type, which means that users cannot have a vector that contains both logical and numeric types. If a user wants to build a mixed vector that contains both integers and characters, then R automatically performs coercion to force that vector to contain elements of only one type.

In the code snippet below, when the two vectors are combined, to maintain the same primitive data type for members in the combined vector, the numeric element values of one vector are coerced into character strings, as specified in the second vector.

```
>draw <- c(23,43, "A",13,"B")
>draw
[1] "23" "43" "A" "13" "B"
```

6.5 | DELETING A VECTOR

A vector can be deleted by assigning NULL to it.

```
> tmp
[1] -3 -2 -1  0  1  2
> tmp <- NULL
> tmp
NULL
> tmp[4]
NULL
```

6.6 | VECTOR ELEMENT SORTING

The `sort()` function can be used to sort the elements of a vector in either ascending or descending order.

```
>tmp <- c(3,8,4,5,0,11, -9, 304)

# Sort the elements of the vector in default ascending order
>sort.result <- sort(tmp)
>sort.result
[1]  -9   0   3   4   5   8  11 304

# Sort the elements in descending order
>revsort.result <- sort(tmp, decreasing = TRUE)
>revsort.result
[1] 304  11   8   5   4   3   0  -9

# Sorting character vectors in default order
>tmpc <- c("Red","Blue","yellow","violet")
>sort.result <- sort(tmpc)
>sort.result
[1] "Blue"   "Red"    "violet" "yellow"

# Sorting character vectors in descending order
>revsort.result <- sort(tmpc, decreasing = TRUE)
>revsort.result
[1] "yellow" "violet" "Red"    "Blue"
```

EXERCISES

Multiple Choice Questions

1. When using the minus operator for subsetting a named vector, you can use the command:
   a. `x1[-c(4,1)]`
   b. `x1[c(-2,4)]`
   c. `x1[c("a","b","c")]`
   d. All of the above
2. How would you subset the first element of a given vector `x <- c(10, 20, 30)`?
   a. `x(1)` b. `x[1]`
   c. `x[0]` d. `X[1]`
3. What is the class of vector x defined as `x <- c(3,4, "A", TRUE)`?
   a. Numeric
   b. Character
   c. Logical
   d. None of the above, it is an error
4. For a vector `x<-1:4` and `y <- 2:3`, if you add x and y, what will be the output?
   a. A numeric vector of 3,5,3,4
   b. A numeric vector of 3,5,5,7
   c. A numeric vector of 1,2,5,7
   d. None of the above
5. Given a vector `x<- c(3,5,1,10,12,6)`. Which of the following will be used to set all the elements of this vector that are less than 5 to be equal to -5?
   a. `x[x<5] <- -5`
   b. `x[x==5] <- -5`
   c. `x[x<5] ==-5`
   d. `x[x==0]`
6. Which one of the following is the correct outcome of the command `c(1,2,3,4)/c(1,2,2,4)*c(2,1,3,2)**c(1,2,3,3)-c(2,2,32,5)`?
   a. `0.0 0.0 -18.5 1.0`
   b. `0.0 -1.0 8.5 3.0`
   c. `-1.000 0.000 -30.875 -4.250`
   d. `Error:...`
7. Which one of the following is the correct outcome of the command `>c(9,16,6,20)/c(3,4)+c(4,2,4,2)^c(2,3)+c(2,4,8,6)/c(2,2)- c(3,8,2,4)*c(3,1)`?
   a. `11 6 16 12`
   b. `9 2 8 6`
   c. `-23 -14 -24 -10`
   d. None of the above
8. Which one of the following commands will give a result without a warning?
   a. `c(1,3,5,7)^c(8,9,4) - c(2,3,4,5)**c(12,3,14,5)- c(240,30, 76,98)/c(8,3)`
   b. `c(1,3,5,7)^c(8,4) - c(2,3,4,5)**c(12,3,14,5)- c(240,30, 76,98)/c(8,3)`
   c. `c(1,3,5,7)^c(8,4) - c(2,3,4,5)**c(12,3,5)- c(240,30, 76,98)/c(8,3)`
   d. `c(1,3,5,7)^c(8,9,4,7) - c(2,3,4,5)**c(12,3,14,5)- c(240,30, 76,98)/c(8,3,7)`
9. Which one of the following is the correct outcome of the command `>sqrt(c(2,6,7,8)*c(4,2,2,4)+c(2,4,2,4)*c(-2,2)+c(1,2,4,4)**c(9,2,4,1))`?
   a. `2.236068 4.898979 16.309506 6.633250`
   b. `3.605551 4.898979 5.099020 6.633250`
   c. `3.605551 2.828427 16.552945 5.291503`
   d. `Error:...`
10. Which one of the following is the correct outcome of the command `>c(1,2,1,2)*-c(1,2,-1,-2)**c(-1,-2,1,2)*-c(1,2,-1,-2)`?
    a. `1 1 1 16`
    b. `1 1 1 -16`
    c. `-1 -16 1 16`
    d. `-1 -1 -1 -16`
11. Which one of the following is the correct outcome of the command `>c(5,6,7,8)%/%4-c(64,64,24,24)%/%c(4,3,5,7)+c(153,646,817,788)%%c(71, 63)`?

a. `4 4 33 31`
b. `-4 -4 -33 -31`
c. `-4 -4 33 31`
d. `4 4 -33 -31`

12. Which one of the following is the correct outcome of the command
```
>min(c(98,88,44,76)**c(-2,
3))/ min(c(49, 44,22,38)
^c(-2,-3))-prod(c(1,2,1,2)
^c(1,2))/max(c(9,4,4,9,26)
*min(c(4,3,2,6)))+max(c
(22,23,24,25)^c(2,3))?
```
a. `-16680439`
b. `16680439`
c. `15633.56`
d. None of the above

13. Which one of the following is the correct outcome of the command
```
>round(prod(c(1,2,1,2)^c(1,
2)) * sum(c(1,2,1,2)^c(2,3))
+prod(c(1,2,1,2)^c(1,2,3,7))
+
ceiling(c(5,6,7,8)^c(2,3)))?
```
a. `-199 -8 -175 288`
b. `825 1016 849 1312`
c. `-825 1016 -849 1312`
d. None of the above

14. Which one of the following is the correct outcome of the command
```
>floor(c(5,6,7,8)^c(2,3))-
ceiling(c(5,6,7,8)^c(2,3))+
ceiling(c(2,3,4,5)^-c(1,-2))
-round(c(5,6,7,8)^c(2,3)) +
floor(c(5,6,7,8)^c(2,3))?
```
a. `51 441 99 1049`
b. `1 9 1 25`
c. `-1 -9 -1 -25`
d. None of the above

15. Which one of the following is the correct outcome of the command
```
>ceiling(c(4,8,4,5)^-c(3,9)
+ sqrt(c(36,16,81,64)**c(2,3
))*sqrt(c(2,3,4,5)^-c(1,2))
+ round(c(4,7,8,9)*round
(c(7,9))))?
```
a. `54 85 97 184`
b. `-2 -41 -15 22`
c. `3 42 16 -21`
d. None of the above

16. Which one of the following is the correct outcome of the command
```
>ceiling(prod(c(2,3,8,9))-
sum(c(2,22,23,24,151)))
- floor(prod(c(2,3,8,9))+
round(c(2,22,23,24,151)))?
```
a. `-220 -200 -199 -198 -71`
b. `640 620 619 618 491`
c. `-224 -244 -245 -246 -373`
d. None of the above

17. Which one of the following is the value of `X2` when the following commands are executed over the R Console?
```
>X1 <- c(23,25,18,24)
>X2 <- sqrt(X1^2)+X1*6/X1^2-
X1**(1/2)+abs(X1)
```
a. `41.46504 45.24000 32.09069 43.35102`
b. `40.94330 44.76000 31.42403 42.85102`
c. `-4.534962 -4.760000 -3.909307 -4.648979`
d. None of the above

18. Which one of the following is the correct outcome of the command
```
>c(21,22,24,34)^c(-3,-
2,2,3)/c(4,3,2,1) + c(2,4,
1,6)%/%c(3,4)*c(2,5,3,6)
+ max(c (20,140,114,215)
^c(1,2)) /min(c(6,2,7,15)
^c(2,2))?
```
a. `5.000027 10.000689 293.000000 39315.000000`
b. `11556.25 11551.25 11844.25 50854.25`
c. `11556.25 11561.25 11844.25 50866.25`
d. None of the above

19. Which one of the following is the correct outcome of the command `>sort (c(15,55,18,32,97,71,82,42, 66), decreasing = FALSE)`?
a. `[1] 1 5 2 3 9 7 8 4 6`
b. `[1] 6 4 8 7 9 3 2 5 1`
c. `[1] 15 18 32 42 55 66 71 82 97`
d. `[1] 97 82 71 66 55 42 32 18 15`

20. Which one of the following is the correct outcome of the command `>order(c(15,55,18,32,97,71,82,42,66), decreasing = FALSE)`?
    a. `[1] 15 18 32 42 55 66 71 82 97`
    b. `[1] 97 82 71 66 55 42 32 18 15`
    c. `[1]1 3 4 8 2 9 6 7 5`
    d. `[1] 5 7 6 9 2 8 4 3 1`
21. Which one of the following is the correct outcome of the command `>mode(c(10, 20, "30", 80+90, "70+90", 16.7, 10*5))`?
    a. Character b. Numeric
    c. List d. Data frame

Answers

1. a	**2.** b	**3.** b	**4.** b	**5.** a	**6.** b	**7.** a	**8.** b	**9.** a	**10.** b
11. c	**12.** c	**13.** b	**14.** b	**15.** a	**16.** c	17.a	**18.** c	**19.** c	**20.** c
21. a									

Programming/Concept-based Questions

1. Write the commands in R for selecting all the vector elements, except a few.
2. Consider a scenario where the user decides to splurge his/her earnings by shopping, spends some money every day, and records the day-wise expenses in a vector. Calculate the day-wise savings using vector subtraction.
3. Perform the following in R:
    a. Create a vector of length 5 containing values as TRUE or FALSE
    b. Create another vector of 4 numeric values
    c. Create a vector containing the names of three students
    d. For each of the vectors created above, check for the class they belong to and their length
4. Create a vector of T1 marks in maths, science and chemistry. Specify a name for the mark value. Create another vector of T2 marks. Find the total marks of a student in T1 and T2.
5. Create a vector of T1 marks in maths, science and chemistry. Specify a name for the mark value. Create another vector of T2 marks. Calculate the improvement in the student's performance.

CHAPTER

7 Matrices

Objectives

At the end of this chapter, you will be able to

- Define a matrix and explain how to create matrices in R
- Explain coercion and subsetting of matrices
- Explain the arithmetic operations on matrices and arrays
- Describe the special matrices in R
- Perform calculation of eigenvalues and eigenvectors of matrices

7.1 | CREATING A MATRIX

A matrix is a two-dimensional R object whose elements contain values of the same atomic data type. Matrices can be created using numeric, character or logical data. A matrix is also a vector in R, but a vector is not a one-column or one-row matrix. The basic syntax for creating a matrix in R is as follows:

```
matrix(data, nrow, ncol, byrow, dimnames)
```

where `data` refers to the input data vector from which the matrix is to be created; `nrow` is the number of rows in the matrix; `ncol` is the number of columns in the matrix; `byrow` is a logical value that indicates how input data should be arranged – TRUE indicates that the input vector elements must be arrange by row; and `dimnames` refers to the names of the rows and columns.

```
> M = matrix( c('aa','aa','ab','ac','ab','aa'), nrow = 2, ncol = 3, byrow
= TRUE)   # Create a matrix.
> print(M)
```

When we execute the above code, we obtain the following output:

```
     [,1]  [,2]  [,3]
[1,] "aa"  "aa"  "ab"
[2,] "ac"  "ab"  "aa"
```

To arrange the data by column:

```
> data<-c(11,23,45,54,23,45)
> m<-matrix(data,nrow=3,ncol=2) # Default fill
method is by column, that is, byrow = FALSE
> m
```

Output:

```
     [,1] [,2]
[1,]   11   54
[2,]   23   23
[3,]   45   45
```

The default fill method of the `matrix()` function is `byrow = FALSE`; that is, it fills data by column rather than by row.

From the above examples, it is clear that the user cannot have logical and numerical values in the same matrix. It is a natural extension of the vector, going from one to two dimensions.

```
>class(m)
[1] "matrix"
```

Apart from the `matrix()` function, there is another easy way to create matrices that is more intuitive. The user can paste vectors together using the `cbind()` and `rbind()` functions. The `cbind()` function – short for column bind – takes the vectors passed and sticks them together as if they were the columns of a matrix. The `rbind()` function – short for row bind – does the same thing but takes the input as rows and makes a matrix out of them.

```
>cbind(11:13, 11:13)
      [,1]  [,2]
[1,]    11    11
[2,]    12    12
[3,]    13    13

>rbind(11:13,11:13)
      [,1]  [,2]  [,3]
[1,]    11    12    13
[2,]    11    12    13


> data<-c(11,23,45,54,23,45)
> m=matrix(data, byrow=TRUE, nrow=2)
> m
     [,1] [,2] [,3]
[1,]   11   23   45
[2,]   54   23   45

> rbind(m,7:9)
      [,1]  [,2]  [,3]
[1,]    11    23    45
[2,]    54    23    45
[3,]     7     8     9

> cbind(m,c(10,11))
     [,1]  [,2]  [,3] [,4]
[1,]   11    23    45   10
[2,]   54    23    45   11
```

We can assign names to columns and rows using the `colnames()` and `rownames()` functions, respectively.

```
> m=matrix(11:16, byrow=TRUE, nrow=2)
> m
      [,1]  [,2]  [,3]
[1,]    11    12    13
[2,]    14    15    16

> rownames(m)<-c("row1","row2")
> m
      [,1]  [,2]  [,3]
row1    11    12    13
row2    14    15    16

> colnames(m)<-c("col1","col2","col3")
> m
      col1  col2  col3
row1    11    12    13
row2    14    15    16
```

We can convert a vector into a matrix using the `as.matrix()` function, as shown below.

```
>c <- c(1,2,3,4,5,6,7,8,9)
>c
 [1] 1 2 3 4 5 6 7 8 9

>c <- as.matrix(c)         # Creates a matrix of dimensions 9 x 1
[,1]
 [1,]    1
 [2,]    2
 [3,]    3
 [4,]    4
 [5,]    5
 [6,]    6
 [7,]    7
 [8,]    8
 [9,]    9
>class(c)
[1] "matrix"
>dim(c)
[1] 9 1
```

The vector `c` has 9 rows and 1 column.

7.2 | COERCION OF MATRIX ELEMENTS

If we try to store different data types in a matrix, coercion automatically takes place. Given below is an example of two different types of data elements in a matrix. Numeric matrix elements are coerced to characters, and thus, the resultant matrix is one that contains only characters.

```
> tmp <- c('a','b','c')
> tmp
[1] "a" "b" "c"
> t1 <- matrix(tmp, nrow=3)
> t1
     [,1]
[1,] "a"
[2,] "b"
[3,] "c"
> t2 <- matrix(1:6,nrow=3)
> t2
     [,1] [,2]
[1,]    1    4
[2,]    2    5
[3,]    3    6
> cbind(t1,t2)
     [,1] [,2] [,3]
[1,] "a"  "1"  "4"
[2,] "b"  "2"  "5"
[3,] "c"  "3"  "6"
```

7.3 | MATRIX SUBSETTING

There may be situations where we want to select a single element or entire sections of a matrix. Individual matrix elements can be accessed using the rules of square-bracket selection.

```
> m<-matrix(sample(1:15,12),nrow=3)
> m
     [,1] [,2] [,3] [,4]
[1,]   14   11    2   12
[2,]   13    9   10    6
[3,]    8    1    5    4
> m[1,3]          # Referencing the element of row 1, column 3
[1] 2
> m[3,2]          # Referencing the element of row 3, column 2
[1] 1
> m[,2]           # Referencing all the elements of column 2
[1] 11  9  1
> m[2,]           # Referencing all the elements of row 2
[1] 13  9 10  6
```

7.4 | MATRIX OPERATIONS

A matrix can be modified by applying various operations on it. Addition, multiplication, inverse and transpose are some commonly used operations.

7.4.1 Transposition

Transposition, using the function `t()`, changes the rows of a matrix to columns and the columns to rows.

```
> t2
     [,1] [,2]
[1,]    1    4
[2,]    2    5
[3,]    3    6
> t(t2)
     [,1] [,2] [,3]
[1,]    1    2    3
[2,]    4    5    6
```

Vectors can also be transposed. Here, a column vector is simply converted into a row vector.

```
> tmp
[1] "a" "b" "c"
> t(tmp)
     [,1] [,2] [,3]
[1,] "a"  "b"  "c"
> dim(t(tmp))
[1] 1 3
```

7.4.2 Inverse Matrices

The inverse of a matrix can be evaluated as:

```
>A <- matrix( c(5, 1, 0,3,-1, 2,4, 1,-1), nrow=3, byrow=TRUE)
  >det(A)
[1] 6
```

The inverse matrix function is available in the `matlib` library. It can be installed using the following command:

```
>install.package("matlib")
```

The basic criterion to be satisfied for a matrix to have an inverse is `det(A)  != 0`. Inverse exists only for non-singular matrices.

```
> library(matlib)
> inv(A)
```

Inverse can also be obtained for square matrices.

```
> m<-matrix(1:6,nrow=2,ncol=3)
> m
     [,1] [,2] [,3]
[1,]    1    3    5
[2,]    2    4    6

> solve(m[,2:3])    # Inverse matrix
     [,1] [,2]
[1,]   -3  2.5
[2,]    2 -1.5
> solve(A)
       [,1]    [,2]   [,3]
[1,] 0.0625  0.0625  0.125
[2,] 0.6875 -0.3125 -0.625
[3,] 0.2500  0.2500 -0.500
```

7.4.3 Matrix Algebra

Matrix algebra is basically the same as scalar algebra (with the exception of division), and obeys the same rules as that of scalar algebra.

Addition The addition of the elements of matrices A and B is only possible if the matrices have the same number of rows and columns (the matrices should have the same shape). Otherwise, it produces an error message.

```
> t1<-matrix(1:6, nrow=3,ncol=2)
> t1
     [,1] [,2]
[1,]    1    4
[2,]    2    5
[3,]    3    6
> t2<-matrix(7:12,nrow=3,ncol=2)
> t2
     [,1] [,2]
[1,]    7   10
[2,]    8   11
[3,]    9   12

> t1+t2
     [,1] [,2]
[1,]    8   14
[2,]   10   16
[3,]   12   18
```

Scalar multiplication This involves multiplying each element of a matrix by a scalar value.

```
> h=.5*t1    # Scalar multiplication
> h
     [,1] [,2]
[1,]  0.5  2.0
[2,]  1.0  2.5
[3,]  1.5  3.0
```

The * operator is used for element-by-element multiplication of identically shaped matrices:

```
>h<-t1*t2
> h
     [,1] [,2]
[1,]    7   40
[2,]   16   55
[3,]   27   72
```

Matrix multiplication In the multiplication of matrices A and B, the use of the %*% operator results in a set of sums and cross-products, which require the number of columns of the first matrix to be equal to the number of rows of the second matrix. The product matrix C will have the same number of rows as the first matrix and the same number of columns as the second matrix. If this condition is false, it produces an error message.

```
> a<-matrix(1:6, nrow=3,ncol=2)
> a
     [,1] [,2]
[1,]    1    4
[2,]    2    5
[3,]    3    6
> b<-matrix(7:12,ncol=3,nrow=2)
> b
     [,1] [,2] [,3]
[1,]    7    9   11
[2,]    8   10   12
> c<- a%*%b      # Matrix multiplication
> c
     [,1] [,2] [,3]
[1,]   39   49   59
[2,]   54   68   82
[3,]   69   87  105

> dim(a)
[1] 3 2
> dim(b)
[1] 2 3
```

7.5 | COMBINING MATRICES

Matrices can be combined using the `cbind()` and `rbind()` functions, which bind matrices together by columns and rows, respectively. They are also used to create a matrix from the given vector data (discussed earlier).

```
>anothermatrix<-matrix(seq.int(2,24,2),nrow=4,dimnames=
list(c("rowfive","rowsix","rowseven","roweight"),c("colone",
"coltwo","colthree")))
> print(anothermatrix)

          colone  coltwo  colthree
rowfive      2      10       18
rowsix       4      12       20
rowseven     6      14       22
roweight     8      16       24

>amatrix<-matrix(1:12,nrow=4,dimnames= list(c("rowone","rowtwo",
"rowthree","rowfour"),c("colfour","colfive","colsix")))
> print(amatrix)
          colfour colfive colsix
rowone       1       5       9
rowtwo       2       6      10
rowthree     3       7      11
rowfour      4       8      12
```

The cbind() and rbind() functions can be used for combining matrices by column and row:

```
>cbind(amatrix,anothermatrix)
        colfour colfive colsix colone coltwo colthree
rowone     1       5       9      2     10       18
rowtwo     2       6      10      4     12       20
rowthree   3       7      11      6     14       22
rowfour    4       8      12      8     16       24

>rbind(amatrix,anothermatrix)
         colfour colfive colsix
rowone      1       5       9
rowtwo      2       6      10
rowthree    3       7      11
rowfour     4       8      12
rowfive     2      10      18
rowsix      4      12      20
rowseven    6      14      22
roweight    8      16      24
```

7.6 | SPECIAL MATRICES

A number of special matrices are available in R. One of them is the diagonal matrix, which has non-zero values along the principal diagonal and 0 everywhere else.

```
# Diagonal matrix
> D <- diag(c(12,11,31), nrow=3, ncol=3)
> D
     [,1] [,2] [,3]
[1,]   12    0    0
[2,]    0   11    0
[3,]    0    0   31
```

The identity matrix is a special form of a diagonal matrix that has 1 along the principal diagonal and 0 everywhere else.

```
# Identity matrix
Iden <- diag(1, nrow=3, ncol=3)
> Iden
     [,1] [,2]  [,3]
[1,]    1    0    0
[2,]    0    1    0
[3,]    0    0    1
```

7.7 | EIGENVECTORS AND EIGENVALUES

Eigenvectors and eigenvalues are used in machine learning and data preparation. R has functions that can be used to compute the eigenvalue and eigenvectors of a given matrix.

```
> t1 <- matrix (.5:1.5, nrow=3, ncol=3)
> t1
     [,1] [,2] [,3]
[1,]  0.5  1.5  0.5
[2,]  1.5  0.5  1.5
[3,]  0.5  1.5  0.5
> eigen(t1)
eigen() decomposition
$values
[1]  2.886001e+00  1.332268e-15 -1.386001e+00

$vectors
           [,1]          [,2]       [,3]
[1,] -0.5284508  7.071068e-01  0.4698295
[2,] -0.6644392  1.580984e-15 -0.7473423
[3,] -0.5284508 -7.071068e-01  0.4698295
```

We can obtain the eigenvalue and eigenvectors using the `eigen()` function. This returns a named list, with eigenvalues as the named values and eigenvectors as the named vectors.

```
>ev <- eigen(t1)
# Extract components
>values <- ev$values
>values
[1]  2.886001e+00  1.332268e-15 -1.386001e+00

>vectors <- ev$vectors
>vectors
           [,1]          [,2]       [,3]
[1,] -0.5284508  7.071068e-01  0.4698295
[2,] -0.6644392  1.580984e-15 -0.7473423
[3,] -0.5284508 -7.071068e-01  0.4698295
```

The eigenvalues are always returned in decreasing order.

7.8 | ARRAYS

An array is a collection of values of similar data type. R provides commands for the easy design and management of arrays. Arrays can be treated as a special case of matrix formation.

While matrices are confined to two dimensions, arrays can be multidimensional. The `array()` function is used to create an array by passing vectors as input and by using the values in the `dim` parameter. The array dimension can be created using the `dim` attribute in the `array()` function. The basic syntax for creating an array in R is as follows:

```
array(data, dim, dimname)
```

where `data` comprises the input values to the vector; `dim` is used to create the dimension; and `dimname` is used to assign a name to `dim`.

You can use the command given below at the R prompt to create an array of two elements, where each element is a 3 x 3 matrix.

```
> a <- array(c('green','yellow'),dim = c(3,3,2))     # Create an array
>print(a)
```

When we execute the above code, we obtain the following result:

```
, , 1
     [,1]     [,2]     [,3]
[1,] "green"  "yellow" "green"
[2,] "yellow" "green"  "yellow"
[3,] "green"  "yellow" "green"
, , 2
     [,1]     [,2]     [,3]
[1,] "yellow" "green"  "yellow"
[2,] "green"  "yellow" "green"
[3,] "yellow" "green"  "yellow"
```

Here is another example.

```
> threedarray<-array(1:24,dim=c(4,3,2),dimnames= list(c("one","two",
"three","four"),c("col1","col2","col3"),c("dim1","dim2")))
> print(threedarray)
, , dim1
```

Output:

```
      col1 col2 col3
one      1    5    9
two      2    6   10
three    3    7   11
four     4    8   12
```

```
, , dim2

      col1 col2 col3
one     13   17   21
two     14   18   22
three   15   19   23
four    16   20   24
```

A matrix can also be created by using the `array()` function. The following two-dimensional array and matrix are identical.

```
>amatrix<-matrix(1:12,nrow=4,dimnames=
list(c("one","two","three","four"),c("col1","col2","col3")))
> print(amatrix)
      col1 col2 col3
one      1    5    9
two      2    6   10
three    3    7   11
four     4    8   12

>twodarray<-array(1:12,dim=c(4,3),dimnames=
list(c("one","two","three","four"),c("col1","col2","col3")))
> print(twodarray)
      col1 col2 col3
one      1    5    9
two      2    6   10
three    3    7   11
four     4    8   12

>identical(amatrix, twodarray)
[1] TRUE
```

7.8.1 Rows, Columns and Dimensions

For both matrices and arrays, various functions work in a similar fashion. The `dim()` function returns a vector of integers of the dimensions of the variable specified.

```
>dim(threedarray)
[1] 4 3 2
>dim(amatrix)
[1] 4 3
```

The `nrow()`, `ncol()`, `rownames()`, `colnames()` and `length()` functions work for both arrays and matrices as follows:

```
>nrow(amatrix)
[1] 4
>ncol(amatrix)
[1] 3
>nrow(threedarray)
[1] 4
>ncol(threedarray)
[1] 3

>length(amatrix)
[1] 12
>length(threedarray)
[1] 24

>rownames(amatrix)
[1] "one"   "two"   "three" "four"
>colnames(threedarray)
[1] "ein"  "zwei" "drei"
```

7.8.2 Array Arithmetic

The standard arithmetic operations (+, –, *, /) work element-wise on matrices and arrays, just as they do on vectors.

```
>amatrix+anothermatrix
      col1 col2 col3
one      3   15   27
two      6   18   30
three    9   21   33
four    12   24   36

>amatrix*anothermatrix
      col1  col2  col3
one      2    50   162
two      8    72   200
three   18    98   242
four    32   128   288

>t(amatrix)
     one two three four
col1   1   2     3    4
col2   5   6     7    8
col3   9  10    11   12
```

The special operators, %*% and %o%, are used for inner and outer matrix multiplication, respectively. In each case, the dimension names are taken from the first input, if such input exists.

```
>amatrix %*% t(amatrix)    # Inner multiplication
      one   two  three  four
one   107   122   137   152
two   122   140   158   176
three 137   158   179   200
four  152   176   200   224

>1:3 %o% 4:6         # Outer multiplication
Or
>outer(1:3,4:6)

     [,1] [,2] [,3]
[1,]    4    5    6
[2,]    8   10   12
[3,]   12   15   18
```

EXERCISES

Multiple Choice Questions

1. Given `y <- matrix(nrow=2,ncol =3,1:6)`, the code to generate matrix y, how would you subset the second row?
   a. `y[nrow=2]` b. `y[2]`
   c. `y[,2]` d. `y[2,]`
2. Which of the following are the uses of matrices?
   a. In solving linear equations
   b. Image processing
   c. Graph theory
   d. All of the above
3. Matrix A when multiplied with Matrix C gives the identity matrix I. What is C?
   a. Identity matrix b. Inverse of A
   c. Square of A d. Transpose of A
4. What would be the output of the following code?
   ```
   > x <- matrix(1:6, 2, 3)
   > x[1, 2]
   ```
   a. 3 b. 2
   c. 1 d. 0
5. What would be the output of the following code?
   ```
   > x <- matrix(1:6, 2, 3)
   > x[1, ]
   ```
   a. 1 3 5 b. 2 3 5
   c. 3 3 5 d. `file`
6. Which of the following code options extracts the second column for the matrix given below?
   ```
   > x <- matrix(1:6, 2, 3)
   ```
   a. `x[2, ]` b. `x[1, 2]`
   c. `x[, 2]` d. All of the above
7. Which of the following is applicable to a matrix?
   a. A matrix is one-dimensional
   b. A matrix has the same number of dimensions as a vector
   c. A matrix is two-dimensional
   d. A matrix is three-dimensional
8. How can a user subset one specific number from a matrix?
   a. Specify the row
   b. Specify the column
   c. Specify the row and the column
   d. Specify the parameter=1
9. What happens when a data sequence cannot fill up a matrix entirely?
   a. R will produce an error
   b. R will fill up the matrix column by column and repeat the data sequence
   c. R will fill up the matrix with NA values
   d. R will fill up a smaller matrix with only the specified data sequence in it

10. Which of the following is the correct outcome of the command `diag(5, nrow=2, ncol=2)`?

    a. `[5 0`
    `5 5]`

    b. `[0 5`
    `5 0]`

    c. `[5 5`
    `5 5]`

    d. `[5 0`
    `0 5]`

11. Which of the following is the correct outcome of the command `t(x)` for `x<-matrix(nrow=3, ncol=2, data=30:35, byrow=T)`?

    a.
    ```
         [,1] [,2] [,3]
    [1,]  30   32   34
    [2,]  31   33   35
    ```

    b.
    ```
         [,1] [,2]
    [1,]  30   31
    [2,]  32   33
    [3,]  34   35
    ```

    c.
    ```
         [,1] [,2]
    [1,]  30   33
    [2,]  31   34
    [3,]  32   35
    ```

    d. NA

12. Which of the following is the correct outcome of X[3 ,] for the matrix specified by `X<-matrix(nrow=3, ncol=3, data=c(10,20,30,40,50, 60,70,80,90), byrow=F)`?
    a. `[1] 30 60 90`
    b. `[1] 30 60 90 10`
    c. `[1] 10 20 30`
    d. None of the above

13. Which of the following is the correct command to obtain the matrix
    [20 30
    50 60
    80 90]
    from the matrix specified by `X<-matrix(nrow=4, ncol=3, data=c(10, 20,30,40, 50,60,70, 80,90, 100,110,120), byrow=T)`?
    a. `X[2:3, 1:3]`
    b. `X[1:3, 2:3]`
    c. `X[1:1, 2:2, 3:3]`
    d. `X[3:3, 2:2, 1:1]`

14. Which of the following is the correct command to obtain the multiplication of two matrices, `x` and `y`, of the same order?
    a. `x**y`
    b. `x*%*y`
    c. `x%*%y`
    d. `x%**%y`

Answers

1. d	**2.** d	**3.** b	**4.** a	**5.** a	**6.** c	**7.** c	**8.** c	**9.** b	**10.** d
11. b	**12.** a	**13.** b	**14.** c						

Programming/Concept-based Questions

1. Perform the following operations in R:
   a. Create a 2 x 3 matrix with values as 5
   b. Create a 2 x 3 matrix with values as 3
   c. Create a 2 x 3 x 2 array with the first level [,,1] populated with `mat1` (5s) and the second level [,,2] populated with `mat2` (3s)
   d. Display the array.
2. Convert vectors into an array of two 3 x 3 matrices. Give the appropriate `dimnames`.
3. Create an array and extract the third row of the second matrix of the array from Q2.
4. Create an array and extract the elements belonging to the first row and third column of the first array.
5. Create a matrix using the `rbind()` and `cbind()` functions.

CHAPTER

8 Lists

Objectives

At the end of this chapter, you will be able to

- Define and create a list in R
- Describe the list operations
- Explain how to access and manipulate the elements of a list
- Explain how to merge and apply functions to a list
- Explain how to create a recursive list and to sort and search lists

8.1 | INTRODUCTION TO LISTS

As we learnt earlier, an atomic vector is one where all the elements are of the same type. A vector that contains elements of different types is called a list. In R programming, a list is an object that contains different element types, such as numbers, strings and vectors. A list can also contain functions or matrices as its elements, making it functionally richer than other existing list utilities.

Lists can be obtained as return values from many functions such as `t.test()` and `lm()`, used in statistical modelling. We can also create customised lists to store useful information, such as grocery lists, shopping lists, lists of books, and so on. Most of these lists are simple and contain nominal and ordinal values, but in many cases, there is a need for storing complex data such as the configuration details of a phone. In such cases, the `list()` function of R can be used.

8.2 | CREATING A LIST

A list can be created using the `list()` function, which takes different R objects and stores their values in the database. In other words, a list is a generic vector that contains other objects as its elements.

For example, in the code given below, the variable `templist` contains copies of three vectors, `one`, `two` and `three`, and a numeric value, 32.

```
>one = c(2, 3, 5)
>two = c("a1", "b1", "c1", "d1", "e1" )
>three = c(TRUE, TRUE, TRUE, FALSE, FALSE )
>templist = list( one, two, three, 32) # x contains copies of one, two,
three
>templist
```

The following output will be generated:

```
[[1]]
[1] 2 3 5
[[2]]
[1] "a1" "b1" "c1" "d1" "e1"
[[3]]
[1] TRUE TRUE  TRUE FALSE FALSE
[[4]]
[1] 32
```

In the following example, a, b and c are called tags, which are optional. Tags make it easy for the user to refer to the components of a list.

```
> list("a" = 2.55, "b" = TRUE, "c" = 1:4)
$a
[1] 2.55
$b
[1] TRUE
$c
[1] 1 2 3 4
```

We can create the same list without tags as well. In such a scenario, numeric indices are used by default.

```
> x <- list(2.55,FALSE,1:4)
> x
[[1]]
[1] 2.55
[[2]]
[1] FALSE
[[3]]
[1] 1 2 3 4
```

Example 8.1: Create a list with a vector, matrix and list as its elements

Code:

```
>list_data<-list(c("Mon","Tue","Wed"),
matrix(c(13,19,15,11,-12,18),nrow=2),
list("color",12.33))
>names(list_data)<-c("First
quarter","AMatrix","Ainner list")
>list_data
```

Output:

```
$`First quarter`
[1] "Mon" "Tue" "Wed"

$`AMatrix`
     [,1] [,2] [,3]
[1,]   13   15  -12
[2,]   19   11   18

$`Ainner list`
$`Ainner list`[[1]]
[1] "color"

$`A inner list`[[2]]
[1] 12.33
```

8.3 | GENERAL LIST OPERATIONS

The `str()` function can be used to obtain the structure of a list. For example, the code given below displays the items of a list, along with their type and value:

```
> x<-list("a" = 2.55, "b" = TRUE, "c" = 1:4)
> str(x)
List of 3
$ a: num 2.55
$ b: logi TRUE
$ c: int [1:4] 1 2 3 4
```

8.4 | ACCESSING THE ELEMENTS OF A LIST

The elements present in a list can be accessed using the index value of that element. For a named list, the elements are accessed based on their names.

For example:

```
>list_data1<-list(c("janu","febu","march"), matrix(c(3,9,5,1,2,8),nrow=2),
list("green",12.36))
>list_data1[1]
[[1]]
[1] "janu" "febu" "march"
```

In the above code, to access the first element from `list_data`, the index value of the list is accessed, that is, `list_data[1]`. Here, the list elements are indexed starting from 1 and not from 0.

The elements of a list can also be accessed by appending the '$' sign to the name of the element. Hence, printing `list_data$AMatrix` gives the output of the second element in the named list given below. We can reference named list members by name instead of numeric index.

```
>list_data1<-list(c("janu","febu","march"),
matrix(c(13,19,15,11,12,18),nrow=2),list("green",12.3))
>names(list_data1)<-c(First quarter","AMatrix","A inner list")
>list_data1$AMatrix
      [,1]  [,2] [,3]
[1,]    13    15   12
[2,]    19    11   18
>list_data1["Amatrix"]    # Gives the same output as above
$AMatrix
      [,1]  [,2] [,3]
[1,]    13    15   12
[2,]    19    11   18
```

We can retrieve a slice from the list elements using an index vector. With an index vector, we can specify the elements that we want to use after slicing the list. Here, a slice contains the first and third members of `list_data`.

```
>list_data<-list(c("janu","febu","march"), matrix(c(3,9,5,1,2,8),nrow=2),
list("green",12.36))
>list_data[c(1,3)]
[[1]]
[1] "janu" "febu" "march"

[[2]]
[[2]][[1]]
[1] "green"

[[2]][[2]]
[1] 12.36
```

8.5 | MANIPULATING THE ELEMENTS OF A LIST

We can add, delete and update a list to manipulate its elements. Elements can be added and deleted only at the end of the list, whereas the update operation can be performed on any element in the list, irrespective of its position.

For example, the code given below creates a list `list_data1`, one element is added, another is deleted at the end and the third element is updated.

```
>list_data1 <- list(c("Jan","febu","march"), matrix(c(3,9,5,1,2,8,4,6),
nrow = 2),list("green",12.36))
>names(list_data1) <- c("First Quarter", "AMatrix", "A Inner list")

# Add an element at the end of the list
>list_data1[4] <- "Newly added element"
>print(list_data1[4])
[[1]]
[1] "Newly added element"

>list_data1
$`First quarter`
[1] "janu" "febu" "march"

$AMatrix
     [,1] [,2] [,3] [,4]
[1,]    3    5    2    4
[2,]    9    1    8    6

$`A inner list`
$`A inner list`[[1]]
[1] "green"
$`A inner list`[[2]]
[1] 12.36

[[4]]
[1] "New element"
```

```
# Remove the last element
>list_data1[4] <- NULL
>list_data1
$`First quarter`
[1] "janu" "febu" "march"

$AMatrix
     [,1] [,2] [,3] [,4]
[1,]    3    5    2    4
[2,]    9    1    8    6

$`A inner list`
$`A inner list`[[1]]
[1] "green"

$`A inner list`[[2]]
[1] 12.3

>list_data1[4]
$<NA>
NULL

# Update the third element
>list_data1[3] <- "newly updated element"
>list_data1
$`First quarter`
[1] "janu" "febu" "march"

$AMatrix
     [,1] [,2] [,3] [,4]
[1,]    3    5    2    4
[2,]    9    1    8    6

$`Ainner list`
[1] "newly updated element"

>list_data1[3]
$`A inner list`
[1] "newly updated element"
```

8.6 | MERGING LISTS

When you merge two or more lists, you place all the lists inside one single list, using the `list()` function.

For example, the code given below creates three lists: `list1`, `list2` and `list3`. These lists are merged into a single `merged.list`:

```
> list1 <- list(1,2,3)
> list2 <- list("Sunday","Monday","Tuesday")> list3<-c(4,5,6)

> # Merge the lists
> merged.list <- list(list1,list2, list3)
> merged.list

[[1]]
[[1]][[1]]
[1] 1

[[1]][[2]]
[1] 2

[[1]][[3]]
[1] 3

[[2]]
[[2]][[1]]
[1] "Sunday"

[[2]][[2]]
[1] "Monday"

[[2]][[3]]
[1] "Tuesday"

[[3]]
[1] 4 5 6
```

8.7 | APPLYING FUNCTIONS TO A LIST

We can apply functions or operations to individual elements ín a list using loops. However, there is a faster way to perform this operation. The `lapply()` function can be used for this purpose. It applies a specified function to the individual values in a list. The syntax is as follows:

```
lapply(LIST, FUNCTION, ...)
```

The following list variable is used for the examples given below:

```
>list1 <- list(observationA = c(1:5, 7:3), observationB=matrix(1:6,
nrow=2))
```

Example 8.2: Find the length of `list1`'s observations

Code:

```
>lapply(list1, length)
$observationA
[1] 10

$observationB
[1] 6
```

Example 8.3: Find the sum of the elements of `list1`'s observations

Code:

```
>lapply(list1, sum)
$observationA
[1] 40

$observationB
[1] 21
```

Example 8.4: Find the quantiles of `list1`

Code:

```
>lapply(list1, quantile)
$observationA
  0%  25%  50%  75% 100%
   1    3    4    5    7

$observationB
  0%  25%  50%  75%  100%
1.00 2.25 3.50 4.75 6.00
```

Example 8.5: Find the maximum of `list1`'s observations

Code:

```
>lapply(list1, max)
$observationA
[1] 7

$observationB
[1] 6
```

8.8 | RECURSIVE LIST

In R programming, we can create recursive lists or lists within lists. The example given below creates a two-component list, where each component is also a list.

```
> list1 <-list(tmp1=18,tmp2=56)
> list2 <-list(w="abc")
> rlist <-list(list1,list2)
> rlist
[[1]]
[[1]]$tmp1
[1] 18

[[1]]$tmp2
[1] 56

[[2]]
[[2]]$w
[1] "abc"

> length(rlist)
[1] 2
```

8.9 | SORTING AND SEARCHING

R has a package called `rlist` that can be installed using the command:

```
install.packages('rlist')
```

This package has many functions for lists such as `sort()`, `search()`, `reverse()`, `subset()`, `extract()`, `which()`, `group()`, `update()`, `insert()`, `rbind()`, `parse()`, `join()` and `match()`. The use of a few of these functions is illustrated below:

```
>install.packages('rlist')
>library(rlist)
> x <- list(p1 = list(type='A',score=list(c1=10,c2=8)),
+           p2 = list(type='B',score=list(c1=9,c2=9)),
+           p3 = list(type='B',score=list(c1=9,c2=7)))
> list.sort(x, type, (score$c2)) # Sort by score$c2 in descending order
$p1
$p1$type
[1] "A"

$p1$score
$p1$score$c1
[1] 10

$p1$score$c2largest element from list in R
[1] 8

$p2
$p2$type
[1] "B"

$p2$score
$p2$score$c1
[1] 9

$p2$score$c2
[1] 9

$p3
$p3$type
[1] "B"

$p3$score
$p3$score$c1
[1] 9

$p3$score$c2
[1] 7
```

```
> list.sort(x, min(score$c1,score$c2))
$p3
$p3$type
[1] "B"

$p3$score
$p3$score$c1
[1] 9

$p3$score$c2
[1] 7


$p1
$p1$type
[1] "A"

$p1$score
$p1$score$c1
[1] 10

$p1$score$c2
[1] 8


$p2
$p2$type
[1] "B"

$p2$score
$p2$score$c1
[1] 9

$p2$score$c2
[1] 9


> sort(c(13,11,71,55), decreasing = FALSE, index.return = TRUE)
$x    # Returns the sorted list (in increasing order)
[1] 11 13 55 71

$ix   # Returns the original index of each element
[1] 2 1 4 3
```

Searching in lists can be performed using the `list.search()` method of the `rlist` package. You can search for a specific value or more generally. You can specify the function parameter accordingly. In the example given below, we create a list `x`, which contains elements, and use the `list.search()` function to finds the value specified in its parameters. You can find any value or all values matching a specified parameter.

```
> x <- list(p1 = list(type='A',score=c(c1=9)),
+           p2 = list(type=c('A','B'),score=c(c1=8,c2=9)),
+           p3 = list(type=c('B','C'),score=c(c1=9,c2=7)),
+           p4 = list(type=c('B','C'),score=c(c1=8,c2=NA)))
>
> x
$p1
$p1$type
[1] "A"

$p1$score
c1
 9

$p2
$p2$type
[1] "A" "B"

$p2$score
c1 c2
 8  9

$p3
$p3$type
[1] "B" "C"

$p3$score
c1 c2
 9  7

$p4
$p4$type
[1] "B" "C"

$p4$score
c1 c2
 8 NA

> ## Search exact values
> list.search(x, identical(., 'A'))
$p1.type
[1] "A"

> list.search(x, identical(., c('A','B')))
$p2.type
[1] "A" "B"
```

```
> list.search(x, identical(., c(9,7)))
named list()
> list.search(x, identical(., c(c1=9,c2=7)))
$p3.score
c1 c2
 9  7

> ## Search all equal values
> list.search(x, all(. == 9))
$p1.score
c1
 9

> list.search(x, all(. == c(8,9)))
$p2.score
c1 c2
 8  9

> list.search(x, all(. == c(8,9), na.rm = TRUE))
$p2.score
c1 c2
 8  9

$p4.score
c1 c2
 8 NA

> ## Search any equal value
> list.search(x, any(. == 9))
$p1.score
c1
 9

$p2.score
c1 c2
 8  9

$p3.score
c1 c2
 9  7

> list.search(x, any(. == c(8,9)))
$p1.score
c1
 9
```

```
$p2.score
c1 c2
 8  9

$p4.score
c1 c2
 8 NA
```

Example 8.6: Write a function for bubble sorting of data

Code:

```
>basic_sort = function(v) {
  n <- length(v)
  for (i in 1:(n-1)) {
    for (j in (i+1):n) {
      if (v[i] > v[j]) {
        tmp = v[i]; v[i] = v[j]; v[j] = tmp
      }
    }
  }
  return(v)
}
>x<-c(3,2,4,1)
>basic_sort(x)
[1] 1 2 3 4
```

Example 8.7: Write a function for linear searching of data

Code:

```
>seq_search = function(v, t) {
  n <- length(v)
  for (i in 1:n) {
    if (abs(v[i] == t) ) {
      return(i)
    }
  }
  return(0)
}
>x<-c(3,2,4,5,1,8)
>v=20
>seq_search(x,v)
[1] 0
>v=2
>seq_search(x,v)
[1] 2
```

Example 8.8: Write a function to implement selection sort and insertion sort

Code: Selection sort

```
>sels <- function(x) {
  n <- length(x)
  for (i in 1:(n - 1)) {
    min <- i
    for (j in (i + 1):n) {
      if (x[j] < x[min]) {
        min <- j
      }
    }
    if (min != i) {
      temp   <- x[i]
      x[i]   <- x[min]
      x[min] <- temp
    }
  }
  x
}
```

Output:

```
d<-c(5,6,4,13,7)
sels(d)
[1]  4  5  6  7 13
```

Code: Insertion sort

```
>ins <- function(A){
    for (j in 2:length(A)) {
    key <- A[j]
    i = j - 1
    while (i > 0 && A[i] > key) {
      A[(i + 1)] <- A[i]
      i <- i - 1
    }
    A[(i + 1)] <- key
  }
  A
}
```

Output:

```
>ins(c(5,4,13,7,3,56))
[1]  3  4  5  7 13 56
```

Example 8.9: Write a function to implement binary search

Code:

```
>bin_search <- function(v, t) {
  lo = as.integer(1)
  hi = length(v)
  while (lo <= hi) {
    mid = as.integer(round((lo + hi) / 2))
# Always even!
    cat("lo, mid, hi = ", lo, mid, hi, "\n")

    if (v[mid] == t){
      return(mid)
    }
    else if (v[mid] < t) {
      lo = mid + 1
    }
    else {
      hi = mid - 1
    }
  }
    return(0)
  }
```

Output:

```
>   bin_search(c(11,
12, 13, 14,16),12)
lo, mid, hi =  1 3 5
lo, mid, hi =  1 2 2
[1] 2
```

EXERCISES

Multiple Choice Questions

1. Which one of the following is the correct outcome of the command `x[[3]]`, where `x <-list (c("class1", "class2", "class3"), seq(from=50, to=57), rep(28:30, each=3))`?
   a. `[1] "class1" class2" "class3"`
   b. `[1] 50 51 52 53 54 55 56 57`
   c. `[1] 28 28 28 29 29 29 30 30 30`
   d. `[1] "class3" 52 28`
2. Which one of the following is the correct outcome of the command `x[[2]][2]`, where `x <-list (c("class1", "class2", "class3"), seq(from=50, to=57), rep(28:30, each=3))`?
   a. `[1] "class2"`
   b. `[1] 51`
   c. `[1] 29`
   d. `[1] 50 51 52 53 54 55 56 57`
3. Which one of the following is the correct outcome of the command `x[2][2]`, where `x <-list (c("class1", "class2", "class3"), seq(from=50, to=57), rep(28:30, each=3))`?
   a. `51`
   b. `29`
   c. `NULL`
   d. `"class2"`
4. Which one of the following is the correct outcome of the command `x[2]`, where `x <-list (c("class1", "class2", "class3"), seq(from=50, to=57), rep(28:30, each=3))`?
   a. `[1] "class3"`
   b. `[1] 28 28 28 29 29 29 30 30 30`
   c. `[1] 52`
   d. `[1] 50 51 52 53 54 55 56 57`
5. Consider the list `z <- list(x1 = "class", x2 = 20:25)`. Which of the following is the correct command to change the element `x2` to `y2`?
   a. `names(z)[2]= y2`
   b. `names(z)[2]= "y2"`
   c. `names(y)[2]= "z2"`
   d. `names(y)[2]= z2`
6. Consider the list `z <- list(x1= "class", x2 = 20:25)`. Which of the following is the correct outcome of the command `z["x2"]`?
   a. `[1] "class"`
   b. `[1] "20:25"`
   c. `[1] 25 24 23 22 21 20`
   d. `[1] 20 21 22 23 24 25`

Answers

1. c	2. b	3. c	4. d	5. b	6. d

Programming/Concept-based Questions

1. Create a list called `skills`, which contains `top`, `con` and `prop`. Name the list elements as `topics`, `context` and `properties` using `names()`. Use the `str()` function to display the structure.
2. Create a list `list_tmp <- list(observationA1 = c(1:5, 7:3), observationB1=matrix(1:6, nrow=2))` and perform the following:
   a. Use `lapply()` to find the classes of `list_tmp's` sub-variables.

b. Create a function `derivative <- function(x) { log10(x) + 1 }`. Apply this to `list_tmp`.
c. Find the unique values and range in `list_tmp`.
d. Use `unlist()` and `lapply()` to convert `list_tmp` to a vector.

3. Use predefined lists for letters and month names and create your own list containing data from these.
4. Create list `> x = list("a"=6, "b"=9, "c"=3)`. Write the R command to sum all the elements of this list.

CHAPTER

9 Data Frames

Objectives

At the end of this chapter, you will be able to

- Define and create data frames in R programming language
- Extract data from data frames
- Expand data frame rows and columns, using the `cbind()` and `rbind()` functions
- Merge and sort data frames
- Apply functions to data frames using the `lapply()` and `sapply()` functions

9.1 | INTRODUCTION TO DATA FRAMES

R is a statistical programming language where data sets are used. Data sets typically comprise observations or instances that have some variables associated with them. For example, consider a data set of five people, where each person is an instance and the properties of each person, such as name, age and whether they have children, are the variables. A matrix cannot be used to store such information in R, as name would be a character and age would be numeric and these different values cannot be accommodated in a single matrix.

Data frame is the most significant concept in R programming. It is a fundamental data structure used to store data sets; it is similar to a spreadsheet that has rows and columns, where each column can be a different vector. Hence, it is not necessary to have a data frame composed only of numbers – it can include numbers, characters, text, and so on.

Thus, it combines the features of vectors, matrices and lists. A data frame contains the same type of data in each of its columns, like vectors, but is also two-dimensional, like matrices, and it can hold a combination of numeric, character and logical data, like lists. A pictorial representation of a comparison of vector, matrix, array and data frame is shown in Fig. 9.1

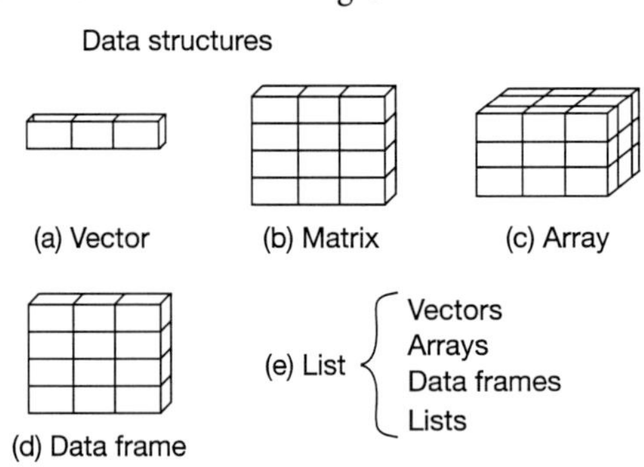

Fig. 9.1: Pictorial representation of various data objects in R

9.2 | CREATING A DATA FRAME

Data frames are tabular data objects that are two-dimensional, like matrices. The columns of a matrix should have the same data type, but in data frames, one column can be numeric while another can have character values, the next column can be logical or factor, and so on. Data frame can also be defined as a list of vectors of the same length. The column names of a data frame should be non-empty, the columns should contain the same number of data items and the row names should be unique.

Data frames are created using the `data.frame()` function.

```
> BMI <- data.frame(
   gender = c("Male", "Male","Female"),
   height = c(152, 171.5, 165),
   weight = c(81,93, 78),
   Age = c(42,38,26)
)                        # Create a data frame
> print(BMI)
```

When we execute this code, the following output will be produced:

```
   gender  height  weight  Age
1  Male    152.0   81      42
2  Male    171.5   93      38
3  Female  165.0   78      26
```

Example 9.1: Create a data frame of employees

Code:

```
> id<-1:10
> age <- c(18,19,20,22,23,30,32,33,34,45)
>name<- c("sandhya","latesh","Puja","rishika","aman","gagan","Malti",
"Tanu","Mithu","Tvisha")
> data <- data.frame(id,age,name)
> data
```

Output:

```
   id  age    name
1   1   18 sandhya
2   2   19  latesh
3   3   20    Puja
4   4   22 rishika
5   5   23    aman
6   6   30   gagan
7   7   32   Malti
8   8   33    Tanu
9   9   34   Mithu
10 10   45  Tvisha
```

9.3 | GENERAL OPERATIONS ON DATA FRAMES

Some commonly used operations on data frames such as obtaining its structure, summarising and extracting data are discussed in this section.

9.3.1 Obtaining the Structure of a Data Frame

The `str()` function can be used to view the structure of a data frame.

For example, the code given below displays the number of columns, column type and values in each column in the data frame:

```
> str(BMI)
'data.frame':   3 obs. of  4 variables:
 $ gender: Factor w/ 2 levels "Female","Male": 2 2 1
 $ height: num  152 172 165
 $ weight: num  81  93  78
 $ Age   : num  42  38  26
```

You can obtain the number of rows and columns in a data frame using the functions `nrow()` and `ncol()`, respectively. To print both the rows and the columns, the `dim()` function can be used; it returns the dimension of the object.

```
> dim(data)
[1] 10  3
> nrow(data)
[1] 10
> ncol(data)
[1] 3
>str(data)
'data.frame':    10 obs. of  3 variables:
 $ id  : int  1 2 3 4 5 6 7 8 9 10
 $ age : num  18 19 20 22 23 30 32 33 34 45
 $ name: Factor w/ 10 levels "aman","gagan",..: 8 3 6 7 1 2 4 9 5 10
```

9.3.2 Viewing a Summary of Data

The `summary()` function gives the nature of the data stored in a data frame by providing its statistical summary.

For example, the code given below displays the minimum, maximum, mean, median, first quartile and third quartile values for each variable of the data frame:

```
> print(summary(BMI))
    gender      height           weight           Age
 Female:1   Min.   :152.0   Min.   :78.0   Min.   :26.00
 Male  :2   1st Qu.:158.5   1st Qu.:79.5   1st Qu.:32.00
 Median :165.0   Median :81.0   Median :38.00
 Mean   :162.8   Mean   :84.0   Mean   :35.33
 3rd Qu.:168.2   3rd Qu.:87.0   3rd Qu.:40.00
 Max.   :171.5   Max.   :93.0   Max.   :42.00
```

9.3.3 Extracting Data

During visualisation, you may have to deal with large pieces of information that may contain thousands/millions of rows. To ensure that all of the data can be seen, you can use the `head(data frame variable name)` function, which displays the first six rows of the data frame. The opposite of this function is `tail(data frame variable name)`, which displays the last six rows in the data frame.

```
> head(data)
  id age    name
1  1  18 sandhya
2  2  19  latesh
3  3  20    Puja
4  4  22 rishika
5  5  23    aman
6  6  30   gagan

> tail(data)
   id age   name
5   5  23   aman
6   6  30  gagan
7   7  32  Malti
8   8  33   Tanu
9   9  34  Mithu
10 10  45 Tvisha
```

Data frames combine the features of matrices and lists. To subset a data frame from both matrix and list, the following syntax is used:

```
>data[10,2]  # Age of Tvisha
[1] 45
>data[10,"age"]
[1] 45
>data[["age"]]  # Or, you can use data[[2]]
 [1] 18 19 20 22 23 30 32 33 34 45
```

Single brackets, '[' and ']', are used for subsetting matrices, while double brackets '[[' and ']]' and the dollar sign '$' are used to select list elements.

The $ sign is used to extract data from a specific column from a data frame.

```
> result<-data.frame(BMI$gender,BMI$Age)
> print(result)
  BMI.gender BMI.Age
1       Male      42
2       Male      38
3     Female      26

> result<-BMI[1:2,]                  # Extract the first two rows
> print(result)
  gender height weight Age
1   Male  152.0     81  42
2   Male  171.5     93  38

> result<-BMI[c(1,3),c(1,2)]         # Extract the first and third rows
with the first and second columns
> print(result)
  gender height
1  Male    152
2 Female   165
```

9.4 | EXPANDING A DATA FRAME

You can expand a data frame by adding columns and rows to it. To add a column, new variable, new row or new observation to an existing data frame, the dollar sign or the double square brackets can be used.

9.4.1 Adding a Column

A vector for salary needs to be created and added to the existing BMI data frame as a new column. The `cbind()` function can also be used for this purpose.

```
> BMI$salary<-c(10000,20000,30000)
> print(BMI)
  gender height weight Age salary
1   Male  152.0     81  42  10000
2   Male  171.5     93  38  20000
3 Female  165.0     78  26  30000

> salary<-c(10000,20000,30000)
> cbind(BMI,salary)
  gender height weight Age salary
1   Male  152.0     81  42  10000
2   Male  171.5     93  38  20000
3 Female  165.0     78  26  30000
```

9.4.2 Adding a Row

New rows of the same structure can be added to an existing data frame using the `rbind()` function.

```
>newBMI<-data.frame(gender=c("Female"),height=c(175),weight=c(94),
Age=c(42),salary=c(40000))
> finalBMI<-rbind(BMI,newBMI)
> print(finalBMI)

  gender  height  weight  Age  salary
1  Male    152.0      81   42   10000
2  Male    171.5      93   38   20000
3  Female  165.0      78   26   30000
4  Female  175.0      94   42   40000
```

9.4.3 Merging Data Frames

Two data frames can be merged based on the column names they have in common, using the `merge()` function.

```
>merge(x, y, by, by.x, by.y, sort = TRUE)
```

where `x` and `y` are the data frames to be merged; `by.x` and `by.y` are the specifications of the common columns and `sort = TRUE` results in sorting by column.

By default, the data frames are merged based on the common column names, but separate column names can be specified in the `by.x` and `by.y` parameters. The rows are, by default, lexicographically sorted in the common columns, but are otherwise in the order in which they occurred in `x`. The columns comprise the common columns followed by the remaining columns in `x` and then those in `y`. If the matching involves row names, an extra column, `Row.names`, is added to the left, and in all cases, the result has no special row names.

For example, the code given below merges the data frames `teacher` and `subjects` by different parameters:

```
> teacher <- data.
frame(name=c("SA","SSG","NA"),age=c(55,35,45),retired=c("yes","no","no"))
> teacher
  name age retired
1   SA  55     yes
2  SSG  35      no
3   NA  45      no
> subjects <- data.frame(shortname=c("SA","SA","SSG","SSG","NA"),
teschingsubject=c("Stats","AIML","SSD","DM","DBMS"))
> subjects
  shortname teschingsubject
1        SA           Stats
2        SA            AIML
3       SSG             SSD
4       SSG              DM
5        NA            DBMS
> merge(teacher,subjects,by.x="name",by.y="shortname")
  name age retired teschingsubject
1   NA  45      no            DBMS
2   SA  55     yes           Stats
3   SA  55     yes            AIML
4  SSG  35      no             SSD
5  SSG  35      no              DM
> merge(subjects,teacher,by.x="shortname",by.y="name")
  shortname teschingsubject age retired
1        NA            DBMS  45      no
2        SA           Stats  55     yes
3        SA            AIML  55     yes
4       SSG             SSD  35      no
5       SSG              DM  35      no
```

More merge operations can be tested as follows:

```
merge(df1, df2, by="common_key_column")      # Equivalent to inner join in
databases
merge(df1, df2, by="common_key_column", all=TRUE)   # Equivalent to outer
join in databases
merge(df1, df2, by="common_key_column", all.x=TRUE) # Equivalent to left
outer join in databases
merge(df1, df2, by="common_key_column", all.y=TRUE) # Equivalent to right
outer join in databases
```

9.5 | APPLYING FUNCTIONS TO DATA FRAMES

As data frames are a special case of lists, the `lapply()` and `sapply()` functions can be used. When `lapply()` is called on a data frame, each of the frame's columns and return values will be placed in a list. The `sapply()` function tries to simplify the output of `lapply()`, as it returns the whole data frame after applying the functions specified in `sapply()`.

For instance, we can use `lapply()` on the BMI data frame created earlier. The output from `lapply()` and `sapply()` are very different as `lapply()` applies functions on individual columns and returns the individual columns of the data frame, whereas `sapply()` applies functions on the data frame as a whole and returns the whole data frame:

```
> lapply(BMI, sort)
$gender
[1] Female Male   Male
Levels: Female Male

$height
[1] 152.0 165.0 171.5

$weight
[1] 78 81 93

$Age
[1] 26 38 42

> sapply(BMI,sort)
     gender height weight Age
[1,]      1  152.0     78  26
[2,]      2  165.0     81  38
[3,]      2  171.5     93  42
```

Example 9.2: Write the R commands to display the values of age in a data frame in ascending order

Code:

```
> sort(data$name)
 [1] aman    gagan   latesh  Malti   Mithu   Puja    rishika sandhya Tanu
[10] Tvisha
Levels: aman gagan latesh Malti Mithu Puja rishika sandhya Tanu Tvisha

>sort(data$age, decreasing=TRUE)
 [1] 45 34 33 32 30 23 22 20 19 18
```

EXERCISES

Multiple Choice Questions

1. Data frames can be converted to a matrix by calling ______:
   a. `matr()` b. `mat()`
   c. `matrix()` d. All of the above
2. What would the following code print?
   ```
   >x<-data.frame(foo=1:4,
   bar=c(T,T,F,F))
   >ncol(x)
   ```
   a. 2 b. 4
   c. 7 d. All of the above
3. Which two methods can be used to add a column stored in a vector to the user's data frame?
   a. The `cbind()` function
   b. Single square brackets
   c. The dollar sign or double square brackets
   d. The `rbind()` function
4. Which type of data structure will users use when they want to store a data set?
   a. Matrix b. Vector
   c. List d. Data frame
5. ________ generates summary statistics of different variables in the data frame, possibly within strata.
   a. `rename()` b. `summarize()`
   c. `set()` d. `subset()`
6. Which of following functions is used to test the missing observation in a data frame?
   a. `missing()` b. `na()`
   c. `is.na()` d. `NA.miss()`
7. ________ is a function in R to obtain the number of observations in a data frame:
   a. `n()` b. `ncol()`
   c. `nrow()` d. `nob()`
8. The difference between a data frame and a matrix in R is:
   a. Data frame can store heterogeneous input while matrix cannot
   b. Matrix can store heterogeneous input while data frame cannot
   c. Both can store heterogeneous input
   d. Both cannot store heterogeneous input

Answers

1. c	**2.** a	**3.** a	**4.** d	**5.** b	**6.** c	**7.** c	**8.** a

Programming/Concept-based Questions

1. Create a data frame called `planet-info` from vectors and perform the following in R:
   a. Check the structure of `planet-info`
   b. Print data for `mars`
   c. Print the diameter of `mercury`
   d. Select the last four elements from the `diameter` column
   e. Select planets with diameter <1
   f. Sort the elements of the `diameter` vector
   g. Select the first three elements from the `rotation` column
2. Create a data frame called `writers-df` from vectors:
   a. Assign `c("age-at.death","age-as.writer","name","surname","gender", "death")` as the names of `writers-df`
   b. Assign column names and row names
   c. Check how many rows and columns are present in `writers-df`

3. Using the data set `demo (demo.csv)`, perform the following operations:
   a. Retrieve the data set to a variable `emp-demo`
   b. What is the class of each column of the data set?
   c. Print the summary and interpret it
4. Create two data frames and merge them using R commands.
5. Create a data frame for marriage and perform the following:
   a. Find the mean and median age at the time of marriage
   b. Find the minimum and maximum age of marriage in the data frame
6. If you have a data frame `df <- data.frame(a = c(1, 2, 3), b = c(4, 5, 6), c(7, 8, 9))`. Write the commands to perform the following:
   a. To select `c(4, 5, 6)`
   b. To select 1
7. Create a 2 x 3 matrix and convert it to a data frame.
8. Create the following data frame and then invert `Sex` for all individuals.

	Age	Height	Weight	Sex
Alex	25	117	57	F
Lilly	31	163	69	F
Mark	23	190	83	M
Oliver	52	179	75	M
Martha	76	163	70	F
Lucas	49	183	83	M
Caroline	26	164	53	F

CHAPTER

10 Factors and Tables

Objectives

At the end of this chapter, you will be able to

- Create factors and ordered factors using the `factor()` function
- Explain the `summary()` and `table()` functions applied on factors
- Work with factor levels and labels using the `labels()` and `levels()` functions
- Change factor levels
- Work with tables, creating and visualising table data and perform cross-tabulation of data
- Explain the functions related to tables such as `prop.table()` and `margin.table()`

10.1 | INTRODUCTION TO FACTORS

As we mentioned earlier, there are three kinds of variables in R programming: categorical, ordinal and interval. In statistical modelling, categorical variables are those that can take on a finite number of values. Since R is a statistical programming language, there exists a specific data structure for this, called the factor. Factors deal with non-numeric data values, which can be nominal or categorical.

10.2 | CREATING A FACTOR

A categorical variable is one that has categories, but there is no order to the categories. For example, Gender is a categorical variable with Male and Female being the possible values. Blood Type is another categorical variable with A, B, AB or O as values. In these cases, there is no intrinsic order to the possible values that the variable can take.

An ordinal variable is a categorical variable, but there is an intrinsic order to the possible values that the variable can take. Categorical variables are used as part of the definition of the factors involved in programming. A factor is a statistical data type that stores categorical variables and is used in statistical modelling. Factors can be ordered or unordered. Factors are stored as a vector of integer values with a set of character values. Factors are more descriptive and self-describing than integers; for example, having a variable that has values Male and Female is more meaningful than a variable that has values 1 and 2.

The `factor()` function is used to create factors.

For example:

```
> t1 <- factor(c("good","good","bad","bad","good","nice"))
> t1
[1] good good bad  bad  good nice
Levels: bad good nice

> table(t1)
t1
 bad good nice
   2    3    1
```

10.3 | FACTOR LEVELS

Factors are very similar to character vectors, but integers can be used in factors. Each factor value is associated with an integer, which corresponds to a category or level. Factors contain a predefined set of values, known as levels, which are sorted alphabetically. For instance, if a factor contains three values, it has three levels.

```
>review <- factor(c("good", "good", "bad", "nice"))
```

R will assign 1 to the level `bad` and 2 to the level `good` and 3 to `nice` (because b comes before g, and g comes before n, even though the first element in this vector is `good`). The `levels()` function can be used to check the level of a factor.

```
>levels(review)    # To find out the distinct values and their order
[1] "bad" "good" "nice"
>nlevels(review)    # To find out the number of distinct values
[1] 3

> apple_colors <- c('green','green','yellow','red','red','red','green')
>factor_apple <- factor(apple_colors)
>levels(factor_apple)
> print(nlevels(factor_apple))
```

When we execute this code, the following output will be produced:

```
Levels: green red yellow
[1] 3
```

10.3.1 Changing the Order of Levels

When a data set is received, it may be noticed that it contains factors with specific factor levels. However, sometimes, the names of these levels may need to be changed for clarity or for other reasons. R allows programmers to perform this task using the `levels()` function. If we apply the `factor()` function again with a new order of levels, we can change the order of the levels in a factor.

```
> review <- factor(c("good", "good", "bad",
"nice","bad","bad","nice","good"))
> review
[1] good good bad  nice bad  bad  nice good
Levels: bad good nice

# Apply the factor function with the required order of levels
>new_review <- factor(review, levels=c("good","nice","bad"))
> new_review
[1] good good bad  nice bad  bad  nice good
Levels: good nice bad

>bloodgrp <-c("B","AB","O","A","O","O","A","B")
>bloodgrp_factor <-factor(bloodgrp)
>bloodgrp_factor
[1] B  AB O  A  O  O  A  B
Levels: A AB B O

>levels(bloodgrp_factor)<-c("BG_A","BG_AB","BG_B","BG_O")
>bloodgrp_factor
[1] BG_B  BG_AB BG_O  BG_A  BG_O  BG_O  BG_A  BG_B
Levels: BG_A BG_AB BG_B BG_O
```

A combination of `levels()` and `labels()` can also be used to manually specify arguments when factors are created. With `levels()`, the order can be specified, while with `labels()`, a new name for the categories can be specified.

```
>factor(bloodgrp, levels=c("O","A","B","AB"),labels=c("BG_A","BG_
AB","BG_B","BG_O"))
[1] BT_B  BG_O  BG_A  BG_AB BG_A  BG_A  BG_AB BG_B
Levels: BG_A BG_AB BG_B BG_O
```

10.3.2 Generating Factor Levels

Factor levels can be generated using the `gl()` function. The input for this function is two integers that indicate how many levels are required and how many times each level should be generated. The syntax for this is as follows:

```
gl(a,b,labels)
```

where `a` is an integer indicating the number of levels; `b` is an integer indicating the number of repetitions; and `labels` is a vector of labels.

For example:

```
>review<-gl(3, 4, labels = c("good", "very good","nice"))
> review
 [1] good      good      good      good      very good very good very good
 [8] very good nice      nice      nice      nice
Levels: good very good nice
```

10.4 | SUMMARISING A FACTOR

The generic function `summary()` can be used on factors as well, to produce a summary of the results. It gives a quick overview of the contents of a variable. The `table()` function gives similar output as the `summary()` function for factors.

For example:

```
> bloodgrp<-c("B","AB","O","A","O","O","A","B")
>bloodgrp_factor <-factor(bloodgrp)
>summary(bloodgrp_factor)
 A AB  B  O
 2  1  2  3

>table(bloodgrp_factor)
blood_factor
 A AB  B  O
 2  1  2  3

> summary(blood)
   Length     Class      Mode
        8 character character
>table(blood)
blood
 A AB  B  O
 2  1  2  3
```

10.5 | ORDERED FACTORS

There are many variables where a natural order exists; sometimes, programmers may have to deal with factors that do have natural ordering among their categories. In this case, programmers must make sure that this information is passed to R. In the domain of categorical variables, there exists a difference between nominal categorical variables and ordinal categorical variables.

For example:

```
>tshirts<-c("L","S","M","M","S","L","L","S")
>tshirts_factor <-factor(tshirts, ordered=TRUE,levels=c("S","M","L"))
>tshirts_factor
[1] L S M M S L L S
Levels: S < M < L
```

It is possible to compare ordered factors in R.

```
>tshirts_factor[2]>tshirts_factor[3]
FALSE
>tshirts_factor[2]<tshirts_factor[3]
TRUE
```

10.6 | CONVERTING FACTORS

Factors can be explicitly converted to text or numbers using the `as.character()` or `as.numeric()` functions.

For example:

```
> review <- factor(c("good", "good", "bad",
"nice","bad","bad","nice","good"))
> review
[1] good good bad  nice bad  bad  nice good
Levels: bad good nice
```

We can use `as.character()` to convert a factor to a character vector.

```
> as.character(review)
[1] "good" "good" "bad"  "nice" "bad"  "bad"  "nice" "good"
```

The `as.numeric()` function can be used to convert a factor to a numeric vector. It returns the numeric codes that represent the factor levels. For example, "good" corresponds to 2, "bad" corresponds to 1, and "nice" corresponds to 3.

```
> as.numeric(review)
[1] 2 2 1 3 1 1 3 2
```

Converting factors to integer results can be confusing. So it should be used carefully, especially when the factor values are themselves integers. For example, if you have a vector that indicates some performance test scores of students as the values `c(79, 78, 90, 78, 79)`, which is in a factor:

```
> numbers <- factor(c(79, 78, 90, 78, 79))

> str(numbers) # Internal representation of numbers
 Factor w/ 3 levels "78","79","90": 2 1 3 1 2
```

Internally, factor values 78, 79 and 80 are stored as 1, 2 and 3 factor levels.

So, to convert numbers to character vector, we use the `as.character()` function. The output will be as follows:

```
> as.character(numbers)
[1] "79" "78" "90" "78" "79"
```

However, if we use the `as.numeric()` function, we will obtain a vector of the internal level representations of the factor and not the original values:

```
> as.numeric(numbers)
[1] 2 1 3 1 2
```

The solution is as follows:

```
> as.numeric(as.character(numbers))
[1] 79 78 90 78 79
```

10.7 | COMMON FUNCTIONS USED WITH FACTORS

Some functions such as `tapply()`, `split()` and `aggregate()` are commonly used with factors.

10.7.1 The `tapply()` Function

The `tapply(x,f,g)` function has `x` as a vector, `f` as a factor or list of factors, and `g` as a function. It splits `x` into groups formed from factors levels, and then the `g()` function is applied on the sub-vectors of `x`.

For example:

```
> marks <- c(75,86,87,65,45,67,89)
> subjects <-c("stats","stats","stats","DM","DM","SSD","SSD")
> tapply(marks,subjects,mean)
      DM       SSD     stats
55.00000  78.00000 82.66667
```

Here, the factor value `stats` occurs at index 1, 2, 3 while factor value `DM` occurs at 4, 5 and factor value `SSD` at 6, 7. Groups are formed based on these levels for marks and the mean is calculated. The mean for `stats` is the mean of the 1, 2, 3 values in the `marks` vector; that is, (75 + 86 + 87)/3. For `DM`, we need to find the mean of the 4, 5 values in the `marks` vector; that is, (65 + 45)/2. For `SSD`, we need the mean of the 6,7 values in the `marks` vector; that is, (67 + 89)/2.

Here is an example with two or more factors, where each factor yields a set of groups, and the groups are ANDed together.

- Male and under 25 years
- Female and under 25 years
- Male and over 25 years
- Female and over 25 years

The code for this is given below:

```
>d <- data.frame(list(gender=c("M","M","F","M","F","F"),
+
age=c(43,57,20,34,32,23),income=c(55600,87000,36450,72400,157000,43650)))
> d
  gender age income
1      M  43  55600
2      M  57  87000
3      F  20  36450
4      M  34  72400
5      F  32 157000
6      F  23  43650
> d$over25 <- ifelse(d$age > 25,1,0)
> d
  gender age income over25
1      M  43  55600      1
2      M  57  87000      1
3      F  20  36450      0
4      M  34  72400      1
5      F  32 157000      1
6      F  23  43650      0

> tapply(d$income,list(d$gender,d$over25),mean)
      0         1
F 40050 157000.00
M    NA  71666.67
```

10.7.2 The `split()` Function

The `split()` function is used to form groups from factors. The basic form is `split(x,f)`, with `x` being a vector or data frame and `f` being a factor or a list of factors. For the above example, the `split()` function can be applied as follows:

```
>d <- data.frame(list(gender=c("M","M","F","M","F","F"),
+
age=c(43,57,20,34,32,23),income=c(55600,87000,36450,72400,157000,43650)))
>d
  gender age income over25
1      M  43  55600      1
2      M  57  87000      1
3      F  20  36450      0
4      M  34  72400      1
5      F  32 157000      1
6      F  23  43650      0

> split(d$income,list(d$gender,d$over25))
$F.0
[1] 36450 43650

$M.0
numeric(0)

$F.1
[1] 157000

$M.1
[1] 55600 87000 72400
```

10.7.3 The `aggregate()` Function

The `aggregate()` function calls `tapply()` once for each variable in a group. For example, the median of each variable, grouped by gender in the above example, could be found as follows:

```
d <- data.frame(list(gender=c("M","M","F","M","F","F"),
+
age=c(43,57,20,34,32,23),income=c(55600,87000,36450,72400,157000,43650)))
> d
  gender age income
1      M  43  55600
2      M  57  87000
3      F  20  36450
4      M  34  72400
5      F  32 157000
6      F  23  43650

> aggregate(d[,-1],list(d$gender),median)
  Group.1 age income
1       F  23  43650
2       M  43  72400
```

The first argument, `d[,-1]`, is the entire data frame excluding the first column. The second argument (should be a list) is the Gender factor and the third argument tells R to compute the median on each column generated by sub-grouping.

10.8 | INTRODUCTION TO TABLES AND CREATING TABLES

Sometimes, we are given data in tabular form and need to create a table to store the data. The `as.table()` function can be used for this purpose.

For example, the code given below creates a table of IQ levels high, medium and low for rich, poor, middle class populations:

```
>IQlevel <- matrix(c(54,63,42,92,88,71,68,28,19),ncol=3,byrow=TRUE)
>colnames(IQlevel) <- c("High","Low","Medium")
>rownames(IQlevel) <- c("rich", "poor","middleclass")
>IQlevel<-as.table(IQlevel)
>IQlevel
            High Low Medium
rich          54  63     42
poor          92  88     71
middleclass   68  28     19
```

The table data can be visualised using the chart and graph functions available in R. An example of the `barplot()` function for the above data is shown in Fig. 10.1.

```
> barplot(IQlevel , beside=T, main = "IQlevel by income")
```

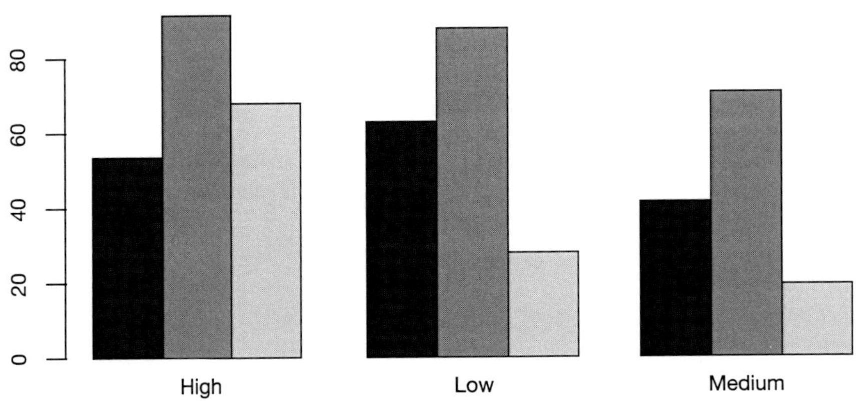

Fig. 10.1: The output of the `barplot()` function for IQ level by income data

10.9 | TABLE-RELATED FUNCTIONS

In R programming, we can perform several functions on tables. The `margin.table()` function calculates the total number of observations in the table. Marginal distribution across rows or columns is also possible using the optional argument (1: across rows, 2: across columns) in the `margin.table()` function.

```
> margin.table(IQlevel)
[1] 525

> margin.table(IQlevel,1)
       rich        poor middleclass
        159         251         115

> margin.table(IQlevel,2)
  High    Low Medium
   214    179    132
```

You can obtain the proportions by combining the commands as follows:

```
>IQlevel/margin.table(IQlevel)
                  High        Low     Medium
rich        0.10285714 0.12000000 0.08000000
poor        0.17523810 0.16761905 0.13523810
middleclass 0.12952381 0.05333333 0.03619048

>margin.table(IQlevel,1)/margin.table(IQlevel)
       rich        poor middleclass
  0.3028571   0.4780952   0.2190476

>  margin.table(IQlevel,2)/margin.table(IQlevel)
     High       Low    Medium
0.4076190 0.3409524 0.2514286
```

Alternatively, we can use the `prop.table()` function as follows:

```
> prop.table(smoke)
                High        Low     Middle
  current 0.14325843 0.12078652 0.06179775
  former  0.25842697 0.07865169 0.05898876
  never   0.19101124 0.06179775 0.02528090

> prop.table(IQlevel,1)    # Row percentage
                 High       Low    Medium
rich        0.3396226 0.3962264 0.2641509
poor        0.3665339 0.3505976 0.2828685
middleclass 0.5913043 0.2434783 0.1652174

> prop.table(IQlevel,2)    # Column percentage
                 High       Low    Medium
rich        0.2523364 0.3519553 0.3181818
poor        0.4299065 0.4916201 0.5378788
middleclass 0.3177570 0.1564246 0.1439394
```

10.10 | CROSS-TABULATION

Cross-tabulation deals with conversion of the raw data representation into a tabular format. The `xtabs()` function can be used for this purpose.

```
>xtabs(freq.data~categories.list, data)
```

This function has two arguments. In the first argument, you can insert the name of the frequency data on the left-hand-side of the tilde (~) sign, while the categories you want to cross-tabulate separated by the plus sign are inserted on the right. The second argument is the name of the data object.

For example, the code given below will tabulate the `iris` data sepal length and petal length of different species:

```
>iris.t = xtabs(Sepal.Length ~ Species + Petal.Length, data = iris)
> iris.t
            Petal.Length
Species         1  1.1  1.2  1.3  1.4  1.5  1.6  1.7  1.9    3  3.3  3.5
3.6
  setosa      4.6  4.3 10.8 33.9 63.9 66.9 34.4 21.6  9.9  0.0  0.0  0.0
0.0
  versicolor  0.0  0.0  0.0  0.0  0.0  0.0  0.0  0.0  0.0  5.1  9.9 10.7
5.6
  virginica   0.0  0.0  0.0  0.0  0.0  0.0  0.0  0.0  0.0  0.0  0.0  0.0
0.0
            Petal.Length
Species       3.7  3.8  3.9    4  4.1  4.2  4.3  4.4  4.5  4.6  4.7  4.8
4.9
  setosa      0.0  0.0  0.0  0.0  0.0  0.0  0.0  0.0  0.0  0.0  0.0  0.0
0.0
  versicolor  5.5  5.5 16.6 28.9 17.1 22.9 12.6 25.1 41.3 19.2 32.2 12.7
13.2
  virginica   0.0  0.0  0.0  0.0  0.0  0.0  0.0  0.0  4.9  0.0  0.0 12.2
18.0
            Petal.Length
Species         5  5.1  5.2  5.3  5.4  5.5  5.6  5.7  5.8  5.9    6  6.1
6.3
  setosa      0.0  0.0  0.0  0.0  0.0  0.0  0.0  0.0  0.0  0.0  0.0  0.0
0.0
  versicolor  6.7  6.0  0.0  0.0  0.0  0.0  0.0  0.0  0.0  0.0  0.0  0.0
0.0
  virginica  18.0 43.0 13.2 12.8 13.1 19.7 38.2 20.3 20.4 13.9 13.5 22.3
7.3
            Petal.Length
Species       6.4  6.6  6.7  6.9
  setosa      0.0  0.0  0.0  0.0
  versicolor  0.0  0.0  0.0  0.0
  virginica   7.9  7.6 15.4  7.7
```

Table 10.1 shows the overall use of data types in the case of homogeneous or heterogeneous 1-D, 2-D or n-D data.

Table 10.1: Use of data types in homogeneous and heterogeneous 1-D, 2-D and n-D data

	Homogeneous	Heterogeneous
1-D	Atomic vector	List
2-D	Matrix	Data frame
n-D	Array	

EXERCISES

Multiple Choice Questions

1. Which of the following are categorical variables?
   a. Blood type
   b. Weight of a person
   c. Gender
   d. Height of a person
2. What argument in R should users use to impose an order on a factor?
   a. `rank=TRUE`
   b. `rank=true`
   c. `ordered=TRUE`
   d. `ordered=true`
3. What would be the output of the following code:
   ```
   >x<-factor(c("yes","yes","no
   ","no","yes"))
   >table(x)?
   ```
   a. `no yes` b. `yes no`
   c. `NO YES` d. All of the above
4. Which of the following is a valid assignment?
   a. `>x<-factor(c("yes","yes"," no","no","yes"))`
   b. `>x<-fact(c("yes","yes","no", "no","yes"))`
   c. `>x<-factor(factor("yes","y es","no","no","yes"))`
   d. None of the above
5. Which one of the following is the correct outcome of the command `>factor(c(10,10,20,20, 30,30))?`
   a.
   ```
   [1] 10 10 20 20 30 30
   Levels: 10 20 30
   ```
   b.
   ```
   [1] 10  20  30
   Levels: 10 20 30
   ```
   c.
   ```
   [1] 10 20 30
   Levels: 10 10 20 20 30 30
   ```
   d.
   ```
   [1] 10 10 20 20 30 30
   Levels: 10 10 20 20 30 30
   ```
6. Which one of the following is the correct outcome of the following commands?
   ```
   >data = c(4,4,2,2,6,6,9)
   >factor(data)
   >levels(data) = c('A','B',
   'C','D')
   >data
   ```
   a.
   ```
   [1] 4 4 2 2 6 6 9
   attr(,"levels")
   [1] "A" "B" "C" "D"
   ```
   b.
   ```
   [1] 4 2 6 9
   attr(,"levels")
   [1] "A" "B"  "C"  "D"
   ```
   c.
   ```
   [1] A A B B C C D
   Levels: 1 2 3
   ```
   d.
   ```
   [1] B A C D
   attr(,"levels")
   [1] "2" "4"  "6"  "9"
   ```
7. Which one of the following is the correct outcome of the command `>x = factor(c(10,20,20,50,10, 20,10,50,60,60), levels = c(10, 20,50,60),ordered=TRUE >x?`
   a.
   ```
   [1] 10 < 20 < 50 < 60
   Levels: 10 20 20 50 10 20
   10 50 60 60
   ```

b. `[1] 10 20 50 60`
`Levels: 10 20 20 50 10 20 10 50 60 60`

c. `[1] 10 20 20 50 10 20 10 50 60 60`
`Levels: 10 < 20 < 50 < 60`

d. `[1] 10 20 20 50 10 20 10 50 60 60`
`Levels: 1 < 2 < 5 < 6`

8. Which one of the following is the correct outcome of the command
`>factor( c(rep("head",3), rep("tale", 4)))?`

a. `[1] head tale`
`Levels: head head head tale tale tale tale`

b. `[1] head head head head tale tale tale`
`Levels: head tale`

c. `[1] tale tale tale tale head head head`
`Levels: head tale`

d. `[1] head head head tale tale tale tale`
`Levels: head tale`

9. Which one of the following is the correct outcome of the command
`>unclass(factor( c("high school", "graduation", "post graduation", "graduation", "graduation", "high school", "post graduation", "high school", "post graduation"), levels=c("high school", "graduation", "post graduation") ))?`

a. `[1] 1 2 3 2 1 3 1 3`
`attr(,"levels")`
`[1] "high school" "graduation" "post graduation"`

b. `[1] 3 2 1 2 3 1 3 1`
`attr(,"levels")`
`[1] "post graduation" "graduation" "high school"`

c. `[1] 1 2 3`
`attr(,"levels")`
`[1] "high school" "graduation" "post graduation”`

d. `[1] 3 2 1`
`attr(,"levels")`
`[1] "post graduation" "graduation" "high school"`

10. Which one of the following is the correct outcome of the command
`> as.factor(c(1, 2, 2, 3, 3, 3, 4, 4, 5, 5, 5) )?`

a. `[1] 1 2 3 4 5`
`Levels: 1 2 3 4 5`

b. `[1] 5 5 5 4 4 3 3 3 2 2 1`
`Levels: 5 4 3 2 1`

c. `[1] 1 2 2 3 3 3 4 4 5 5 5`
`Levels: 1 2 3 4 5`

d. `[1] 1 2 2 3 3 3 4 4 5 5 5`
`Levels: 5 4 3 2 1`

Answers

1. a, c	**2.** c	**3.** a	**4.** a	**5.** a	**6.** a	**7.** c	**8.** d	**9.** a	**10.** c

Programming/Concept-based Questions

1. Perform the following using R commands:

a. Create a character vector of 10 elements with sizes small, medium, and large

b. Convert the vector to a factor and place it in an object called `sizes`

c. Identify the class of object `sizes`

d. Display the contents of object `sizes`

e. Use the `nlevels()` function to see how many levels there are in `sizes` and insert them in a table using the `table()` function
f. Use the `plot()` function to plot the factors

2. Create an ordered factor `emp_salary` of employees on `salary` order. Generate its summary and write the R commands to find the employees whose salary is less than 20,000.
3. Create a table of university data that stores data about students admitted in the last five years for Humanities, BCA and Engineering. Perform the following:
   a. Plot data year-wise and stream-wise
   b. Display the total students (all streams) admitted each year
   c. Display the total students admitted in BCA, Humanities and Engineering in the last five years
   d. Calculate and display the proportions
4. If `s1 <- factor(sample(letters, size=5, replace=TRUE))` and `s2 <- factor(sample(letters, size=5, replace=TRUE))`, write an R expression that will concatenate `s1` and `s2` in a single factor with 10 elements.
5. Let `x <- data.frame(q=c(2, 4, 6), p=c("a", "b", "c"))`. Write an R statement that will replace levels `a`, `b` and `c` with labels `fertiliser1`, `fertliser2` and `fertiliser3`.
6. If `x <- factor(c("high", "low", "medium", "high", "high", "low", "medium"))`, write an R expression that will provide unique numeric values for various levels of `x` with the following output:

```
#   levels value
# 1 high   1
# 2 low    2
# 3 medium 3
```

7. If `x = c(1, 2, 3, 3, 5, 3, 2, 4, NA)`, what are the levels of `factor(x)`?
8. Let `x <- c(11, 22, 47, 47, 11, 47, 11)`. If an R expression `factor(x, levels=c(11, 22, 47), ordered=TRUE)` is executed, what will be the fourth element in the output?

CHAPTER 11

Regular Expressions and String Manipulation in R

Objectives

At the end of this chapter, you will be able to

- Describe how to create regular expressions in R
- Explain the string manipulation functions in R
- Describe the regular expression commands supported by R
- Describe the five categories of regular expressions: metacharacters, sequences, quantifiers, character classes and POSIX character classes

11.1 | INTRODUCTION TO REGULAR EXPRESSIONS

R is a statistical language that mostly deals with numeric vectors, lists and matrices. However, along with such numeric data, string data also needs to be processed. For example, date of birth, patterns and medical data.

To process string data effectively and efficiently, regular expressions are used. A regular expression is a method or mathematical model of strings used for pattern matching. It provides a formula-based approach to matching strings of text. For example, a regular expression `a*` is used to search for all the words in a piece of text that start with the letter 'a'.

Regular expressions are used in systems that find substrings, for data validation and in search engines such as Google or Yahoo to try to retrieve relevant results to a user query.

11.2 | REGULAR EXPRESSIONS AND PATTERN MATCHING

Regular expressions are a set of pattern matching commands used to detect string sequences in text data. Using regular expressions, more text data can be extracted using shorter code. Regular expressions can perform various string processing operations such as string manipulation, search, validation and formatting.

Regular expressions are created using alphabets, numbers, special symbols such as {, [, *, ?, etc. to represent a wider scope than a specific word or text. Regular expressions are defined as look-alike character strings to find substrings in text. They are widely used in search engines, document processing, text processing, bioinformatics, attack detection and other pattern matching applications.

Literal metacharacters: To introduce metacharacters (such as [ ], ( ), |, *, +, ? and {) as characters/literals in an expression, they should be preceded by a backslash (\). For example, backslash is a metacharacter and to identify it as a literal metacharacter, it should be preceded by another backslash, that is, "\\". Some metacharacters along with their patterns are listed in Table 11.1.

Table 11.1 Metacharacters with patterns

Pattern	Metacharacter
\\	\
\[	[
\.	.
*	*

Repetition of pattern is represented by the expression along with a repetition metacharacter such as ?, * or +.

- ?: Matches either an empty string or anything that the pattern matches
- +: Matches anything that 1 or more occurrences of the pattern match
- *: Matches anything that 0 or more occurrences of the pattern match
- [ab]: a or b
- (ab): Sequence ab

For example:
(efg)?: ε *or* efg *but nothing else*
[ef]+: e *or* f *or* ee *or* fe *or* ef *or ...*
(efg)***:** ε *or* efg *or* efgefg *or ...*

11.3 | STRING MANIPULATION

R contains many functions for string manipulation. These functions can process regular expressions as well. The main differences between string manipulation functions and regular expressions are as follows:

- String manipulation functions perform simple tasks such as splitting a string, extracting the subsequence, and so on, but regular expressions can perform more complicated tasks such as extracting email IDs or DNA strings and packets having certain patterns.
- String manipulation functions process strings in a specific manner only, whereas regular expressions are very flexible.

11.3.1 String Manipulation Functions

In R, a string is any value enclosed within quotes (" "). It can even comprise numbers. R considers strings under the character class.

For example, the code given below explains the use of `paste()`, `cat()` and other functions used for string manipulation:

```
text <- "Nagpur"
typeof(text)
[1] "character"
cint  <- c("33","34","36")
typeof (cint)  # To check data type
[1]  "character"
```

The `paste()` function is used to concatenate sets of strings. It can be used to create or re-structure variable names. For example, if you want to create `variable3` combining two strings `Variable1` and `Variable2`. Here, the hyphen acts as a separator and a combining character.

```
variable3 <- paste("Variable1","Variable2",sep = "-")
variable3
[1] "Variable1-Variable2"
```

In the above output, the double quotes show that the string belongs to the character class. To print and concatenate strings without quotes, you can use the `cat()` function. In the `stringr` package, the `str_c()` or `str_join()` functions can be used to join strings without quotes.

```
cat(text,"INDIA",sep = "-")
Nagpur-INDIA
```

The `toString()` function allows you to convert any non-character value to a string.

```
toString(355)
[1] "355"
```

Now, let us examine some of the commonly used functions and their alternatives available in the `stringr` package to modify strings (Table 11.2).

Table 11.2 Commonly used string functions in R and their alternatives in the `stringr` package

Function	Description	Alternative function in `stringr`
`nchar()`	Finds the length of the string	`str_length()`
`tolower()`	Converts all characters to lowercase	`str_to_lower()`
`toupper()`	Converts all characters to uppercase	`str_to_upper()`
`chartr()`	Replaces each character in a string	`str_replace()`
`substr()`	Extracts a part of a string	`str_sub()`
`setdiff()`	Determines the difference between two vectors	
`setequal()`	Checks if the two vectors are the same	
`strsplit()`	Splits a string based on a criterion	`str_split()`
`sub()`	Finds and replaces the first match in a string	
`gsub()`	Finds and replaces all matches in a string	`str_replace()`

To install the `stringr` package to perform string operations, the following command is used:

```
install.packages("stringr", repos='http://cran.us.r-project.org')
library("stringr")
string <- "Hello World"
> strwrap(string) # Wrap string if it cannot fit in line
[1] "Hello World"

> nchar(string) # Count number of characters
[1] 11
> str_length(string)
[1] 11
# Convert to lower
> tolower(string)
[1] "hello world"
> str_to_lower(string)
[1] "hello world"
> # Convert to upper
> toupper(string)
[1] "HELLO WORLD"
> str_to_upper(string)
[1] "HELLO WORLD"

# Obtain difference between two vectors
> setdiff(c("monday","tuesday","wednesday"),c("monday","tuesday",
"friday"))
[1] "wednesday"
# Check if strings are equal
setequal(c("monday","tuesday","thursday"),c("monday","tuesday",
"thursday"))
[1] TRUE

# Abbreviate strings
abbreviate(c("monday","tuesday","wednesday"),minlength = 4)
   monday   tuesday wednesday
   "mndy"    "tsdy"    "wdns"
# Split strings
strsplit(x = c("ID-101","ID-102","ID-103"),split = "-")
[[1]]
[1] "ID"  "101"
[[2]]
[1] "ID"  "102"
[[3]]
[1] "ID"  "103"
```

These functions, when used with regular expressions, can perform more complex search operations.

11.3.2 Regular Expression Commands

R supports string processing using regular expression functions such as `sub()`, `gsub()`, `grep()`, `grepl()`, `regexpr()`, `gregexpr()` and `strsplit()`.

Regular expression commands perform various operations on text such as matching and sub-string extraction. To use regular expressions, the available base `regex` functions are `grep()`, `regexpr()`, `grepl()`, `gregexpr()`, `regexec()` and `regmatches()` (Table 11.3).

Table 11.3 Regular expression commands in R for string manipulation

Function	Description
`grep()`	Returns the index of the matched string
`grepl()`	Returns the Boolean value (T/F) of the matched string
`regexpr()`	Returns the index of the first match
`gregexpr()`	Returns the index of all matches
`regexec()`	A hybrid of `regexpr()` and `gregexpr()`
`regmatches()`	Returns the matched string at a specified index; used in conjunction with `regexpr()` and `gregexpr()`

The `grep()` function: This function searches for a pattern in a given string and returns its matching index.
The `grep(pattern,x)` function: It searches for a specified sub-string pattern in the vector string x and returns the match in a vector x of strings.

For example, the expression `[ei]` refers to any string that contains the letters e or i; it returns the index in vector string.

```
> grep("[ei]",states("Maharashtra","Rajasthan", "Himachal
Pradesh","Orissa"))

[1] 3 4
```

Here, elements 3 and 4 of the `states` vector, that is, "Himachal Pradesh" and "Orissa", contain either e or i.
In addition to searching for a set of letters, `grep()` can be used to search for a pattern.
"o.e" :: Searches for a sub-string starting with 'a', followed by any letter and then 'e'.
I..n :: Searches for a sub-string consisting of an 'I', followed by any two characters and then 'n'.

Regular expressions in R can be divided into the following categories:

- Metacharacters
- Sequences
- Quantifiers
- Character classes
- POSIX character classes

Metacharacters Text formulae can be created using metacharacters. They are used for generalisation of characters. They are special symbols/operators. These characters include ., *, \, |, (,), [,], {, }, $, + and ? (Table 11.4).

As they are special symbols, by default they are considered as metacharacters. If you want these characters to be part of a string, they must be prefixed with a backslash (\). For example, "1+2" should be written as "1\+2".

Table 11.4 Metacharacters in R and their description

Metacharacter	Description
.	Checks for period as a single character
?	Makes the symbol that occurs before it as optional
$	Checks the end of input
|	Alternates between checking the character occurring before or after the symbol
[]	Checks for any character in square brackets
[^]	Negates any set of characters followed by ^ in square brackets
*	Checks for zero or more occurrences
+	Checks for one or more occurrences
{n,m}	Matches n, m times
(abc)	Matches characters in the same sequence
\	Allows you to match reserved characters; it directs the compiler to treat a reserved character as a character and not as an operator

The code given below explains how to detect and replace a string ("interest%", in this example) and substring using the `grep()` and `gsub()` functions.

```
dt <- c("interest%","interest")  # Create a set of strings
> grep(pattern = "interest\\%",x = dt,value = T) # Display strings having
interest%
[1] "interest%"

# Detect all strings having special character ? $
> dt <- c("Why?","Dollar$")
Search for pattern ? or $
> grep(pattern = "[a-z][\\?-\\$-\\&]",x = dt,value = T)
[1] "Why?"    "Dollar$"
# Replace special character ? $  with empty space
gsub(pattern = "[\\?-\\$]",replacement = "",x = dt)
[1] "Why"    "Dollar"
```

If you want to consider a double backslash in a string, you must prefix it with another double backslash to ensure that R treats it as a character and not as a regular expression. Given below is an example to replace a double backslash with a hyphen:

```
gsub(pattern = "\\\\",replacement = "-",x = "India\\Canada")
[1] "India-Canada"
```

Quantifiers Quantifiers are immensely powerful as they represent search in the form of a formula, that is, regular expression. Quantifiers are mainly used to repetitively apply formulae a certain number of times. Quantifiers exercise their power on the characters to their immediate left. They match everything except a newline character, '\n' (Table 11.5).

Table 11.5 Quantifiers in R and their description

Quantifier	Description
.	Matches everything
?	Matches at most once
*	Matches zero or more occurrences of the character or formulae to the left
+	Matches one or more occurrences of the character or formulae to the left
{n}	Matches n times; the item must have consecutive repetition at place – for example, Anna
{n, }	Matches n or more number of times
{n,m}	Matches greater than or equal to n times and less than m times

These quantifiers can be used along with metacharacters to quantify the search and return of complex patterns. Two types of quantifiers are available:

- **Greedy:** This matches as many times as its repetition. The symbols .+ and .* are greedy quantifiers (zero or more occurrences).
- **Non-greedy:** This matches for a fixed number of times or fixed characters. The symbols .? and {n} are non-greedy quantifiers.

Given below are examples of greedy and non-greedy quantifiers.

(a) Given a number, apart from the starting digit, extract this number till the next digit '1' is detected. The desired result is 101.

```
x<- "101000010010"
regmatches(number, gregexpr(pattern = "1.*1",text = x))
[[1]]
[1] "10100001001"
```

The greedy match starts from the first digit, continues to search for '1' and moves on till the end of the string is encountered. Hence, it returns the result "10100001001".

```
regmatches(number, gregexpr(pattern = "1.?1",text = x))
[[1]]
[1] "101"
```

This searches for the first '1', then any number (single digit) followed by '1', thus returning "101".

(b) Display the list of names consisting of zero or more occurrences of 'e' and then display names having 't' one or more times.

```
names <- c("alex","anna","steven","crissy","puerto","cristian","garcia","rudy")
> # Does not matter if e is a match
> grep(pattern = "e*",x = names, value = T)
[1] "alex"     "anna"     "steven"    "crissy"    "puerto"    "cristian" "garcia"
[8] "rudy"
# It  matches for  't ' character one or more times
grep ( pattern = "t+",x = names ,value = T)
[1] "steven"   "puerto"   "cristian"
# Must match n two times

grep(pattern = "n{2}",x = names,value = T)
[1] "anna"
```

Sequences Sequences are patterns in a given string. They are represented by '\' followed by a specific character. They are case-sensitive and uppercase is the reverse of lowercase. Given below are a few sequences in R (Table 11.6). They can be combined with quantifiers.

Table 11.6 Sequences in R and their description

Sequences	Description
\d	A digit character
\D	A non-digit character
\s	A space character
\S	A non-space character
\w	A word
\W	A non-word
\b	A word boundary
\B	A non-word boundary

For example, the code below checks digits (numeric) and non-digit characters in a string using sequences:

```
string <- "I went  to Canada  20 times"
To check digit
> gsub(pattern = "\\d+",replacement = "_",x = string)
[1] "I went to Canada  _ times">
regmatches(string,regexpr(pattern = "\\d+",text = string))
[1] "20"
To check non digit
gsub(pattern = "\\D+",replacement = "_",x = string)
[1] "_20_"
```

Character classes Character classes are used in conjunction with quantifiers to match sets of characters enclosed in square brackets, []. They describe the match pattern, that is, the set or sequence or the character class that is allowed in the sequence. The caret symbol (^) symbol is used to negate the expression and extract the text, excluding the specified pattern. Some of the types of character classes used in `regex()` are given in Table 11.7.

Table 11.7 Character classes used in `regex()` and their description

Characters	Description
[aeiou]	Matches lowercase vowels
[AEIOU]	Matches uppercase vowels
[0123456789]	Matches any digit
[0-9]	Matches digits
[a-z]	Matches lowercase letters
[A-Z]	Matches uppercase letters
[a-zA-Z0-9]	Matches any of the above classes
[^aeiou]	Matches everything except letters
[^0-9]	Matches everything except digits

For example, to extract numbers and text separately, the following code can be used:

```
string <- "200  people got killed in the mumbai attack. 140 got severely
injured"
# Extract numbers 0 to 9 continuously one or more occurrences
regmatches(x = string,gregexpr("[0-9]+",text = string))
[[1]]
[1] "200" "140"
# Extract without digits using caret
regmatches(x = string,gregexpr("[^0-9]+",text = string))
[[1]]
[1] "  people got killed in the mumbai attack. "
[2] " got severely injured"
```

POSIX character classes POSIX character classes are the same as character classes but have additional features. POSIX can group a category such as lowercase, uppercase, alphabet, alphanumeric and punctuation using keywords such as lower, alnum, digit, etc. They are enclosed within double square brackets ([[ ]]). A caret before an expression negates the expression value. Some POSIX character classes in R are listed in Table 11.8.

Table 11.8 POSIX character classes in R and their description

POSIX characters	Description
[[:lower:]]	Matches lowercase alphabet
[[:upper:]]	Matches uppercase alphabet
[[:alpha:]]	Matches alphabet
[[:digit:]]	Matches digits
[[:space:]]	Matches space characters, such as tab, newline, vertical tab, space, etc.
[[:blank:]]	Matches blank characters (same as previous), such as space and tab
[[:alnum:]]	Matches alphanumeric characters, such as AB12, ID101, etc.
[[:cntrl:]]	Matches control characters (non-printable characters), such as \t (tab), \n (newline), \e (escape), \f (form feed), etc.
[[:punct:]]	Matches punctuation characters
[[:xdigit:]]	Matches hexadecimal digits (0–9 A–E)
[[:print:]]	Matches printable characters like punctuation, alphanumeric, space, etc.
[[:graph:]]	Matches graphical characters, such as [[:alpha:]] and [[:punct:]]

For example, to extract digits and text using the POSIX character classes, the following code can be used:

```
string <- c("I can  sleep 10 hours\n, a day","I sleep 8 hours\n a
day.","You sleep how many\t hours ?")
# Get digits
unlist(regmatches(string,gregexpr("[[:digit:]]+",text = string)))
[1] "10" "8"
# Remove punctuation
> gsub(pattern = "[[:punct:]]+",replacement = "",x = string)
[1] "I can  sleep 10 hours\n a day" "I sleep 8 hours\n a day"
[3] "You sleep how many\t hours "
# Remove spaces
gsub(pattern = "[[:blank:]]",replacement = "-",x = string)
[1] "I-can--sleep-10-hours\n,-a-day" "I-sleep-8-hours\n-a-day."
[3] "You-sleep-how-many--hours-?"
# Remove control characters
gsub(pattern = "[[:cntrl:]]+",replacement = " ",x = string)
[1] "I can  sleep 10 hours , a day" "I sleep 8 hours  a day."
[3] "You sleep how many  hours ?"
# Remove non-graphical characters
gsub(pattern = "[^[:graph:]]+",replacement = "",x = string)
[1] "Icansleep10hours,aday" "Isleep8hoursaday."
"Yousleephowmanyhours?"
```

11.4 | SOLVED EXAMPLES OF REGULAR EXPRESSIONS

Example 11.1: Extract digits from a string of characters

Code:

```
# Extract digits  from text
string <- "My roll number is 1700657"
gsub(pattern = "[^0-9]",replacement = "",x = string)
stringi::stri_extract_all_regex(str = string,pattern = "\\d+") #list
regmatches(string, regexpr("[0-9]+",string))
regmatches(string, regexpr("[[:digit:]]+",string))
```

Output:

```
"1700657"
```

Example 11.2: Remove spaces from a line of strings

Code:

```
# Remove space
gsub(pattern = "[[:space:]]",replacement = "",x = "and going there today
tomorrow")
gsub(pattern = "[[:blank:]]",replacement = "",x = "and going there today
tomorrow")
gsub(pattern = "\\s",replacement = "",x = "and going there today
tomorrow")
```

Output:

```
[1] "andgoingtheretodaytomorrow"
```

Example 11.3: Write a program to extract only alphabets

Code:

```
c2 <- "My date of birth is 24 07 1973"
From the string above, the desired output is "My date of ." You can'birth
is "t
"[[:digit:]]+" regex as it will match all the digits available in the
given string. Instead, in such case, we'll detect the digit boundary to
get the desired result.
gsub(pattern = "\\b\\d+\\b",replacement = "",x = c2)
```

Output:

```
[1] "My date of birth is    "
```

Example 11.4: Find the location of digits in a string

Code:

```
string <- "there were 2 players each in 8 teams"
gregexpr(pattern = '\\d',text = string) #or
unlist(gregexpr(pattern = '\\d',text = "there were 2 players each in 8 teams"))
```

Output:

```
[1] 12 30
```

Example 11.5: Extract information available inside parentheses (brackets) in a string

Code:

```
string <- "What are we doing tomorrow ? (laugh) Play soccer (groans) (cries)"
gsub("[\\(\\)]","",regmatches(string, gregexpr("\\(.*?\\)", string))[[1]])
```

Output:

```
[1] "laugh"  "groans" "cries"
```

Here, we have used the lazy matching technique. First, using `regmatches()`, we have extracted the parentheses with words such as `(cries)  (groans)  (laugh)`. Then, we have removed the brackets using the `gsub()` function.

Example 11.6: Extract only the starting digit in a range

Code:

```
x <- c("75 to 79", "80 to 84", "85 to 89")
gsub(" .*\\d+", "", x)
```

Output:

```
[1] "75" "80" "85"
```

Example 11.7: Extract email addresses from a given string

Code:

```
string <- c("My email address is abc@boeing.com","my email address is def@
jobs.com","aescher koeif","paul renne")
unlist(regmatches(x = string, gregexpr(pattern = "[[:alnum:]]+\\@
[[:alpha:]]+\\.com",text = string)))
```

Output:

```
[1] "abc@boeing.com" "def@jobs.com"
```

Example 11.8: Write a function that tests whether a string is a palindrome

You need to install the `stringr` package for this. Use `>install.packages("stringr")` for this purpose.

Code:

```
>is_palindrome <- function(word) {
       library(stringr)
       word <- str_to_lower(word)
       split_word <- unlist((str_split(word, pattern = "")))
       reverse_word <- split_word[str_length(word):1]
       paste_word <- paste(reverse_word, collapse = "")
       cat(word == paste_word)
   }
```

Output:

```
> is_palindrome("civIc")
TRUE
> is_palindrome("civic")
TRUE
> is_palindrome("civi")
FALSE
> is_palindrome("great")
FALSE
> is_palindrome("great day")
FALSE
>is_palindrome("da ad")
TRUE
```

EXERCISES

Multiple Choice Questions

1. ____________ provides the necessary string operators in R:
   a. `str`
   b. `forecast`
   c. `stringr`
   d. None of the above
2. What will be the output of this code:
   `> paste("a", "b", se = ":")?`
   a. "a+b"
   b. "a=b"
   c. "a b :"
   d. None of the above
3. What will be the output of this code:
```
> f <- function(num = 1) {
        x <- "Hello India!\n"
       for(i in seq_len(num)) {
                cat(x)
         }
        chars <- nchar(x) * num
         chars
  }> f()?
```
   a. Hello India!
      [1] 13
   b. Hello India!
      [1] 14
   c. Hello India
      [1] 15
   d. None of the above
4. Dealing with strings is an important part of text analytics and splitting a string is often one of the common tasks performed while creating tokens, etc. What will be the output of the following commands?
```
A<-paste("alpha","beta",
"gamma",sep=" ")
B←paste("phi","theta",
"zeta", sep="")
parts←strsplit(c(A,B), split=" ")
```
   a. alpha b. beta
   c. gamma d. phi
   e. theta f. zeta
5. What will be the output of the following command:
   `grepl("neeraj",c("dheeraj", "Neeraj","neeraj","is", "NEERAJ"))?`
   a. [FALSE TRUE FALSE FALSE TRUE]
   b. [FALSE FALSE TRUE FALSE FALSE]
   c. [FALSE TRUE TRUE FALSE FALSE]
   d. Unexpected input in grepl

Answers

1. c	**2.** a	**3.** b	**4.** c	**5.** a

Programming/Concept-based Questions

1. Write a program in R to clean an individual string by removing any characters that are not letters and additional spaces between words, and by lowercasing all letters, tokenising the processed text and returning a set of isolated words.
2. For the above question, calculate the total number of words, total number of unique words and sets of unique words.
3. Write a program to extract digits from a text.
4. Write a program to extract email IDs from a text and convert all gmail.com to yahoo.com.

CHAPTER

12 S3 and S4 Classes and Objects

Objectives

At the end of this chapter, you will be able to

- Define classes and objects in R using S3 and S4
- Explain the concept of generic functions
- Describe how to create a user-defined function
- Describe how to use methods from S3 and S4

12.1 | INTRODUCTION TO S3 AND S4 CLASSES AND OBJECTS

The R language supports the implementation of object-oriented concepts using the S3 and S4 systems. These systems allow the user to create objects and classes and make use of the concepts of inheritance, encapsulation and packages. An object is a collection of attributes and methods, while a class is the blueprint for an object. The original S language also used the S3 and S4 class structures.

S4 has the ability to add a safety feature to R, by preventing accidental access to class components. In S3, methods are defined in the same way as in any object-oriented programming language, but they are called in a different way.

In S3, no formal definition is required to define a class. We can create an S3 object by setting the class attributes. These attributes can be accessed and modified using the $ symbol. In S4, the `setClass()` function is used to create a class while the `new()` function is used to create an object. The class attributes are accessed and modified using the @ symbol.

S3 and S4 have their own properties and features and vary in implementation. You can choose S3 or S4 based on the requirements of your application.

12.2 | S3 CLASSES

S3 implements generic-function object-oriented programming. This is different from object-oriented programming languages such as C++, C# and JAVA, which implement message passing. In this approach, the methods defined in the classes perform the main functionality. Objects of classes are created and methods are then called using these objects. For example, the command `canvas.drawRect("blue")` – here, `canvas` is the object, `drawRect()` is the calling method and message passing takes place with "blue" as the parameter.

In S3, a generic function and not an object decides which method needs to be called. Methods are defined in the same way as in message-passing object-oriented programming, but they are called in a different way.

S3 is an R object with class attributes; that is, it is associated with a class object. A class is a vector of elements. Functions are declared using type parameters and are called generic functions.

A class can be inherited from another class, and also used to specify the order of execution. To create an S3 class, we must first create a list with members and make a copy of the list to be returned.

Following is an example of the creation of an S3 object of class `studentX`. First, we create a list with the `class` attribute set. The name of the object is assigned using `class(list)`. The values of all the attributes of the S3 object can be displayed as given below:

```
> s <- list(sname = "Ram", sage = 22, sGPA = 3.5)
> class(s) <- "studentX"
> s

$sname
[1] "Ram"
$sage
[1] 22
$sGPA
[1] 3.5
```

The `attr()` function is used to display the name of the object.

```
attr(,"class")
[1] "studentX"
```

12.2.1 Constructors

Constructors are used to initialise the members of a class. They can also be used to add our own integrity checks on some members of a class.

Constructors can be created using the same function name as the class name (though this is not necessary). They automatically initialise the class members at the time of object creation. The constructor function for the `studentX` class can be created as follows:

```
studentX<-function (sn,sa,sg)
```

If we want to add some integrity checks on the members, these checks needs to be defined in the constructor function. For example, a list of permissible values can be assigned to the object using the `attr()` function.

```
attr(value, "class") <- "studentX"

# Creating  a constructor for the  class "studentX"
studentX <- function(sn,sa,sg) {
# Adding integrity checks
if(sg > 4 || sg < 0)  stop("sGPA must be between 0 and 4")
data <- list(sname = sn, sage = sa, sGPA = sg)
# Class can be set either by using function class() or attr()
attr(value, "class") <- "studentX"
data
}
```

In the example given below, we create an object using a constructor and display the values.

```
> s <- studentX("Paul", 30, 2.8)
> s
$sname
[1] "Paul"
$sage
[1] 30
$sGPA
[1] 2.8
attr(,"class")
[1] "studentX"
> class(s)
[1] "studentX"

> s <- studentX("Paul", 26, 5)
Error in studentX("Paul", 26, 5) : sGPA must be between 0 and 4
```

12.2.2 Methods and Generic Functions

Generic functions do not perform any computation but encapsulate a generic concept, such as print, plot, residuals and summaries. The implementation of a generic function for a particular class of object is called a method. Polymorphism means that the same function can lead to different operations for different classes. You can apply `plot()`, for example, to many different types of objects, obtaining a different type of plot for each. The same is true for `print()`, `summary()` and many other functions.

In this manner, we obtain a uniform interface to different classes. Generic functions are used to implement polymorphism in OOPs. For example, if you are writing code that performs a print operation, the generic function `print()` can be used along with the object you wish to print. You need not worry about the type of the object you wish to print.

The values of the members of a class can be displayed by writing the class name.

```
> s
$sname
[1] "Paul"
$sage
[1] 30
$sGPA
[1] 2.8
>>attr(,"class")
[1] "studentX"
```

`print()` is a generic function to print objects of various types. Actually, they are implemented as different methods specific to an object. You can display these methods by executing the code:

```
> methods(print)
.
.
[4] print.aovlist*
  [5] print.ar*
  [6] print.Arima*
,
,
[194]
```

Some of these functions are not visible (marked with asterisk) but they provide functionality.

To print our object of class `studentX` with the `print()` generic function, the system will search for a method of the form `print.studentX()`, but no such method is defined in R. Therefore, R will call `print.default()`. If no defined method match is found, control goes to `default()`. All generic functions have an associated `default()` method to handle such cases. The command `methods(class="default")` can be used to display the list of generic functions that provide a fallback default method.

```
> methods(class="default")
.............
[5] ansari.test     anyDuplicated   aperm           ar.burg

[157]..
```

12.2.3 Creating a User-defined Method for a Generic Function

We can write our own method for a generic function by using the command, `genericfunction.classname<- function (obj)`. For example, to implement a generic-function method of print to display data from class `student`, we can use the following code:

```
print.studentX <- function(obj) {
cat ( obj$sname, "\n")
cat ( obj$sage, "years old\n")
cat ( "GPA:", obj$sGPA, "\n")
}
```

To print the values of the object `studentX` using the `print()` generic function:

```
>print.studentX(s)
Paul
30 years old
GPA: 2.8
```

12.2.4 Creating a User-defined Generic Function

Generic functions such as `print()` and `plot()` can also be defined by the user. The structure of a pre-defined generic function like print/plot is given below:

```
> print
```

Output:

```
   function (x, ...)
   UseMethod("print")
   <bytecode: 0x0674e230>
   <environment:
namespace:base>
```

```
> plot
```

Output:

```
function (x, y, ...)
UseMethod("plot")
<bytecode: 0x04fe6574>
<environment:
namespace:graphics>
```

Here, `UseMethod ()`is implemented and the parameter `name of GF` is passed to it. `UseMethod()` implements all the background details. For example, to create a new generic function called `grades()`, the `grades <- function(obj)` definition should include an implementation of `UseMethod()`.

```
grades <- function(obj) {
UseMethod("grades")
}
```

The methods of a generic function need to be implemented. Let us implement the default method by using `function()`, assigned to generic function `name.method`.

```
grades.default <- function(obj) {
cat("This is a generic function\n")
}
```

Now let us create a method for our class `student`.

```
grades.student <- function(obj) {
cat("Your grade is", obj$GPA, "\n")
}
```

Output:

```
> grades(s)
Your grade is 3.7
```

In this way, we can implement a generic function named `grades()` and later a method for our class.

Example 12.1: Write a program to create a constructor of `studentX` class and a generic function to display the grades

Code:

```
s <- list(name = "Nany", age = 28, GPA = 8.5)
class(s) <- "studentX"
# Constructor
studentX <- function(xn,xa,xg) {
 # To test integrity checks
 if(xg>10 || xg<0)  stop("GPA must be in range of 0 to 10")
 value <- list(name = xn, age = xa, GPA = xg)
 # Assign values to class studentX
 attr(value, "class") <- "studentX"
 value
 }
```

```
s <- studentX("Paul", 26, 8.7)
# Generic function grade
 grades.studentX <- function(obj) {
+ cat("Your grade is in range ", obj$GPA, "\n")
+ }
 grade(s)
```

Output:

```
Your grade is in range  8.7
```

12.2.5 Extended Example: A Class for Storing Upper Triangular Matrices

An upper triangular matrix stores non-zero values only above the diagonal. This saves storage space. We will implement this using the S3 class.

$$\begin{pmatrix} 1 & 5 & 12 \\ 0 & 6 & 9 \\ 0 & 0 & 2 \end{pmatrix}$$

First, we need to create an object of class `upt` from the full matrix, `inmatrix`. This function is a constructor that creates an instance of the given class, eventually returning that instance. The `for` loop fills in `retrn$mat` by column and stores the diagonal and above-diagonal elements of the matrix. `retrn$idx` shows where in the matrix the various columns begin. The `sumseries()` function returns the summation from 1 to *i*.

Code:

```
upt <- function(inmatrix) {
    n <- nrow(inmatrix)
    retrn <- list()
    class(retrn) <- "upt"
    retrn$mat <- vector(length=sumseries(n))
    retrn$ix <- sumseries(0:(n-1)) + 1
    for (i in 1:n) {
       ixi <- retrn$ix[i]
       retrn$mat[ixi:(ixi+i-1)] <- inmatrix[1:i,i]
    }
    return(retrn)
}

sumseries <- function(i) return(i*(i+1)/2)

test <-function()
{
 utm1 <- upt(rbind(1:2,c(0,2)))
 print(utm1)
}

test()
```

Output:

```
     [,1] [,2]
[1,]    1    2
[2,]    0    2
```

12.3 | S4 CLASSES

The S3 class is an older way to create classes in R programming, whereas S4 is a new way. It is more structural compared to S3 classes. The `slot` parameter is used to create variables in S4.

S4 classes have a formal definition and a uniform way to create objects, whereas S3 classes and objects lack a formal definition. This makes code safer and reduces the possibility of mistakes by the programmer.

S3 and S4 are separate systems and can be used independently.

12.3.1 Defining an S4 Class

The `setClass()` function is used to build an S4 class and return a function to create an object of that class. An object of the S4 class can be created using the `new()` function as well as generic functions.

```
setClass(name,slot)
name: Class Name
slot: variable values
```

For example, to define a new class called `studentX` having `sname`, `sage` and `sGPA` as class variables, we can use the following command:

```
setClass("studentX", slots=list(sname="character", sage="numeric",
sGPA="numeric"))
```

12.3.2 Creating S4 Objects

An S4 object can be created using the `new()` function and passing the class name and the slot's value. In S4 functions, member variables are known as slots. Reference slots can be accessed by the using the @ symbol.

For example, to create an S4 object of class `studentX` and set the name as "Shivam", age 21 and SGPA 3.5:

```
> s1 <- new("studentX",sname="Shivam", sage=21, sGPA=3.5)
```

To print values of an object:

```
> s1
An object of class studentX
"sname":
[1] "Shivam"
"sage":
[1] 21
"sGPA":
[1] 3.5
```

To check if an object belongs to S4 or not:

```
> isS4(s1)
[1] TRUE
```

12.3.3 Constructors

The `setClass()` function acts as a constructor used to initialise the values of the class members and returns a generator function. The constructor (generator function) uses the same name as that of the class and includes the initialisation parameters. It creates new objects with the initialised data values.

```
> studentX <- setClass("student", slots=list(sname="character",
sage="numeric", sGPA="numeric"))
> studentX
```

For example, to create S4 objects using the generator function:

```
> studentX(sname="Shivam", sage=25, sGPA=3.8)
```

Output:

```
An object of class "student"
Slot "name":
[1] "Shivam"
Slot "age":
[1] 25
Slot "GPA":
[1] 3.8
```

12.3.4 Accessing Slots

The slot of an object can be accessed using `@.object_name`. The @ member variable is used to display or edit values.

```
> s1@sname
```

Output: `[1] "John"`

```
> s1@sGPA
```

Output: `[1] 3.8`

```
> s1@sage
```

Output: `[1] 25`

You can reassign or access a slot by using the `object_name@` member variable and a value can be assigned to it.

```
> s1@sage <- 22
> s1
```

Output:

```
An object of class "student"
Slot "sname":
[1] "John"
Slot "sage":
[1] 22
Slot "sGPA":
[1] 3.8
```

12.3.5 Modifying Slots

The `slot()` function can be used to access or modify slots by assigning new values. The parameters passed with this function are the class name and class member variable.

```
> slot(s1,"sname")
```

Output:

```
[1] "John"
> slot(s1,"sname") <- "Paul"
> s1Output:
   An object of class "studentX"
   Slot "sname":
   [1] "Paul"
   Slot "sage":
   [1] 22
   Slot "sGPA":
   [1] 3.8
```

12.3.6 Methods and Generic Functions of S4

As with the S3 class, methods in the S4 class also belong to generic functions rather than the class or object itself. Working with S4 generic functions is thus very similar to that in S3. You can list all the generic functions and methods available in S4 using the `showMethods()` function.

For example, to list all the generic functions in the S4 class:

Code:

```
> showMethods()
```

Output:

```
   Function: - (package base)
   Function: != (package base)
   ...
   Function: trigamma (package base)
   Function: trunc (package base)
```

To check if a function is generic or not:

```
isS4(Name of function) : returns true or false.

> isS4(print)
[1] FALSE

> isS4(show)
[1] TRUE
```

We can list all the methods of a generic function by using showMethods(generic function name).

To list all the methods of the show() generic function:

```
> showMethods ( show )
```

Output:

```
Function: show (package methods)
object="ANY"
object="classGeneratorFunction"
...
object="standardGeneric"
(inherited from: object="genericFunction")
object="traceable"
```

12.3.7 Creating a User-defined Method

We can write user-defined methods using the setMethod() function, if default or built-in definitions do not serve our purpose.

For example, the user-defined code for the show() generic function can be implemented as follows:

```
setMethod("show","studentX",function(object) {
cat ( object@sname, "\n")
cat ( object@sage, "years old\n")
cat ("SGPA:", object@sGPA, "\n")
}
```

To assign a name to an object, along with the initial values to class members, we can use the following code:

```
> s <- new("studentX",sname="Shivam", sage=22, sGPA=3.7)
> s
```

Output:

```
Shivam
22 years old
SGPA: 3.7
```

```
# Create new class S4
s <- new("studentX",name="John", age=22, GPA=3.7)

> setMethod("show",
+ "studentX", function(object) {
+ cat( object@sname, "\n")
+ cat( object@sage, "years old\n")
+ cat("SGPA:", object@sGPA, "\n")
+ }
+ )
> s
```

Output:

```
John
22 years old
GPA: 3.7
```

EXERCISES

Multiple Choice Questions

1. S3 is a message-passing object-oriented programming class:
   a. True b. False
2. In R, __________ decides which method to call.
   a. Object
   b. Class
   c. Generic function
   d. All of the above
3. An S3 class can be created by
   a. First creating a list with members
   b. Using `setClass()`
   c. Using `new()`
   d. None of the above
4. The `new()` function is used for
   a. Creating an S4 class
   b. Creating an S4 object
   c. Creating an S3 class
   d. Creating an S3 object
5. A constructor of an S4 class can be created using
   a. `new()`
   b. `setClass()`
   c. `slot()`
   d. `setMethod()`

Answers

1. b	2. c	3. a	4. b	5. b

Programming/Concept-based Questions

1. How many types of base objects are present in R?
2. Describe the difference in behaviour in these two calls.

```
set.seed(1014)
some_days <- as.Date("2017-01-31") + sample(10, 5)

mean(some_days)
  #> [1] "2017-02-05"
mean(unclass(some_days))
  #> [1] 17202
```

3. Draw a Venn diagram illustrating the relationships between functions, generics and methods.
4. Write a constructor for `diffyear` objects. Assume attributes of your own and initialise them.
5. Create an S3 class for student information: name, age, class, address. Add a method to display the details of students who are older than 18.
6. What is an S4 generic function? Create an S4 class for the problem stated in Q5.

CHAPTER 13

Accessing Input and Output

Objectives

At the end of this chapter, you will be able to

- Explain input and output processing in R
- Read data from the keyboard and from a file
- Write output to the monitor and to files
- Create different types of files and modify them using file functions
- Create and set up directories

13.1 | INTRODUCTION TO FILES AND INPUT/OUTPUT

Often, we may need to store data permanently and process the data stored in various file formats such as .csv, .dat, .txt and .xml. Using the R programming language, you can read from and write into various file formats. This becomes especially important in the context of Big Data, where information is stored in different file formats and acts as a source of input and the repository of output.

Many data sets such as data from social media, images, medical data and bioinformatics are available online in the public domain for analysis. Therefore, reading this data, processing it and write data in other useful forms is a common activity for researchers. To process a file using the R file handling functions, the file should be present in the current working directory. R can then read it or you can specify the file path.

13.2 | ACCESSING THE KEYBOARD AND MONITOR

R can read data from a user request in the form of input from the keyboard or from files. Similarly, R can write data to the monitor to display it or store the results of processing in a file. All these actions make the program interactive.

R supports input/output access through functions such as `readline()`, `cat()` and `scan()`.

13.2.1 Reading from the Keyboard

To read data from the keyboard, R uses two different functions: `scan()` and `readline()`.

(a) `scan()`: The `scan()` function reads data from the console or a file separated by whitespace and then stores the data in a vector or list. The data can be numeric or character and originate from a file or the keyboard.

For example:

```
> z <- scan()
1: 14
2: 8
3: 3
4: 4
5:
```

Read the four items:

```
> z
[1] 14  8  3  4
```

Default vectors are separated by whitespace (blanks, carriage return/line feeds, horizontal tabs). However, additional separators can be used with the optional `sep` argument.

For example, if we want to treat the newline character as a separator to read each input line as a string, we can use the code given below.

The test.txt file contains the following text:

Hello
I am
John

```
bs <- scan("test.txt",what="")
Read 4 items
> nl <- scan("test.txt",what="",sep="\n")
Read 3 items
> bs
[1] "Hello" "I" "am" "John"
> nl
[1] "Hello" "I am" "John"
> bs[2]
[1] "I"
> nl[2]
[1] "I am"
```

When the default separator, which is a blank, is used, the above file is read as four different elements: Hello, I, am, John. However, when the newline character is used as the separator, the same file will be read as three different elements – the second line, "I am", will be treated as a single string. Individual element `bs[2]` will be "I" and `nl[2]` will be "I am".

To read data from the keyboard, the `scan()` function is used, with an empty string as the terminator. In other words, this function will read the input till a blank line or newline character (an empty string) is encountered. The read data will be assigned to a vector.

For example:

```
> v <- scan("")
1: 14 8 13
4: 3 4
7: 8
8:
```

Read the six items:

```
> v
[1] 14 8 13 3 4  8
```

(b) `readline()`: While the `scan()` function is used to read data word by word, separated by a separator, to read data line by line, we need the `readline()` function. To read a line from the keyboard as a string, the `readline()` function with no argument is used

For example:

```
> w <- readline()
hello R . You are very powerful
> w
[1] "hello R . You are very powerful"
```

The `readline()` function reads one line at a time, but to read all the lines at once in a text file the `readlines()` function is used.

The file test.txt contains the following text:
Nagpur Maharashtra
Jaipur Rajasthan
Ludhiyana Punjab

We can read the file all at once, like this:

```
> city <- readLines("test.txt")
> city
[1] " Nagpur Maharashtra " " Jaipur Rajasthan" " Ludhiyana Punjab"
```

The `readlines()` function reads all three lines at once as a vector in the character mode. One vector element is assigned one line; hence, there will be three lines in three vector elements. If you wish to use `readline()`, you need to execute it iteratively. In this case, it will need to execute three times to read the file text.txt.

13.2.2 Reading from a File

The `readline()` and `scan()` functions read data as characters or strings. To read data that is a combination of alphabetic and numeric data, the `read.table()` function is used. This function reads data into a data frame.

For example, the contents of the file test.txt is given below:

Fname	class
Yashmit	3
Shreya	11
Rishika	9
Tanu	9

We could read the above file along with the header and store this data in a data frame:

```
> data <- read.table("test.txt",header=TRUE)
> data
Fname       class
1  Yashmit     3
2  Shreya      11
3  Rishika     9
4  Tanu        9
```

This is a mix of numeric and character data. So the `scan()` and `readline()` functions would not work here. If you tried using these functions, the `class` column would be read as a character, but we want to process it as a number.

To read data in a matrix from a file, the easiest way is to use the `scan()` function as a parameter in the `matrix()` function and also specify `nrows` and `byrow`. Here, data is read row by row and `nrow` specifies the number of rows to be read.

File: test.txt contains a 4 x 3 matrix:

1	0	1
1	1	1
1	1	0
1	1	0

To read it in matrix form:

```
> data <- matrix(scan("test.txt"),nrow=4,byrow=TRUE)
```

To return the same data as a data frame, you can use `read.table()` and then convert it to a matrix using `as.matrix()`. The general method is given below:

```
read.matrix <- function("test.txt") {
as.matrix(read.table("test.txt"))
}
```

13.2.3 Printing to the Monitor

The output function `print()` prints values to the screen. This can print the value of a variable or an expression to the screen.

```
print(variable name/expression)
>x="hello"
>print(x)
"hello"
```

13.2.4 Creating a Connection

To communicate with any file, a connection needs to be set before reading from the file or writing to it. This connection is automatically created when you call the `file()` or `url()` functions.

```
> ?connection
```

For example, assume that the file test.txt contains the following:

Fname	class
Yashmit	3
Shreya	11
Rishika	9
Tanu	9

We want to read test.txt line by line:

```
> f <- file("test.txt","r")
> readLines(f,n=1)
[1] "Yashmit  3"
> readLines(f,n=1)
[1] "Shreya 11"
> readLines(f,n=1)
[1] "Rishika 9"
> readLines(f,n=1)
[1] "Tanu  9"
> readLines(f,n=1)
character(0) //EOF
```

The `file()` function opens a connection and stores the connection details in a variable, `f`. We can pass `f` to the `readline()` function, which will read the file line by line from the beginning. The file pointer moves automatically to the next line till it reaches the end of file (EOF). We can detect EOF in our code.

We want to read test.txt line by line:

```
> f <- file("test.txt","r")
> readLines(f,n=1)
[1] "Yashmit  3"
> readLines(f,n=1)
[1] "Shreya 11"
> readLines(f,n=1)
[1] "Rishika 9"
> readLines(f,n=1)
[1] "Tanu  9"
> readLines(f,n=1)
character(0) //EOF
```


If you wish to rewind this file, you can establish a connection again or use the `seek()` function to place the file pointer at a specific position.

```
> f <- file("test.txt","r")

> readlines(f,n=2)
[1] "Yashmit 3", "Shreya 11"
> seek(con=f,where=0)
[1] 19
```

The `seek()` function with `where` = 0 refers to position zero or the beginning of the file. After reading the two lines, it will point to 20 – "Yashmit 3" is 9 characters long + 1 newline character + "Shreya 11" is 8 characters long + 1 newline character = 19 will be the current position of the file pointer.

13.3 | FILE FUNCTIONS

When you create a file in R with a specific name, it is created with default permissions and will give a default warning if the operation fails. If `showWarnings = TRUE`, it will give a warning for an unexpected failure.

The basic functions on files are stated below. When you call the file functions, you need to pass the file name as argument if the file is available in the current working directory; otherwise, the full path name must be specified.

```
file.create(..., showWarnings = TRUE)
```

To check if a file already exists, we can use the `file.exists()` function, with the file name as argument:

```
file.exists(...)
```

To remove a file from the system, the `file.remove()` function can be used, along with the file name as argument:

```
file.remove(...)
```

To rename a file, we can use the `file.rename()` function. The location of the file along with the file name should be passed as arguments:

```
file.rename(from, to)
```

To append the contents of file2 to file1, the general form the `file.append()` function is given below:

```
File.append(file1, file2)
```

For example, to append f2.csv to f1.csv:

```
> cat("I am 16 years old \n",file="f1.csv")
> cat("I study in class Xth \n", file="f2.csv")

file.append("f1.csv", "f2.csv")
[1] TRUE
```

The contents of f1.csv will be:

I am 16 years old

I study in class Xth

To copy a file from one location to another, the `file.copy()` function can be used. The general form of the `file.copy()` function is as follows:

```
file.copy("source file","destination folder")
```

For example:

```
file.copy("/home/ccoew/3937.java", "/home/ccoew/R/")
[1] TRUE

> file.exists("filtered.csv")
[1] TRUE
```

If the same file exists at the destination location and you wish to overwrite it, the `overwrite` parameter must be set to TRUE. In addition, if you want to copy all the files in a directory to a destination location, the `recursive` parameter must be set to TRUE. You can also control the copy mode and copy date.

```
file.copy(from, to, overwrite = recursive, recursive = FALSE, copy.mode =
TRUE, copy.date = FALSE)
```

13.3.1 Working with CSV Files

A .csv file is a text file in which the values in the columns are separated by commas. Such files can be edited in Notepad, MS Excel, Works9, etc. Generating and importing .csv files is easy and quick, as is processing them. The CSV format can differentiate between numeric and text values. Column headers are written only once. They consume very little memory.

Let us consider the following data present in a file named input.csv.

Roll No., Name of Student, CLASS TEST-1 (20M), CLASS TEST-2 (20M), CLASS TEST-1 (6M), CLASS TEST-2 (6M), Conduct & Timely (8M), Total (20M)

1,Aditi Yogesh Jamkar,4,0,2,0,6,8
2,Anshuli Rajesh Bobde,6,16,3,6,7,16
3,Avantika Murlidhar Hatmode,16,17,6,6,8,20
4,Devyani Sanjay Gabhane,14,17,5,6,8,19
5,Pali Divya Rajesh,16,16,6,6,8,20
6,Dnyaneshwari Kishor Badarkhe,17,18,6,6,8,20
7,Gauri Shrikant Wyawahare,19,17,6,6,8,20

Creating a .csv file The following command creates a .csv file with the given name, if it does not already exist, and truncates the file if it does exist.

```
file.create("C:\\temp1\\test.csv")
[1] TRUE
file.create("C:\\temp1\\test1.csv", "C:\\temp2\\test2.csv")
[1] TRUE TRUE
```

The `cat()` function can be used to create a new .csv file. Using this function, you can direct the data you want to store to a new file that will be created if such a file does not already exist in the current working directory.

```
[1] "C:/Users/LAPTOP/Documents/curdata"
> cat("I am R language\n",file="test.csv")
```

You can also create a CSV file by importing data from databases.

```
data(iris)
write.table(iris, file = "test.csv", row.names = FALSE, sep = ",")
```

The test.csv file for the code shown above will be created in the current working directory with the following sample contents.

Sepal.Length	Sepal.Width	Petal.Length	Petal.Width	Species
5.1	3.5	1.4	0.2	setosa
4.9	3	1.4	0.2	setosa
4.7	3.2	1.3	0.2	setosa
4.6	3.1	1.5	0.2	setosa
5	3.6	1.4	0.2	setosa
5.4	3.9	1.7	0.4	setosa

While importing data from data sets, you can apply filters using the `subset()` command. You can pass the filter condition in this function.

```
# Create a data frame
cdata <- read.csv("test.csv")
fdata <- subset(cdata, Sepal.Length > 6.0)

# Write filtered data into a new file
write.csv(fdata,"filtered.csv")
ndata <- read.csv("filtered.csv ")
print(ndata)

   Sepal.Length Sepal.Width Petal.Length Petal.Width    Species
51          7.0         3.2          4.7         1.4 versicolor
52          6.4         3.2          4.5         1.5 versicolor
53          6.9         3.1          4.9         1.5 versicolor
55          6.5         2.8          4.6         1.5 versicolor
57          6.3         3.3          4.7         1.6 versicolor
```

R can also create CSV files from existing data frames. The `write.csv()` function is used to create such CSV files.

Reading a .csv file The `read.csv()` function reads a .csv file present in the current working directory. If it is not in the current working directory, the full path must be specified.

```
data <- read.csv("C:\\temp1\\input.csv")
print(data)
```

Roll No.	Name of Student	CLASS TEST-1 (20M)	CLASS TEST-2 (20M)	CLASS TEST-1 (6M)	CLASS TEST-2 (6M)	Conduct & Timely (8M).	Total (20M)
1	Aditi Yogesh Jamkar	4	0	2	0	6	8
2	Anshuli Rajesh Bobde	6	16	3	6	7	16
3	Avantika Murlidhar Hatmode	16	17	6	6	8	20
4	Devyani Sanjay Gabhane	14	17	5	6	8	19
5	Pali Divya Rajesh	16	16	6	6	8	20
6	Dnyaneshwari Kishor Badarkhe	17	18	6	6	8	20
7	Gauri Shrikant Wyawahare	19	17	6	6	8	20

```
mydata1 = read.table("C:\\temp1\\input.csv", header = TRUE, sep = ",")
> print(mydata1)
```

Roll No.	Name of Student	CLASS TEST-1 (20M)	CLASS TEST-2 (20M)	CLASS TEST-1 (6M)	CLASS TEST-2 (6M)	Conduct & Timely (8M)	Total (20M)
1	Aditi Yogesh Jamkar	4	0	2	0	6	8
2	Anshuli Rajesh Bobde	6	16	3	6	7	16
3	Avantika Murlidhar Hatmode	16	17	6	6	8	20
4	Devyani Sanjay Gabhane	14	17	5	6	8	19
5	Pali Divya Rajesh	16	16	6	6	8	20
6	Dnyaneshwari Kishor Badarkhe	17	18	6	6	8	20
7	Gauri Shrikant Wyawahare	19	17	6	6	8	20

We can also use `read.table()` to read data from a .csv file.

The first line of the file contains the variable names of the columns.

The `file.choose()` function opens the File dialog box, from which you can select the file to be opened. If your .txt file has no column names, then you can assign them using `colnames()`.

Contents of input.txt:

```
1   4   0
6   16  3
16  17  6
14  17  5
```

This data does not have column names. Thus, we need to assign the column names "Roll No", “CT1” and "CT2" to the input.txt data set.

```
> f1<- read.table("C:\\desktop\\input.txt", header=F)
> colnames(f1) <- c("Roll No" , "CT1" , "CT2")
> colnames(f1)
[1] "Roll No"  "CT1"  "CT2"
```

The argument `header = F` ensures that there are no column names associated with the data set.

When you read a .csv file, the contents can be retrieved as a data frame. You can then print the number of rows and columns in this data.

```
write.table(iris, file = "test.csv", row.names = FALSE, sep = ",")
> rdata <- read.csv("test.csv")
> print(is.data.frame(rdata))
[1] TRUE
> print(ncol(rdata))
[1] 5
> print(nrow(rdata))
[1] 150
```

Once you read data into the variable `rdata`, you can find the maximum `Sapel.Length` of the `Iris` data column.

```
> mdata <- max(rdata$Sepal.Length)
> mdata
[1] 7.9
```

To obtain details of the row with maximum `Sepal.Length`:

```
> retval <- subset(data, Sepal.Length==mdata)
> print(retval)
    Sepal.Length Sepal.Width Petal.Length Petal.Width   Species
132  7.9          3.8          6.4              2 virginica
```

You can filter data based on any criteria by applying SQL-like queries. For example, to retrieve all the rows whose `Sepal.Length` > 6.0, you can use the command given below

```
fdata <- subset(rdata, Sepal.Length > 6.0)
```

13.3.2 Working with JSON Files

JSON files are mostly created to store IOT sensor data and are becoming increasingly popular. These files store data as text in human-readable format. JSON stands for JavaScript Object Notation. To read JSON files in R, the `rjson` package must be installed and imported.

```
install.packages("rjson")
```

Creating a .json file We can create a JSON file by entering data in a text editor such as Notepad and then saving the file with a .json extension. For example, you can copy the data given below into a text editor and save the file as input.json.

```
{
"Fruit":[ "Apple","Orange","Pear"],
"Size": ["Large","Large","Medium"],
"Color": ["Red","Orange","Green"]
"Cost": ["200","100","150"]
}
```

Reading a .json file First, we need to load the `rjson` package using the `library()` function. To read the contents of a JSON file, the `fromJSON()` function can be used.

```
library("rjson")
result <- fromJSON(file = "input.json")
print(result)
```

Output:

```
$Fruit
[1] "Apple","Orange","Pear"

$Size
[1] "Large","Large","Medium"

$Color
[1] "Red","Orange","Green"
$Cost
[1] "200","100","150"
```

Converting to data frame JSON files read using the above method show data in the form of text entries only. To read cost as a numerical entry, we can use the `as.dataframe()` function for further analysis.

```
library("rjson")
result <- fromJSON(file = "input.json")
json_data_frame <- as.data.frame(result)
print(json_data_frame)
```

When we execute the above code, it produces the following output:

```
  Fruit   Size    Color   Cost
1 Apple   Large   Red     200
2 Orange  Large   Orange  100
3 Pear    Medium  Green   150
```

13.3.3 Working with XML Files

XML stands for Extensible Markup Language, which is similar to HTML. The main difference is that instead of using standard tags, XML uses markup tags. A markup tag describes the structure of the page or data. These tags are meaningful and describe the data.

XML files can be processed by importing and installing the `XML` package. You can load the `XML` package using the `library()` function. This will load all the functions required to process XML files.

```
install.packages("XML")
library("XML")
```

You can load the other required packages by passing "methods" in the `library()` function.

```
library("methods")
```

Creating a .xml file You can create .xml files in any editor such as Notepad or Wordpad and then save it as filename.xml. For example, we can create the following record of a student in the XML format.

```
<CLASS>
   <STUDENT>
      <NAME>SHREYA</NAME>
      <AGE>16</AGE>
      <SUB1>PHYSICS</SUB1>
      <SUB2>COMPUTER</SUB2>
    </STUDENT>

   <STUDENT>
      <NAME>RISHIKA</NAME>
      <AGE>16</AGE>
      <SUB1>COMMERCE</SUB1>
      <SUB2>MATHEMATICS</SUB2>
    </STUDENT>

<STUDENT>
      <NAME>SNEHA</NAME>
      <AGE>17</AGE>
      <SUB1>PHYSICS</SUB1>
      <SUB2>BIOLOGY</SUB2>
    </STUDENT>
<STUDENT>
      <NAME>Ojas</NAME>
      <AGE>16</AGE>
      <SUB1>CHEMISTRY</SUB1>
      <SUB2>COMPUTER</SUB2>
    </STUDENT>
</CLASS>
```

Reading a .xml file You can read an XML file using the `xmlParse()` (file name with path) function.

```
Record1 <- xmlParse( "c:\\test.xml")
print(Record1)
```

Output:

```
<?xml version="1.0"?>
<CLASS>
  <STUDENT>
    <NAME>SHREYA</NAME>
    <AGE>16</AGE>
    <SUB1>PHYSICS</SUB1>
    <SUB2>COMPUTER</SUB2>
  </STUDENT>
  <STUDENT>
    <NAME>RISHIKA</NAME>
    <AGE>16</AGE>
    <SUB1>COMMERCE</SUB1>
    <SUB2>MATHEMATICS</SUB2>
  </STUDENT>
  <STUDENT>
    <NAME>SNEHA</NAME>
    <AGE>17</AGE>
    <SUB1>PHYSICS</SUB1>
    <SUB2>BIOLOGY</SUB2>
  </STUDENT>
  <STUDENT>
    <NAME>Ojas</NAME>
    <AGE>16</AGE>
    <SUB1>CHEMISTRY</SUB1>
    <SUB2>COMPUTER</SUB2>
  </STUDENT>
</CLASS>
```

Converting to data frame You can convert XML data to data frame using the `xmlToDataFrame()` function and passing the file name as argument.

```
> xmldataframe <- xmlToDataFrame("C:\\test.xml")
> xmldataframe
     NAME AGE      SUB1        SUB2
1  SHREYA  16   PHYSICS    COMPUTER
2 RISHIKA  16  COMMERCE MATHEMATICS
3   SNEHA  17   PHYSICS     BIOLOGY
4    Ojas  16 CHEMISTRY    COMPUTER
```

To obtain the number of nodes present in an XML file, we can use the following command:

```
> rnode <- xmlRoot(record1)
> rsize <- xmlSize(rnode)
> print(rize)
[1] 4
```

To obtain the details of the root node 1, you can use the following command:

```
> rnode <- xmlRoot(Record1)
> print(rnode[1])

$STUDENT
<STUDENT>
  <NAME>SHREYA</NAME>
  <AGE>16</AGE>
  <SUB1>PHYSICS</SUB1>
  <SUB2>COMPUTER</SUB2>
</STUDENT>

attr(,"class")
[1] "XMLInternalNodeList" "XMLNodeList"
```

We can obtain the details of the second node in a similar manner:

```
> print(rnode[2])
$STUDENT
<STUDENT>
  <NAME>RISHIKA</NAME>
  <AGE>16</AGE>
  <SUB1>COMMERCE</SUB1>
  <SUB2>MATHEMATICS</SUB2>
</STUDENT>

attr(,"class")
[1] "XMLInternalNodeList" "XMLNodeList"
```

When we execute the above code, it produces the following output:

```
attr(,"class")
[1] "XMLInternalNodeList" "XMLNodeList"
```

To obtain the first element of the first node:

```
> print(rnode[[1]][[1]])
<NAME>SHREYA</NAME>
```

To obtain the third element of the first node:

```
> print(rnode[[1]][[3]])
<SUB1>PHYSICS</SUB1>
```

To obtain the first element of the third node:

```
> print(rnode[[3]][[1]])
<NAME>SNEHA</NAME>
```

13.3.4 Creating and Setting up Directories

To find out and print the current working directory, we can use the `getwd()` function.

```
> print(getwd())
[1] "C:/Users/LAPTOP/Documents"
```

You can create a new directory in the current working directory `curdata` using the `dir.create()` function.

```
> dir.create("curdata")
> print(getwd())
[1] "C:/Users/LAPTOP/Documents"
> list.files()
```

In the above example, the `list.file()` function will list all the files and directories under "C:/Users/LAPTOP/Documents", where the new directory `curdata` has been created.

You can set the current working directory to any new directory using the `setwd()` function.

```
> setwd("C://Users//LAPTOP//Documents//curdata")
> getwd()
[1] "C:/Users/LAPTOP/Documents/curdata"
```

Creating a path to a file You can construct the path to a file from components in a platform-independent way. The following command can be used to achieve this:

```
file.path("test.csv")
[1] "test.csv"
```

The `basename()` function removes all of the path up to and including the last path separator:

```
basename(file.path("test.csv"))
[1] "test.csv"
```

The `dirname()` function returns the part of the path up to but excluding the last path separator, or `"."` if there is no path separator:

```
dirname(file.path("test.csv"))
[1] "."
```

Removing, deleting and renaming a file To remove a file, we must first check that it exists. For example, we need to find out if test.csv exists. We can then remove it using the `file.remove()` function.

```
> file.exists("test.csv")
[1] TRUE
> file.remove("test.csv")
[1] TRUE
> file.exists("test.csv")
[1] FALSE
```

The `file.remove()` function removes the file but the `unlink()` function removes the symbolic reference to the file.

```
unlink("test1.csv")
file.exists("test1.csv")
[1] FALSE
```

We can rename the file in the same directory, which is the current working directory.

```
file.rename("filtered.csv", "newfiltered.csv")
[1] TRUE
```

Extracting file information The `file.info()` function enables you to extract information about a specific file. You need to pass the file name as argument with this function.

```
file.info("test.csv")
size isdir mode                    mtime                  ctime
test.csv 4177 FALSE  666 2013-10-08 12:45:40 2013-10-08 12:45:05
atime exe
test.csv 2013-10-08 12:45:40  no

> file.info("filtered.csv")
             size isdir mode                  mtime                  ctime
filtered.csv 2161 FALSE  666 2019-12-28 15:49:17 2019-12-28 15:49:17
                            atime exe
filtered.csv 2019-12-28 15:49:17  no
```

You can also use this function to list the files of a particular type in a directory/folder.

```
> Sys.glob("*.csv")
[1] "f1.csv"            "f2.csv"            "filtered.csv"     "newfiltered.
csv"
[5] "test.csv"
```

EXERCISES

Multiple Choice Questions

1. Which of the following commands will correctly read the .csv file with five rows in a data frame?
   a. `read.csv('Dataframe.csv')`
   b. `read.csv('Dataframe.csv',header=TRUE)`
   c. `dataframe('Dataframe.csv')`
   d. `read.csv('Dataframe.csv',header=FALSE,sep=',')`
2. The Excel file format is one of the most common formats used to store data sets. It is important to know how to import an Excel file into R. Below is an Excel file in which data has been entered in the third sheet.

Alpha	**125.5**	**0**
Beta	235.6	1
Beta	212.03	0
Beta	211.30	0
Alpha	265.46	1

File name – Dataframe.xlsx

Which of the following codes will read the above data in the third sheet into a data frame in R?

a. `Openxlsx::read.xlsx ("Dataframe.xlsx",sheet=3, colNames=FALSE)`

b. `Xlsx::read.xlsx ("Dataframe.xlsx", sheetIndex=3, header=FALSE)`

c. `XLConnect::readWorksheet FromFile("Dataframe.xlsx", sheet=3,header=FALSE)`

d. All of the above

3. R functionality is divided into a number of ________.

a. Packages
b. Functions
c. Domains
d. All of the above

Answers

1. d	**2.** d	**3.** a

Programming Questions

1. Write an R program to read the header row of a .csv file.
2. Create two .csv files and merge them based on a criterion.
3. Write an R program to delete a column from a .csv file.
4. Create data frames and write them to a file.
5. Create a backup of all the .csv files in a directory.
6. Create a .txt file and .csv file of a student database and filter the entries based on a numerical column.

CHAPTER

14 Graphs in R Programming

Objectives

At the end of this chapter, you will be able to

- Define and create graphs in R
- Create histograms, kernel density plots, dot plots, bar charts, line charts, pie charts, box plots and scatter plots
- Explain how to save a graph as a PDF
- Describe how to create three-dimensional plots

14.1 | INTRODUCTION TO GRAPHS

Graphs are a powerful way to present data in a concise and pictorial manner. Different types of data can be shown graphically in R (Fig. 14.1). One of the main features of R is its ability to handle large volumes of data, and graphs can be a better way of representing that data than just with words and numbers. Some graphs reveal patterns of data that can be used in correct statistical analysis.

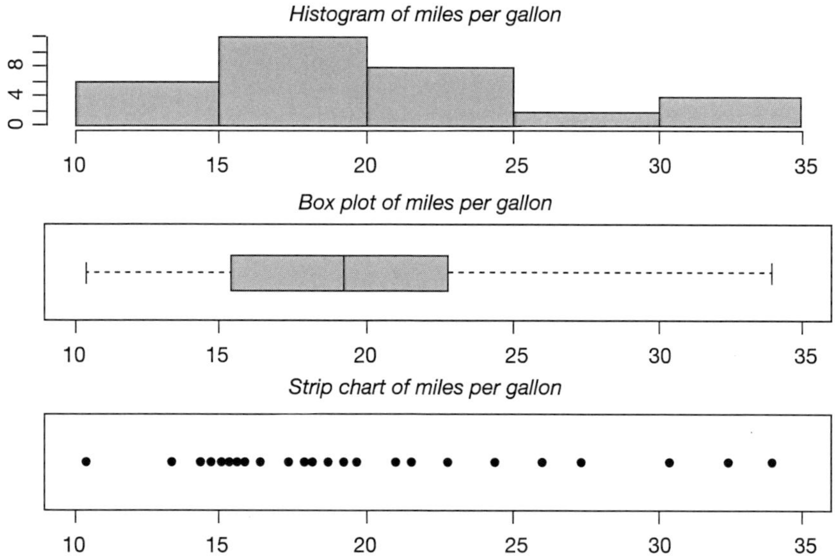

Fig. 14.1: Graphical presentation of data

14.2 | CREATING GRAPHS

In R programming, graphs can be created using the `plot()` function. Each new graph is created in a separate canvas. The shape of the plot depends on the commands and arguments specified by the user.

14.2.1 The `plot()` Function

In R, `plot()` is a generic function passed along with the class of the object to be drawn. It is a placeholder for a family of functions. When we call `plot()` with vectors X and Y, it is interpreted as plotting of the data on the (x,y) plane.

```
>plot(c(11,22,33), c(11,22,33))
```

The above code will create a line from (11, 11) to (22, 22) and to (33, 33) (Fig. 14.2).

You may add labels to an axis using the parameters `xlab` and `ylab`. The range of the x axis and y axis can be given in the first parameter. The parameter `type` = "n" means the graph is empty – there is nothing in the graph itself and no points are plotted, as shown in Fig. 14.3.

```
> plot(c(10,100), c(10,50), type = "n", xlab="days", ylab="Temp")
```

This command states that the range of the x axis should 10–100 and that of the y axis, 10–50 (Fig. 14.3).

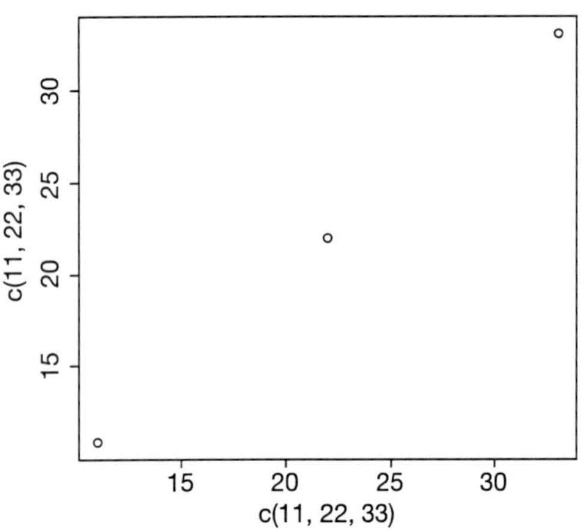

Fig. 14.2: Simple point plot

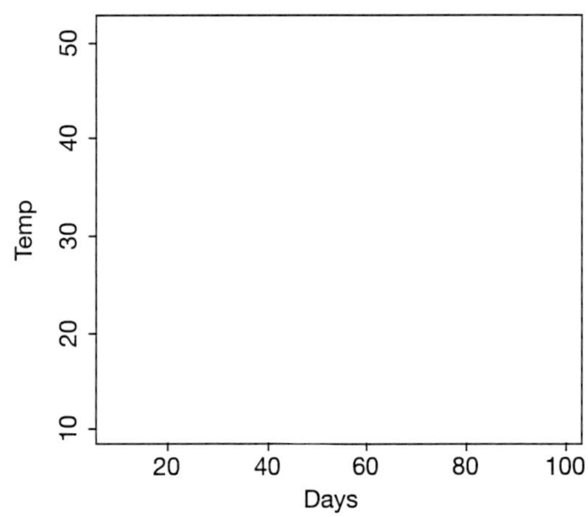

Fig. 14.3: Point plot with labels on the axes and `type` = "n"

14.2.2 Adding Lines: The `abline()` Function

In the previous section, we discussed how to plot the axes and points, and how to specify labels and the range of axes. Now, we can draw a line connecting the points. First we use the linear regression function, `lm()`, to simulate the model and then draw a line using `abline()` by passing the linear regression model as argument (Fig. 14.4).

```
x<-c(11,22,33)
> y<-c(11,22,33)
> plot(x,y)
> lmout <- lm(y ~ x)
>  abline(lmout)
```

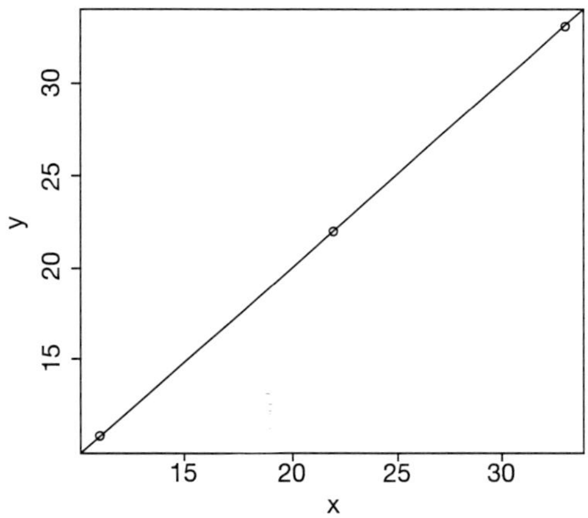

Fig. 14.4: Using the `abline()` function to add a line to the graph

The linear regression function, `lm(c,m)`, has as its arguments the slope and intercept of the fitted line. The equation for the line will be y = m * x + c. The `abline()` function takes the regression model created with `lm()` as its argument. This draws a straight line connecting the points of the regression model.

Alternatively, you can draw a line by specifying type = "1".

```
x<-c(11,22,33)
> y<-c(11,22,33)
> plot(x,y, type="l")
```

14.3 | HISTOGRAMS AND DENSITY PLOTS

All the plots created in the following sections use the `mtcars` database given below.

```
> mtcars
                    mpg cyl  disp  hp drat    wt  qsec vs am gear carb
Mazda RX4          21.0   6 160.0 110 3.90 2.620 16.46  0  1    4    4
Mazda RX4 Wag      21.0   6 160.0 110 3.90 2.875 17.02  0  1    4    4
Datsun 710         22.8   4 108.0  93 3.85 2.320 18.61  1  1    4    1
Hornet 4 Drive     21.4   6 258.0 110 3.08 3.215 19.44  1  0    3    1
Hornet Sportabout  18.7   8 360.0 175 3.15 3.440 17.02  0  0    3    2
Valiant            18.1   6 225.0 105 2.76 3.460 20.22  1  0    3    1
Duster 360         14.3   8 360.0 245 3.21 3.570 15.84  0  0    3    4
Merc 240D          24.4   4 146.7  62 3.69 3.190 20.00  1  0    4    2
Merc 230           22.8   4 140.8  95 3.92 3.150 22.90  1  0    4    2
Merc 280           19.2   6 167.6 123 3.92 3.440 18.30  1  0    4    4
Merc 280C          17.8   6 167.6 123 3.92 3.440 18.90  1  0    4    4
Merc 450SE         16.4   8 275.8 180 3.07 4.070 17.40  0  0    3    3
Merc 450SL         17.3   8 275.8 180 3.07 3.730 17.60  0  0    3    3
Merc 450SLC        15.2   8 275.8 180 3.07 3.780 18.00  0  0    3    3
Cadillac Fleetwood 10.4   8 472.0 205 2.93 5.250 17.98  0  0    3    4
```

14.3.1 Histograms

The `hist(y)` function in R is used to create histograms, where `y` is a numeric vector of the values (frequency of values) to be plotted.

```
# Simple histogram shown in Fig. 14.5 with default parameters
>hist(mtcars$mpg)
```

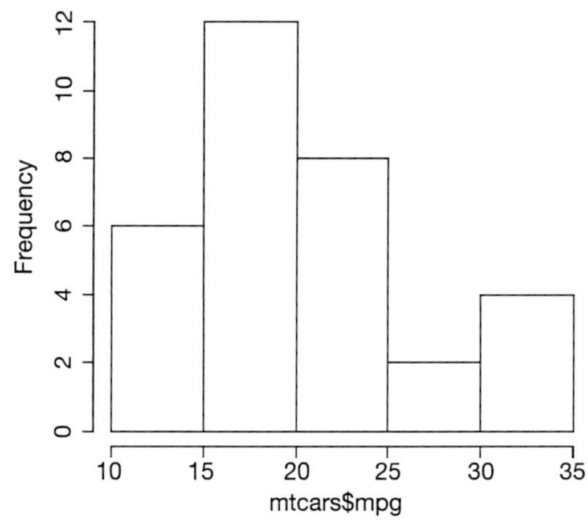

Fig. 14.5: Simple histogram of the `mtcars` data set's `mpg` variable

In this function, the `breaks` parameter can be used to specify the number of bins. Minimum to maximum range values divided in equal parts are called bins or the class interval. In addition, the columns `color`, `x title`, `y title` and `graph title` can be specified. You can colour the bars of the graph by specifying the colour using the `col` parameter. Figure 14.6 shows the histogram for 10 bins and green colour.

```
hist(mtcars$mpg, breaks=10, col="green")
```

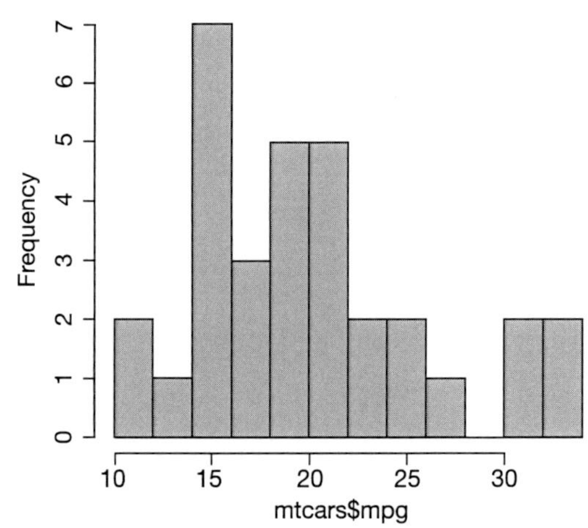

Fig. 14.6: Histogram of the `mtcars mpg` variable with different bins

You can draw a normal curve using the `dnorm()` function, which takes the minimum, maximum and mean of x values as arguments.

```
x <- mtcars$mpg
h<-hist(x, breaks=12, col="green", xlab="MPG",
main="Histogram and Normalized Distribution")
xvalue<-seq(min(x) ,max(x) ,length=30)
yvalue<-dnorm(xvalue, mean=mean(x),sd=sd(x))
yvalue <- yvalue*diff(h$mids[1:2])*length(x)
lines(xvalue, yvalue, col="red", lwd=4)
```

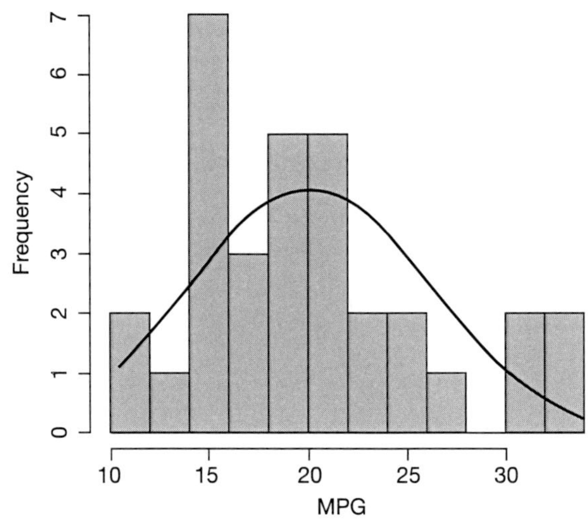

Fig. 14.7: Histogram and normalised distribution

The shape of the distribution can be roughly determined because it is affected by the number of bins used in the histogram, as shown in Fig. 14.7.

14.3.2 Kernel Density Plots

Kernel density plots can directly draw the distribution of a data. The `plot(density(y))` function can be used to create the plot, where y is a numeric vector.

```
# Kernel density plot on field mpg of mtcars data, as shown in Fig. 14.8
# To obtain the data of interest
data <- density(mtcars$mpg)
plot(data) # plots the real distribution
```

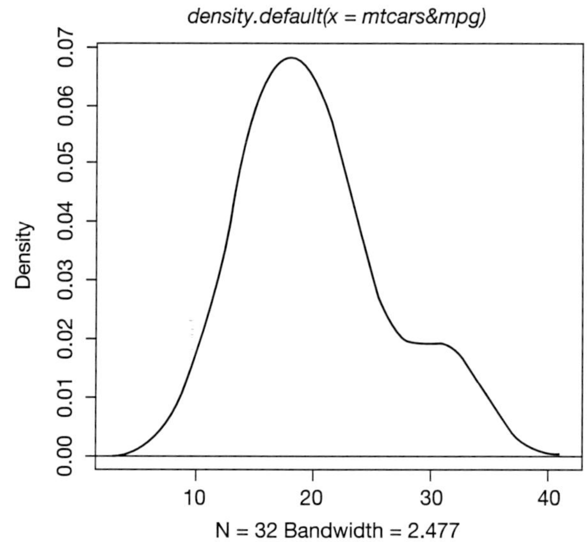

Fig. 14.8: Density plot of the `mtcars mpg` variable

```
# To colour the density plot green
data <- density(mtcars$mpg)
plot(data, main="Kernel Density of  mtcars data")
polygon(data, col="green", border="red")
```

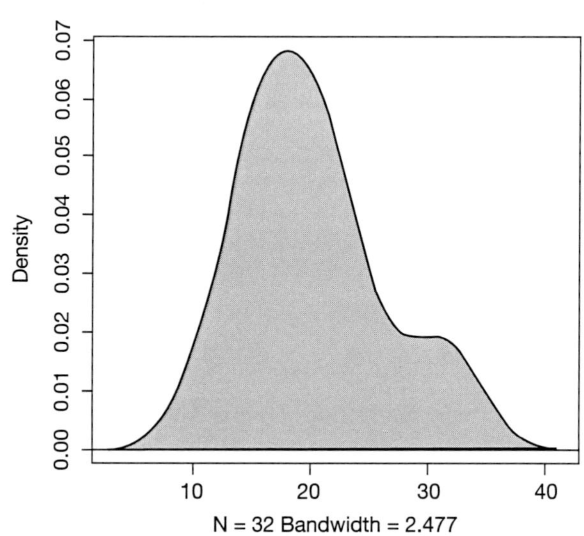

Fig. 14.9: Kernal density plot of the `mtcars mpg` variable

14.4 | DOT PLOTS

A dot plot is a two-dimensional plot that draws dots of specific x, y coordinates. Dot plots can be created using the `dotchart(data, labels=)` function, where `data` is a numeric vector and `labels` is a vector of labels to be displayed on the axes. The `groups=` option can be added to specify how data should be grouped; the `gcolor=` option controls the colour of the group labels; while the `cex` option controls the size of the labels.

```
# Dot plot on field mpg of mtcars data, as shown in Fig. 14.10
dotchart(mtcars$mpg, labels=row.names(mtcars), cex=.9,main="Dot Plot for
Car Models", xlab="Miles Per Gallon")
```

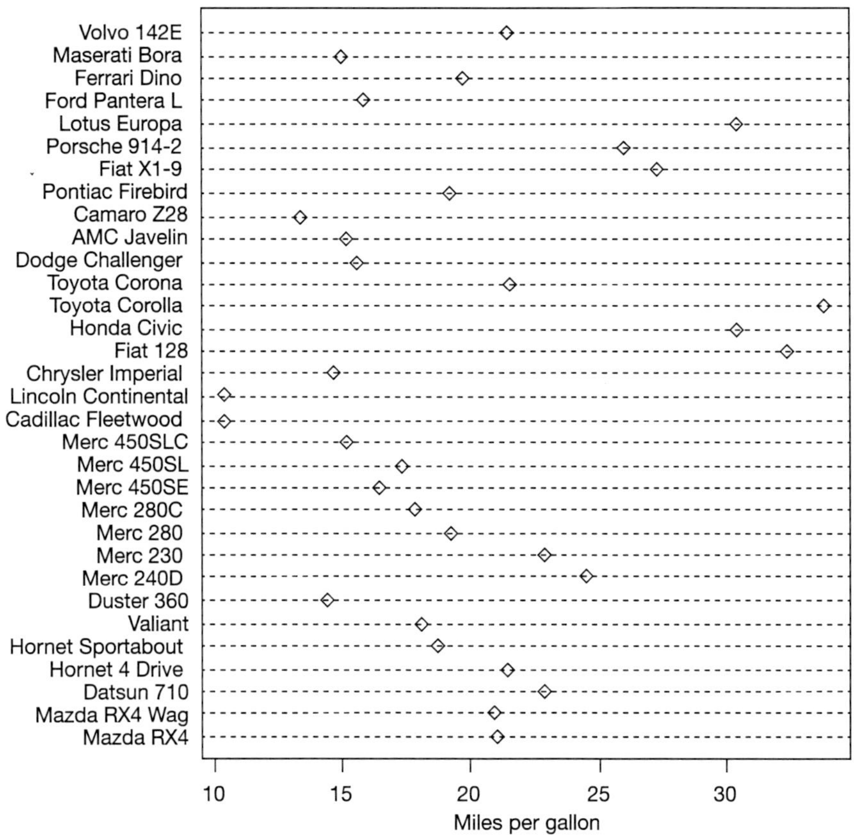

Fig. 14.10: Dot plot for car models

Given below is the code to create a dot plot and group the data based on field `cyl`, shown in Fig. 14.11. This factor will level (group) the data and bring similar data together. Level 4 of `cyl` is to be coloured red, and so on. The data is sorted on `mpg`, group on `cyl` and colour by `cylinder`. The code first sorts (orders) `mtcars` based on the `mpg` field. It then groups data based on the `cyl` column.

```
xcar <- mtcars[order(mtcars$mpg),]
# Factor on cyl to group data
xcar$cyl <- factor(xcar$cyl)
xcar$color[xcar$cyl==4] <- "green"
xcar$color[xcar$cyl==6] <- "red"
xcar$color[xcar$cyl==8] <- "yellow"
dotchart(xcar$mpg,labels=row.names(xcar),cex=.9,groups= xcar$cyl,
main="car Models dot plot grouping on cyn",xlab="MPG", gcolor="black",
color=xcar$color)
```

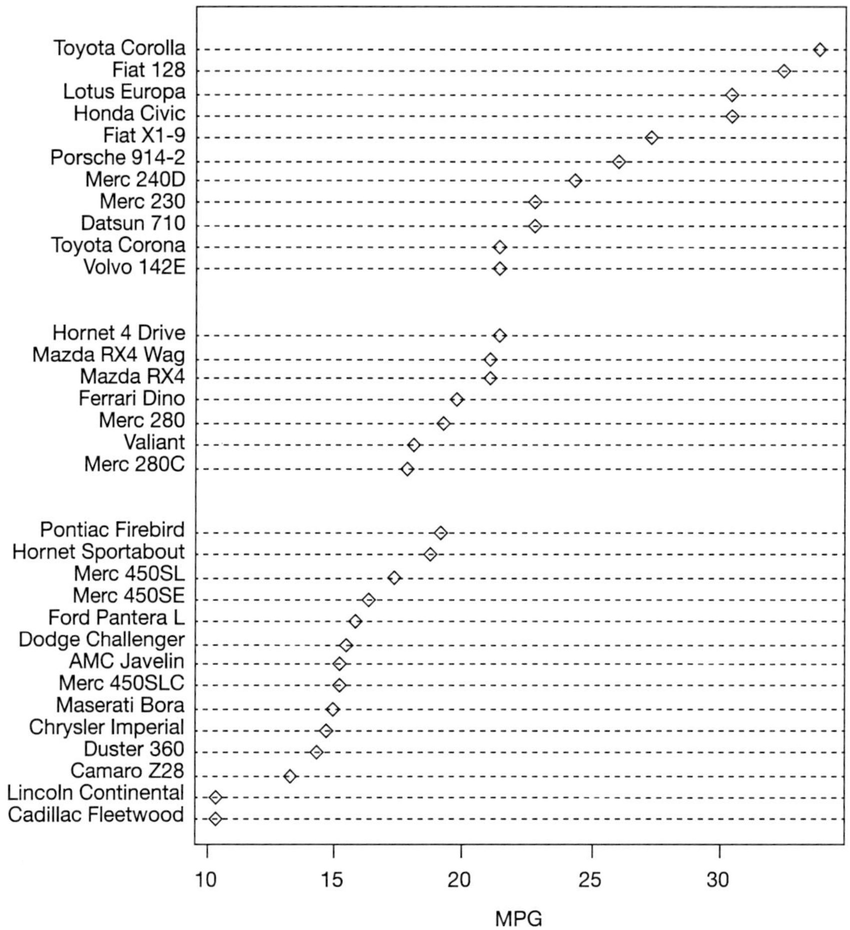

Fig. 14.11: Car model dot plot grouping on `cyl`

14.5 | BAR PLOTS

The bar chart is suitable for showing data that falls into discrete categories. The horizontal axis represents the different categories and the vertical axis represents the number of cases (frequencies) of the characteristics. Bar charts are flexible and can show items in various groupings.

The `barplot(y)` function can be used to create bar plots, where `y` is a vector or matrix. This function takes as its arguments the vector or matrix data, title and axis labels. The code given below creates a bar plot based on the `gear` field of `mtcars`. The `table(gear)` function counts the frequency of data in the `gear` field of `mtcars` while `barplot()` creates a bar graph (histogram) on the `gear` field.

```
# Simple bar plot on gear field of mtcars. X axis has data values and y
has frequency, as shown in Fig. 14.12
cnt <- table(mtcars$gear)
barplot(cnt, main="Car Distribution",xlab="Number of Gears")
```

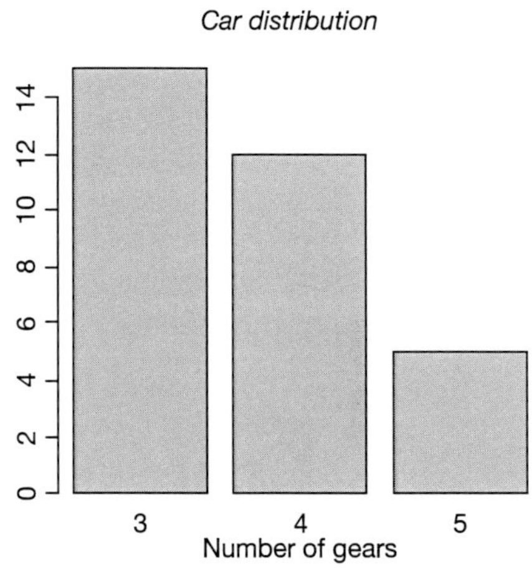

Fig. 14.12: Bar plot of `gear` variable of `mtcars`

We will now create the same graph horizontally and label the levels of data.

```
# Horizontal bar plot with horiz, add labels with names.arg, as shown in
Fig. 14.13
cnt <- table(mtcars$gear)
barplot(cnt, main="Car Gear Histogram", horiz=TRUE,
names.arg=c("3 Gears", "4 Gears", "5 Gears"))
```

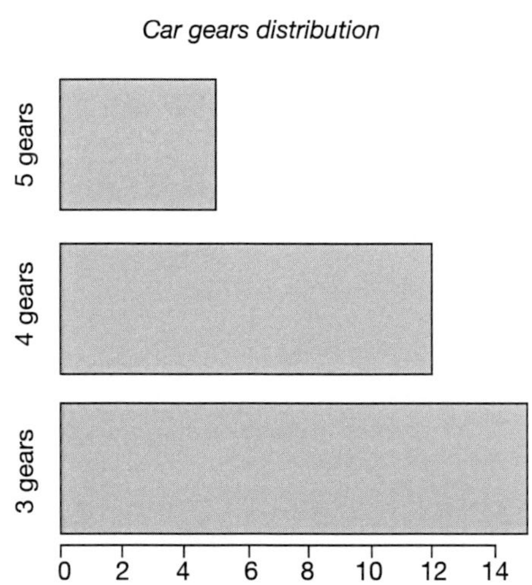

Fig. 14.13: Horizontal bar plot with labels of the `gear` variable of `mtcars`

You can display multiple categories on a single plot. Stacked bars and group bars enable you to display several groups of categories.

14.5.1 Stacked Bar Plot

If you want to display bars in groups of categories stacked one over the other, then you can choose to plot a stacked bar. You can select the first group of data and then pass it to the `barplot()` function, as the first parameter. The other parameters are `set label`, `color` and `legend`.

Given below is the code to plot a stacked bar based on the `gear` and `VS` fields, as shown in Fig. 14.14.

```
cnt <- table(mtcars$vs, mtcars$gear)
barplot(cnt, main="Car Distribution Stacked Bars by Gears and
VS",xlab="Number of Gears", col=c("green","red"),
legend = rownames(cnt))
```

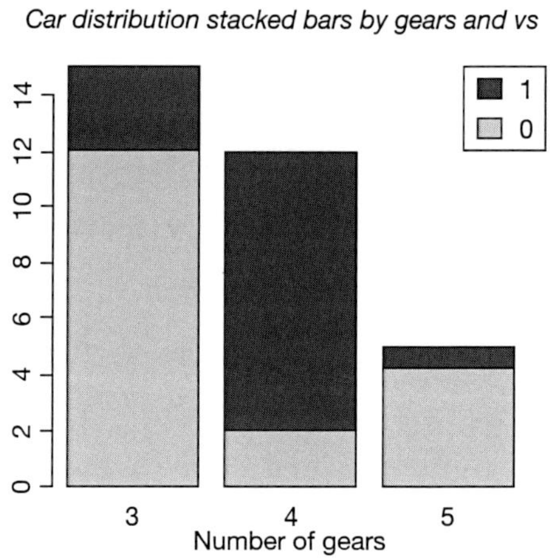

Fig. 14:14: Stacked bar plot

14.5.2 Grouped Bar Plot

The default bar chart is a stacked bar plot. If you wish to display groups horizontally beside each other instead of stacked, then you can use the group bar plot. This can be accomplished by setting `beside=true` in the `barplot()` function. Given below is the code to display the bar chart for two display groups, `VS` and `gear`, next to each other, as shown in Fig. 14.15.

```
cnt <- table(mtcars$vs, mtcars$gear)
barplot(cnt, main="Car Distribution Group Bars by Gears and
VS",xlab="Number of Gears", col=c("green","red"),
legend = rownames(cnt), beside=TRUE)
```

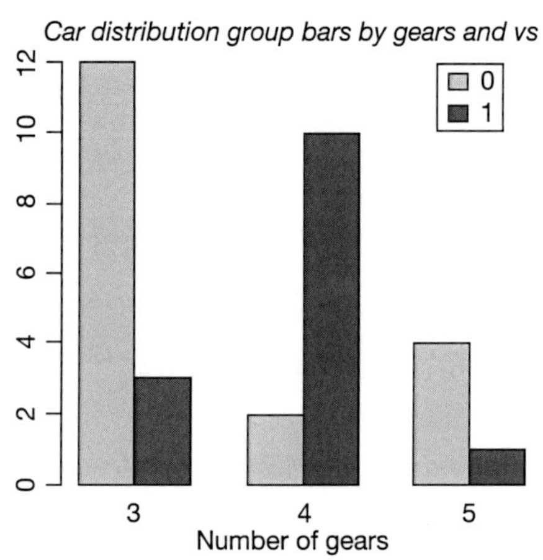

Fig. 14.15: Grouped bar plot

14.6 | LINE CHARTS

Line charts are used to record data over time. Often, data is collected over a period of time. Line charts or scatter plots are the best way to represent this data, where the y axis reflects the magnitude of the data and the x axis reflects the time. Joining this data over time can reveal data trends.

Line charts are created using the `lines(x, y, type=)` function, where `x` and `y` are numeric vectors and `type` can take the character values listed in Table 14.1.

Table 14.1 Character values for the `type` parameter

Type	Description
P	Displays only points
L	Connects points with lines but the points are not shown
O	Overlaps the line with points
B	Shows broken lines
H	Shows vertical lines like in a histogram
N	Shows no points or lines

The `lines()` function draws lines on a graph, but it cannot produce the graph itself. Usually, it follows a `plot(x, y)` command, which produces the graph. The `line()` function can specify the type of line graph that will be plotted by the `plot()` command, which plots the `(x,y)` points of a graph with axes, titles, and so on, as shown in Fig. 14.16.

For example, to create and set up a graph but without plotting the points:

```
# Use the type="n" option in the plot( ) command, plot shown in Fig. 14.16
# Generate some data and store in x
x <- c(1:5); y <- x
# Plotting symbol and red colour
par(pch=24, col="red")
# All plots 2 rows and 3 columns on one page
par(mfrow=c(2,3))
options = c("p","l","o","b","s","h")
for(i in 1:length(options)){
headopt = paste("type=",options[i])
plot(x, y, type="n", main=headopt)
lines(x, y, type=options[i])
}
```

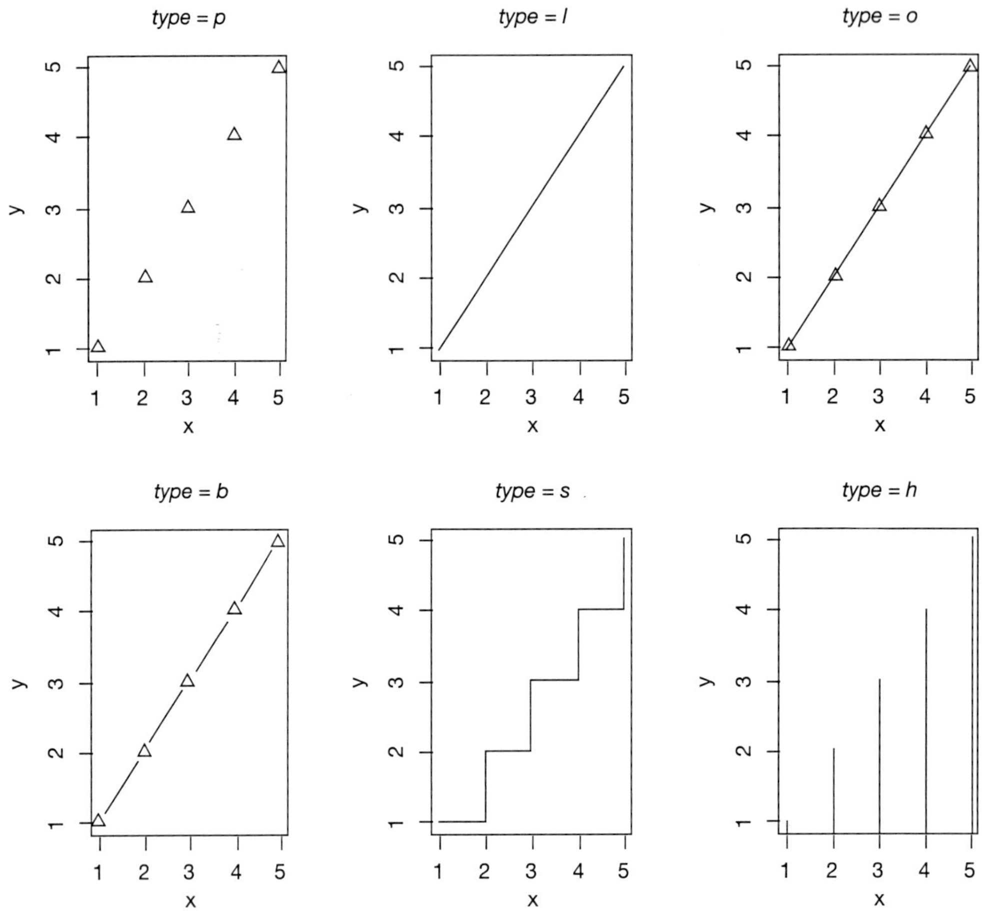

Fig. 14.16: Line plots of different types without points

Next, we can use the same code but draw points by removing `type=n` in `plot()`, as shown in Fig. 14.17.

```
# Generate some data
x <- c(1:5); y <- x
# Plotting symbol and red colour
par(pch=22, col="red")
# All plots 2 rows and 3 columns on one page
par(mfrow=c(2,3))
opts = c("p","l","o","b","s","h")
for(i in 1:length(options) ) {
headopt = paste("type=",opts[i])
plot(x, y, main=headopt)
lines(x, y, type=options[i])
}
```

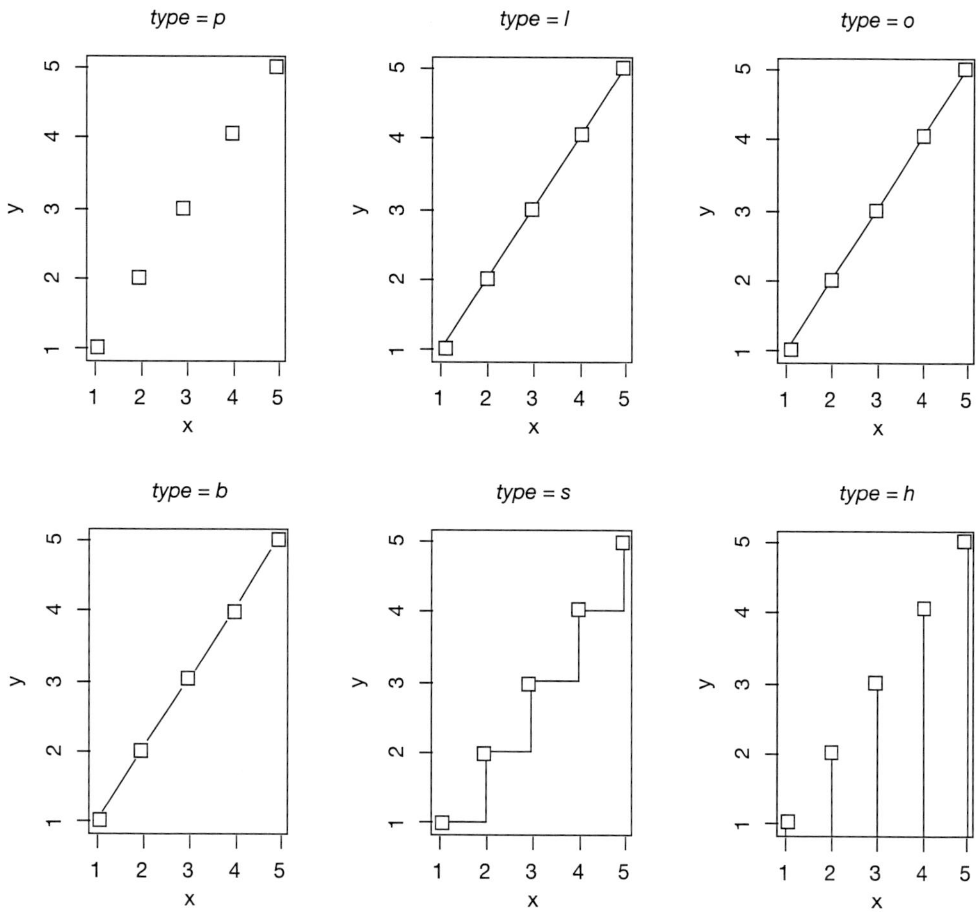

Fig. 14.17: Line plots of different types with the points plotted

To demonstrate the creation of a more complex line chart, let us plot the growth of five orange trees based on the fields, age and circumference. The built-in data set `Orange` can be displayed as follows:

```
> Orange
   Tree  age circumference
1     2  118            30
2     2  484            58
3     2  664            87
4     2 1004           115
5     2 1231           120
6     2 1372           142
7     2 1582           145
8     4  118            33
9     4  484            69
10    4  664           111
11    4 1004           156
12    4 1231           172
```

The code to plot the line graph of `age` versus `circumference` group by tree number is shown below and the plot itself in Fig. 14.18. This code works on the built-in data set `Orange` which has three columns: `Tree`, `age`, `circumference`.

```
# Line charts to compare orange tree data
# Convert data to numeric and sort on Tree field
Orange$Tree <- as.numeric(Orange$Tree)
# Calculate maximum of Tree field
noftrees <- max(Orange$Tree)
# Get the range of values for the age and circumference field on x and y
axis respectively
xaxis <- range(Orange$age)
yaxis <- range(Orange$circumference)
# Set up the plot Age Vs Circumference
plot(xaxis, yaxis, xlab="Age (in days)",ylab="Circumference (in mm)" )
# Generate 5 random colours of rainbow
colors <- rainbow(noftrees)
# Generate sequence between 1 and 5
ltype <- c(1:noftrees)
# Generate sequence between 18 and 23
pchar <- seq(18,18+noftrees,1)

# Add lines joining points
for (i in 1:noftrees) {
# Create group on Tree field
treeg <- subset(Orange, Tree==i)
lines(treeg$age, treeg$circumference, type="b", lwd=1.5, lty=ltype[i],
col=colors[i], pch=pchar[i])
}

# Add title to graph
title("Orange Tree Growth", "Line plots")
# Add a legend
legend(xaxis[1], yaxis[2], 1:noftrees, cex=0.8, col=colors,
pch=pchar, lty=ltype, title="Tree Number")
```

Intermediate variable values

```
> xaxis
[1]  118 1582
> colors
[1] "#FF0000FF" "#CCFF00FF" "#00FF66FF" "#0066FFFF" "#CC00FFFF"
> noftrees
[1] 5
> ltype
[1] 1 2 3 4 5
> pchar
[1] 18 19 20 21 22 23
> treeg
   Tree  age circumference
22    5  118            32
23    5  484            62
24    5  664           112
25    5 1004           167
26    5 1231           179
27    5 1372           209
28    5 1582           214
```

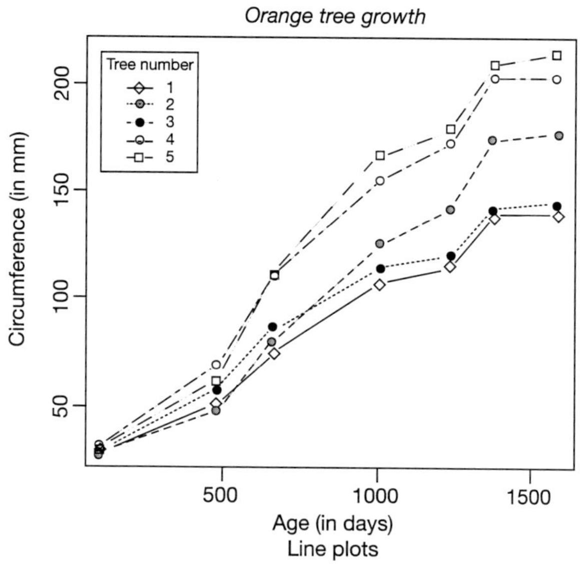

Fig. 14.18: Line plot `age` vs `circumference` group by tree number

14.7 | PIE CHARTS

Pie charts are useful for the graphical representation of nominal and ordinal data. They display categories and their values. Areas/Values are represented in proportion to the total as slices of a circle or pie. For example, you may have data that shows the placement of students in various companies. The pie chart enables you to know how many students are placed in a company. Each company placing students is represented by a slice of the pie. The bigger the slice or area, the bigger the contribution to the total placement. The pie chart takes a series of data values and determines the relative proportion of each item towards the total.

Pie charts are created using the `pie(x, labels=)` function, where x is a non-negative numeric vector indicating the area of each slice and `labels` is used to name the areas in the pie.

The example given below shows how to generate the number of placements in companies. The company names are stored in the vector `lbls`. The `pie()` function accepts data, labels and title.

```
# Pie chart to represent placement of students by companies, as shown in
Fig. 14.19
portions <- c(10, 12,4, 15, 8)
lbls <- c("TCS", "Persistent", "Capgemini", "Cognizant", "L&T")
pie(portions, labels = lbls, main="Pie Chart of placements")
```

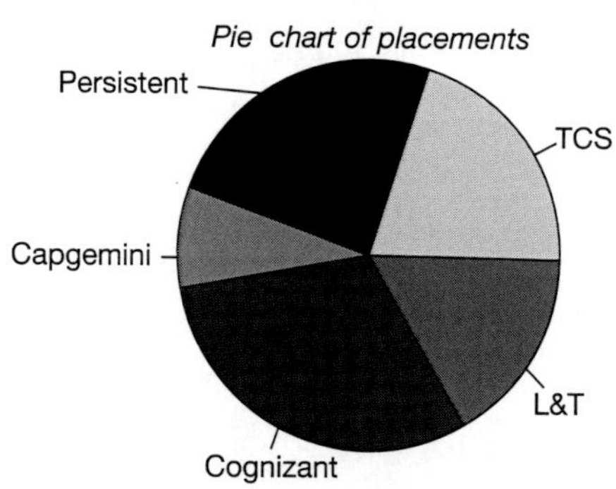

Fig. 14.19: Pie plot

```
# Pie chart with annotated percentages, as shown in Fig. 14.20
portions<- c(10, 12,4, 15, 8)
lbls <- c("TCS", "Persistent", "Capgemini", "Cognizant", "L&T")
per<- round (portions/sum(portions)*100)
# Add percents to labels
lbl <- paste(lbl, per)
# Add % to labels
lbl <- paste(lbl,"%",sep="")
pie(portions ,labels = lbl, col=rainbow(length(lbl)), main="Pie Chart of
Placement in Companies")
```

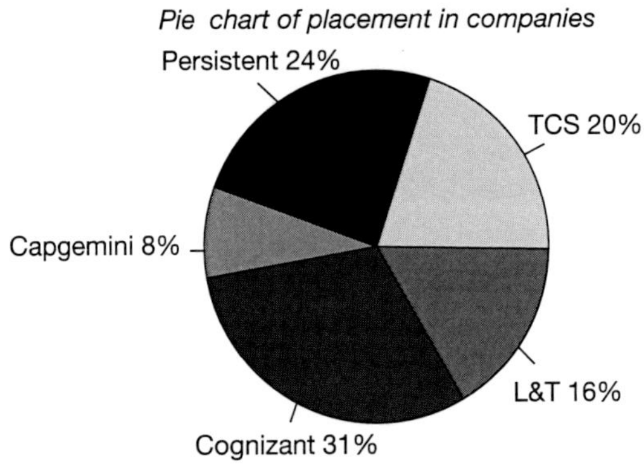

Fig. 14.20: Pie plot with annotations

The pie chart shown in Fig. 14.21 was created from the data frame `iris`, which is built into R, and is given below:

```
> iris
    Sepal.Length Sepal.Width Petal.Length Petal.Width   Species
1            5.1         3.5          1.4         0.2    setosa
2            4.9         3.0          1.4         0.2    setosa
3            4.7         3.2          1.3         0.2    setosa
4            4.6         3.1          1.5         0.2    setosa
5            5.0         3.6          1.4         0.2    setosa
6            5.4         3.9          1.7         0.4    setosa
7            4.6         3.4          1.4         0.3    setosa
8            5.0         3.4          1.5         0.2    setosa
```

```
# Takes data frame iris and display the species in form of pie chart,
shown in Fig. 14.21.
data <- table(iris$Species)
# Combine  string
lbl <- paste(names(data), "\n", data, sep="")
pie(data, labels = lbl, main="Pie Chart of Species\n (with sample sizes)")
>lbl
[1] "setosa\n50"     "versicolor\n50" "virginica\n50"
> data
   setosa versicolor  virginica


       50         50         50
```

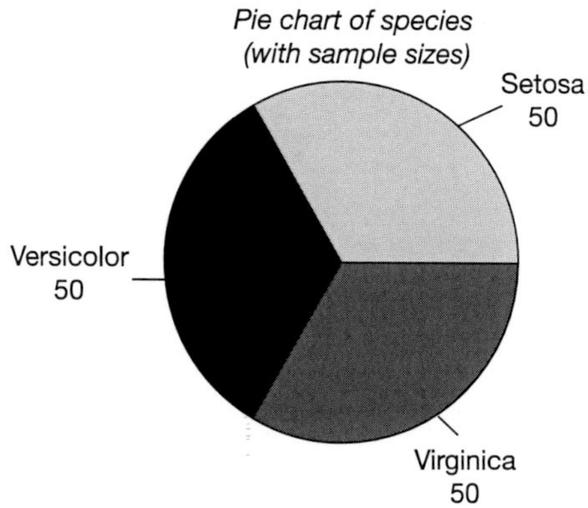

Fig. 14.21: Pie plot on `iris` data

14.8 | BOX PLOTS

The box plot is a way to visualise a lot of information in a compact manner and is more useful when there are multiple samples. The box plot shows the maximum, minimum, median value and quartiles. It can also be used to visualise outliers in a single sample. The `boxplot()` command can be used to visualise a box plot, based on complex data.

Box plots can be created to display different parameters for a variable or many variables by group. The function is of the form `boxplot(y, data=)`, where `y` is a formula to form groups and `data=` denotes the source of the data such as data frame. You can use a formula such as `f1~f2(group)`, where `f1` is generated for each value of the group on `f2`. The parameter `horizontal=TRUE` is used for orientation about the horizontal axis.

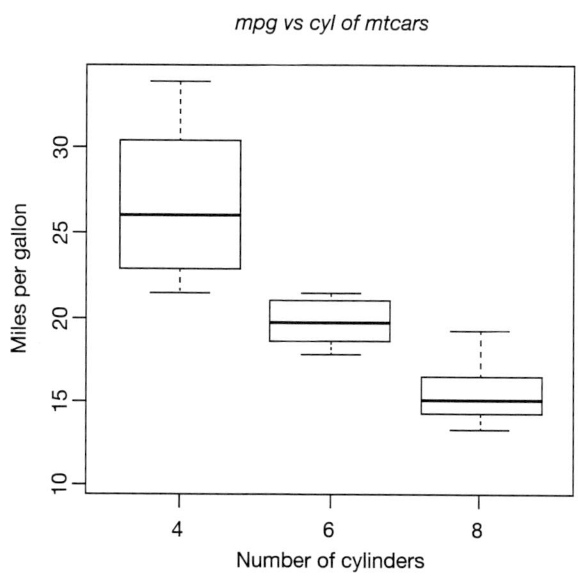

Fig. 14.22: Box plot on `mtcars` data

The whiskers show the maximum and minimum values and the middle stripe shows the median, while the box represents the upper and lower hinges.

Notched box plots narrow the box around the median to offer a rough guide to the significance difference in medians. We can create notch graphs on the following ToothGrowth data, as shown in Fig. 14.23.

```
> ToothGrowth
   len supp dose
1  4.2   VC  0.5
2 11.5   VC  0.5
3  7.3   VC  0.5
4  5.8   VC  0.5
5  6.4   VC  0.5
```

```
# Formulae is defined on len,supp,dose and data source is ToothGrowth
boxplot(len ~ supp * dose, data=ToothGrowth, notch=TRUE,
col=(c("yellow","green")), main="Tooth Growth notch graph",
xlab="Supplement Vs Dose")
```

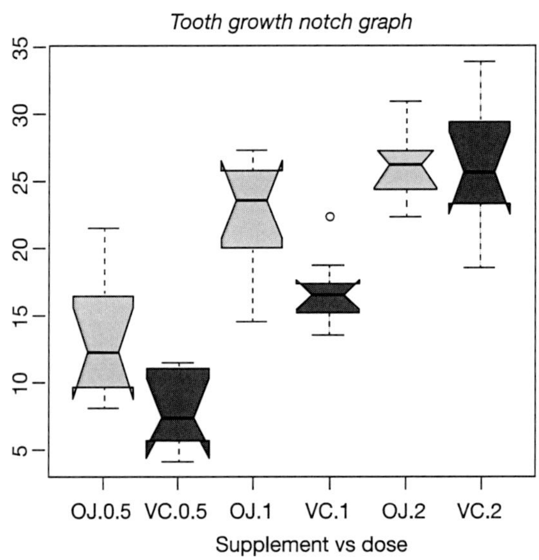

Fig. 14.23: Notched box plot

14.9 | SCATTER PLOTS

Drawing the given points on a graph creates a scatter plot. It broadly shows the distribution of data. It helps us identify whether data is linearly or non-linearly distributed.

14.9.1 Simple Scatter Plots

The basic `plot()` command is used to draw a scatter plot between two variables. It represents the relationship between the two variables. Many statistical routines include a `plot()` function to produce a specialised graph. It is the simplest way of implementing statistical methods such as regression, prediction and curve fitting.

R has different types of scatter plots. The basic type can be created by the `plot(x, y)` function, where `x` and `y` are numeric vectors to plot values on the x and y axes. The `attach()` command attaches a database to the R search path. By using the `attach()` function, database searching in R can be accessed by simply calling the names of objects. The `attach()` command thus attaches the source of data. It will become the default data to the instructions that follow and you can directly use any field (say `mpg`) without writing `field$database name` (`mpg$mtcars`) every time. An example of a scatter plot is shown in Fig. 14.24.

```
# Attach database mtcars and draw a scatter plot between wt and mpg
attach(mtcars)
plot(disp , mpg, main="Displacement Vs mpg",
 xlab=" Displacement ", ylab="Miles Per Gallon ", pch=20)

 # Add regression lines
abline (lm ( mpg~disp), col="darkgreen")
# Lower line  blue colour
lines ( lowess( disp, mpg), col="blue")
```

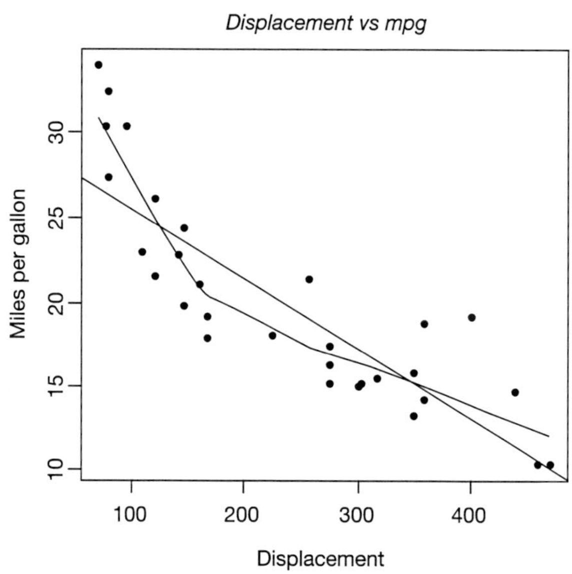

Fig. 14.24: Scatter plot

14.9.2 Scatter Plot Matrices

The scatter plot can consider matrix values. Multiple fields can be plotted on the same screen using the `pairs ()` function.

```
# Scatter plot on one screen, as shown in Fig. 14.25
pairs(~mpg+cyl+disp+hp, data=mtcars, main="Paired Scatterplot Graph")
```

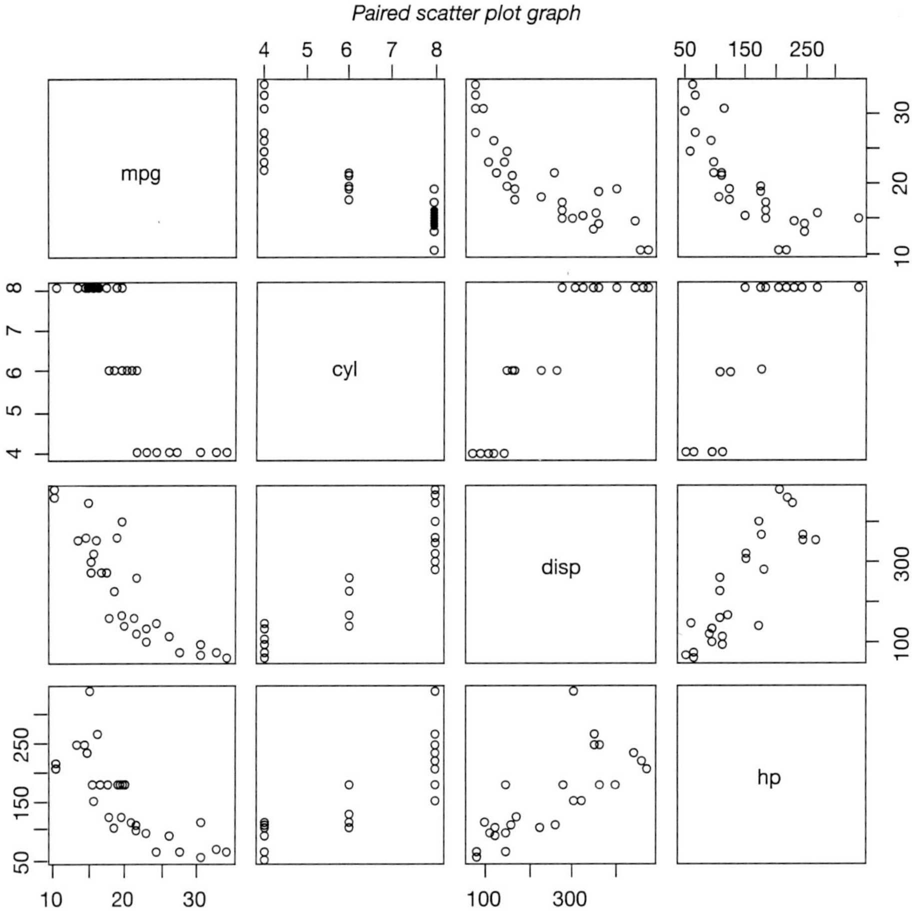

Fig. 14.25: Scatter plot matrix

14.10 | SAVING GRAPHS TO A FILE

We can save the scatter plot we have generated in the PDF format. The graph can be directed to a device: the monitor or the current working directory. The `pdf(file name)` command will open the device to save subsequent plots in the PDF format. The `plot()` function is the same as discussed above. You can draw any plot using the relevant `plot()` command. At the end, the device should be turned off.

The code given below directs the graph to a PDF in the current working directory instead of the screen.

```
# Saving graph to rplot.pdf file in current working directory, as shown in
Fig. 14.26
pdf("rplot.pdf")
x1 <- rnorm(900)
y1 <- rnorm(900)
plot(x1,y1, main="Store Scatter plot  in PDF",
col=rgb(0,150,0,49,maxColorValue=255), pch=18)
dev.off()
```

The scatter plot will be stored in the form of a PDF in the current working directory.

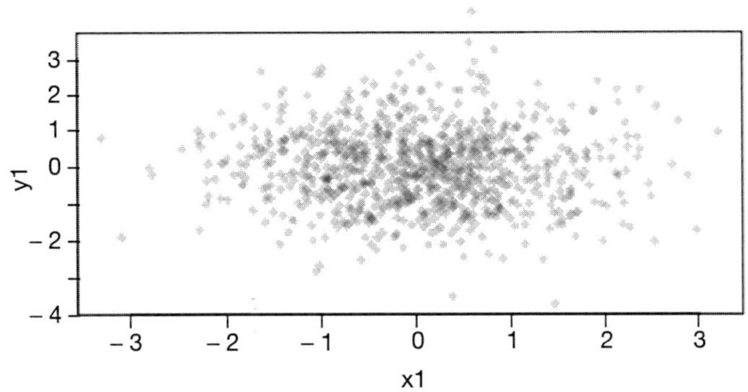

Fig. 14.26: Scatter plot in PDF

14.11 | CREATING THREE-DIMENSIONAL PLOTS

Three-dimensional scatter plots can be created using functions such as `persp()` and `wireframe()` or `cloud()`. To use these functions, you need to import the `lattice` library.

In the code given below, the `grid()` function creates a data frame consisting of two columns named `x` and `y`. The range of the variables `a` and `b` is set as 1 to 10 and 1 to 15. The `expand.grid()` command creates a data frame of dimension `x,y` with the range of values as 1 to 10 and 1 to 15; that is, a total of 150 values. The `z` dimension is then calculated based on the expression values of `x` and `y`. We then use the `wirefame(x,y,z)` command to draw the three-dimensional plot, as shown in Fig. 14.27.

```
library(lattice)
a <- 1:10
b <- 1:15
eg <- expand.grid(x=a,y=b)
eg$z <- eg$x^2 + eg$x * eg$y
wireframe(z ~ x+y, eg)
```

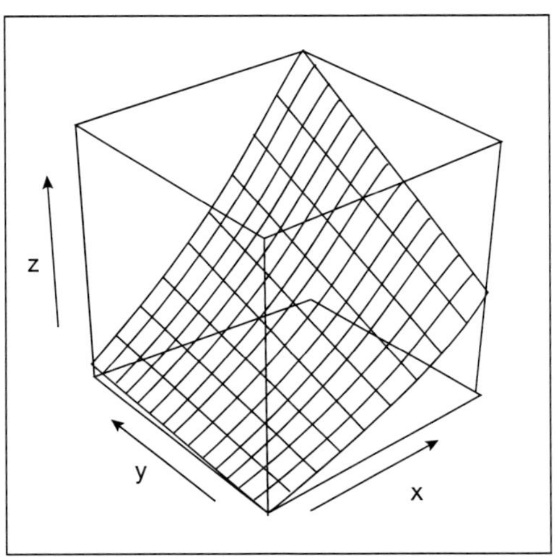

Fig. 14.27: Three-dimensional plot

EXERCISES

Concept-based Questions

1. The normal distribution drawn in a graph depends on
   a. Median and Standard Deviation
   b. Mean and Standard Deviation
   c. Mean only
   d. Standard Deviation only
2. The cumulative frequency is a ________ frequency.
   a. Fixed
   b. Decreasing
   c. Increasing
   d. None of the above
3. The process of systematically arranging data in rows and columns is called
   a. Array b. Tabulation
   c. Arrangement d. Classification
4. While constructing graphs of frequency distribution, the number of classes are decided by
   a. Range of data
   b. Number of observations
   c. Size of class
   d. None of the above
5. The graph of frequency distribution in data is represented as
   a. Scatter plot b. Curve
   c. Historiogram d. Histogram
6. The sum of angles in a pie chart is
   a. 90° b. 180°
   c. 360° d. 270°
7. If the class interval of a class is double in size than the others in the histogram, then the width of that bar will be
   a. Half b. Double
   c. Quarter d. One
8. A set of adjacent ________ is a histogram.
   a. Squares b. Triangles
   c. Rectangles d. Points
9. The principle of analytic graphics is
   a. Do not plot more than two variables at a time
   b. Make judicious use of colour in your scatter plots
   c. Show box plots only
   d. Represent causality, mechanism and explanation

Answers

1. b	2. c	3. b	4. c	5. d	6. d	7. c	8. c	9. d

Programming Questions

1. The data given below shows the number of registrations in different years in different courses.

Sr. No.	Year	Humanities	Science	Commerce
1	2010	580	640	876
2	2011	1020	3590	564
3	2012	800	900	1000
4	2013	6578	6543	1290
5	2014	2567	1289	5430

a. Show the total number of students in a bar plot based on year-wise registrations.
b. Show the data as a subdivided bar plot.

2. The tax revenue department collected tax in 2017–18 under various heads, as given below. Create a pie chart showing the given data.

Tax heads	Professional tax	Service tax	GST	Income tax
Tax collected (in crores)	6524	6543	8976	1768

3. Following are the ages of 50 students. Display the frequency distribution in a histogram by using the rule: First k for which $2^k > n$. Display the value of k for the given data.

18	19	19	19	20	20	18	17	16	17
19	18	18	18	19	18	17	17	17	18
17	17	18	19	17	16	19	18	19	20
18	18	18	18	19	19	19	19	17	17
17	17	17	16	16	20	16	117	18	20

4. The following table shows the frequency of daily item sales. Construct a histogram for the data given below:

Class interval (Daily sales)	Frequency
0–100	4
100–200	12
200–300	13
300–400	10
400–500	6

5. Write the set of instructions to draw an empty R plot on the screen.
6. Assume that you created a plot. Write the set of instructions to set the x and y axis labels and title of the plots.
7. In a plot, write the set of instructions to add or change the plot's legend. Assume the data for writing the instructions.
8. How can you add a grid to a graph? What more information is visible by adding the grid?
9. Write a function and its parameter to adjust the size of points in a plot.
10. How can you fit a curve? Assume any R data and write the R commands to fit a curve and display it.
11. Create a graph as per Q10 and save it to PDF on a CD.
12. How can you pair multiple plots on a screen?
13. How can you display lines and points on a graph?
14. How can you set the aspect ratio and size of a plot?

CHAPTER 15 R Apply Family

Objectives

At the end of this chapter, you will be able to

- Describe the `apply()` family of functions in R used to manipulate groups or slices of data
- Explain how to use the `lapply()` function on lists
- Explain how to use the `sapply()` function on data frames and obtain a vector or matrix as output
- Discuss how to filter data by writing user-defined functions and pass these functions to `sapply()` or `lapply()`
- Explain how to use the `tapply()` function to compute group-wise mean, median, etc.
- Explain how to use the `rep(X, times)` function to repeat an operation a certain number of times
- Explain how to use the `mapply()` function to perform multivariate apply of functions on data
- Explain the similarities and differences between the `vapply()` and `sapply()` functions

15.1 | INTRODUCTION TO THE APPLY FAMILY

The apply family of functions in R is used to manipulate groups or slices of data from matrices, lists or data frames. You can perform aggregate functions row-wise or column-wise or in other ways as well. You can also perform manipulations in repetitive ways without using the `for` loop explicitly.

This family of R functions comprises `apply()`, `lapply()`, `mapply()`, `vapply()` and `tapply()`. These functions are applied on different types of data and produce results in different ways.

15.2 | THE `apply()` FUNCTION

The `apply()` function requires three parameters: the data, way of performing the manipulation and the function to be applied. The `apply()` function performs aggregation of data row-wise, column-wise or both on arrays and matrix data. The output is a vector, list or array.

```
>apply(X, MARGIN, FUN)
```

where `X` represents the data (matrix/array); `MARGIN` can be 1 (row-wise manipulation), 2 (column-wise manipulation) or C(1,2) (row-wise and column-wise manipulation); and `FUN` is the aggregate function to be applied on the data.

For example, let us create a 5 x 6 matrix and use the `apply()` function to calculate the column-wise sum, which is stored in the variable, `s_mat`.

First, we initialise a matrix with values from 1 to 10 and form 5 rows and 6 columns. Then, we use the `apply()` function to calculate the column-wise (second parameter = 2) sum and the values are stored in `s_mat`.

```
mat <- matrix(C<-(1:10),nrow=5, ncol=6)
mat
s_mat<- apply(mat, 2, sum)
s_mat
```

Output:

```
> mat
     [,1] [,2] [,3] [,4] [,5] [,6]
[1,]    1    6    1    6    1    6
[2,]    2    7    2    7    2    7
[3,]    3    8    3    8    3    8
[4,]    4    9    4    9    4    9
[5,]    5   10    5   10    5   10
> s_mat
[1] 15 40 15 40 15 40
```

15.3 | THE lapply() FUNCTION

The `lapply()` function is used on lists. It takes two parameters: data and the aggregation function.

This function returns output in the form of list.

```
lapply(X, FUN)
```

where X is the data frame, list or vector and FUN is the function applied on the data.

For example, to convert a list from uppercase to lowercase letters, we can use the code given below:

```
>mupper <- c("SUPER 30","SPIDERMAN","BHIM","SHOLE")
>mlower <-lapply(mupper, tolower)
>str(m_lower)
```

Output:

```
List of 4
 $ : chr "super 30"
 $ : chr "spiderman"
 $ : chr "bhim"
 $ : chr "shole"
```

Here is another example, where we create three lists and display the sum of the elements of each list:

```
>A <- c(1:5)
>B<-c(1:8)
>C<-c(1:3)
>mlist<-list(A,B,C)
   >lapply(mlist,sum)
```

Output:

```
[[1]]
[1] 15

[[2]]
[1] 36

[[3]]
[1] 6
```

15.4 | THE sapply() FUNCTION

The `sapply()` function takes two parameters: data – which is either list, vector or data frame and returns a vector or matrix – and the aggregate function.

```
sapply(X, FUN)
```

where `X` is the list, vector or data frame and `FUN` is the aggregate function, such as mean, sum, median, etc.

```
> mtcars
               mpg   cyl disp   hp   drat  wt     qsec   vs am  gear carb
Mazda RX4      21.0  6   160.0  110  3.90  2.620  16.46  0  1   4    4
Datsun 710     22.8  4   108.0  93   3.85  2.320  18.61  1  1   4    1
```

Using the `mtcars` data set, let us find the minimum and maximum of all the columns. To calculate the maximum or minimum of any column, we can use the `max()` and `min()` functions and pass the column name as parameter.

```
>max(mtcars$mpg)                                    # Compute max of column mpg
# 33.9
>min(mtcars$mpg)                                    # Compute max of column mpg
# 10.4
```

However, the `sapply()` function can compute the maximum or minimum of all columns in one step.

```
>sapply(mtcars, max)
mpg     cyl    disp     hp       drat   wt     qsec    vs     am     gear
33.900  8.000  472.000  335.000  4.930  5.424  22.900  1.000  1.000  5.000
  carb
  8.000
>sapply(mtcars, min)
mpg     cyl    disp    hp      drat   wt    qsec    vs     am     gear   carb
10.400  4.000 71.100  52.000  2.760  1.513 14.500  0.000  0.000  3.000  1.000
```

15.5 | SLICING A VECTOR

We can slice a vector or data frame using the `sapply()` and `lapply()` functions based on certain criteria by writing the functionality in a user-defined function.

For example, we may like to slice only values below the mean for all the columns. The function code given below will filter the same and is used with the `sapply()` function on the `mtcars` database.

```
>below_avg <- function(y) {
    avgg <- mean(y)
    return(y[y > avgg])
}
>dt_s<- sapply(mtcars, below_ave)
```

Output:

```
> dt_s
$mpg
 [1] 21.0 21.0 22.8 21.4 24.4 22.8 32.4 30.4 33.9 21.5 27.3 26.0
30.4 21.4

$cyl
 [1] 8 8 8 8 8 8 8 8 8 8 8 8 8 8

$disp
 [1] 258.0 360.0 360.0 275.8 275.8 275.8 472.0 460.0 440.0 318.0
304.0 350.0
[13] 400.0 351.0 301.0

$hp
 [1] 175 245 180 180 180 205 215 230 150 150 245 175 264 175 335

$drat
 [1] 3.90 3.90 3.85 3.69 3.92 3.92 3.92 4.08 4.93 4.22 3.70 3.73
4.08 4.43 3.77
[16] 4.22 3.62 4.11

$wt
 [1] 3.440 3.460 3.570 3.440 3.440 4.070 3.730 3.780 5.250 5.424
5.345 3.520
[13] 3.435 3.840 3.845 3.570

$qsec
 [1] 18.61 19.44 20.22 20.00 22.90 18.30 18.90 18.00 17.98 19.47
18.52 19.90
[13] 20.01 18.90 18.60

$vs
 [1] 1 1 1 1 1 1 1 1 1 1 1 1 1 1

$am
 [1] 1 1 1 1 1 1 1 1 1 1 1 1 1

$gear
 [1] 4 4 4 4 4 4 4 4 4 4 4 5 5 5 5 5 4

$carb
 [1] 4 4 4 4 4 3 3 3 4 4 4 4 4 6 8
```

15.6 | THE tapply() FUNCTION

The `tapply()` function computes group-wise mean, median, minimum, etc. The first parameter of this function is the data/column for which you want to apply a function and the second parameter is the group-by information.

```
>tapply(X, INDEX, FUN = NULL)
```

where `X` is the data frame or vector, `INDEX` specifies the basis of the grouping and `FUN` indicates the function to be applied to the group of values.

The `tapply()` function is thus used to calculate the summary of data group-wise. For instance, you may want to calculate the median of `mpg` values for groups of cylinders. Here, the groups of cylinders are 4, 6 and 8 and the `mpg` median values for each `cyl` group will be displayed.

```
>data(mtcars)
> tapply(mtcars$mpg,mtcars$cyl,median)
   4    6    8
26.0 19.7 15.2
```

15.7 | THE rep() FUNCTION

The `rep(X, times)` function replicates the `X` vector a certain number of times, as specified in the second parameter.

```
>X<-c(1,2,3,4)
> rep(X,2)
[1] 1 2 3 4 1 2 3 4
```

We need to specify the number of repeats in the second parameter.

```
> rep(X, each=2)
[1] 1 1 2 2 3 3 4 4
```

The vector `X` can be extracted using the `sapply()` or `lapply()` functions given above.

15.8 | THE mapply() FUNCTION

The `mapply(FUN, more arguments)` function enables you to perform a 'multivariate' apply using a single command. It is a multivariate version of the `sapply()` function.

In the code given below, the `rep()` function is applied to data 2, 4, 6, 8 four times.

```
> Q=mapply(rep,c(2,4,6,8),4)
> Q
     [,1] [,2] [,3] [,4]
[1,]    2    4    6    8
[2,]    2    4    6    8
[3,]    2    4    6    8
[4,]    2    4    6    8
```

15.9 | THE vapply() FUNCTION

The general syntax of the `vapply()` function is given below:

```
>vapply(X, FUN, FUN.VALUE)
```

where `X` is the vector, `FUN` is the function to be applied on the vector and `FUN.VALUE` is the expected output – for example, a Boolean or an integer.

This function takes a vector as input, applies a function to it and returns the output in the data type specified by `FUN.VALUE`.

```
>X<-1:10
>X1<-vapply(X, function(x) {x + 10}, numeric(1))
>X2<-vapply(X, function(x) {x < 10}, logical(1))
> X1
 [1] 11 12 13 14 15 16 17 18 19 20
> X2
 [1]  TRUE  TRUE  TRUE  TRUE  TRUE  TRUE  TRUE  TRUE  TRUE FALSE
```

The `vapply()` function is similar to the `sapply()` function. The difference is that the former enables you to specify the type of the output.

In the code given above, we display numeric data by adding +10 to the original data, while in the second command, the function checks if the value is less than 10 and returns the output as a Boolean TRUE/FALSE.

EXERCISES

Multiple Choice Questions

1. ________ loops over a list and evaluates a function on each element.
   a. `apply()`
   b. `lapply()`
   c. `sapply()`
   d. `mapply()`
2. Select the incorrect statement:
   a. Multi-line expressions with curly braces are not that easy to sort through when working on the command line
   b. `lappy()` loops over a list, iterating over each element in that list
   c. `lapply()` does not always return a list
   d. You cannot use `lapply()` to evaluate a function multiple times, each with a different argument
3. Which of the following is a multivariate version of `lapply()`?
   a. `apply()`
   b. `lapply()`
   c. `sapply()`
   d. `mapply()`
4. The `lappy()` function takes ________ arguments in R language.
   a. Two b. Three
   c. Four d. Five
5. ________ applies a function over the margins of an array.
   a. `apply()`
   b. `lapply()`
   c. `tapply()`
   d. `mapply()`

Answers

1. a	2. c	3. d	4. c	5. a

Programming/Concept-based Questions

1. What is the advantage of using the apply family of functions in R?
2. Take a 5 x 5 matrix and calculate the maximum, minimum and average of each column.
3. Take any built-in database, group it based on a column and display the group-wise summaries.
4. Take an input vector, apply a function to it and finally assign `FUN.VALUE`, that is, the expected type of output data.
5. Slice data and send it to the apply family of functions.

CHAPTER

16 The R Profiler

Objectives

At the end of this chapter, you will be able to

- Define the role of the R profiler
- Explain how to use the `system.time()` function
- Explain how to start and end the R profiler
- Describe how `summaryRprof()` is used

16.1 | INTRODUCTION

The R profiler helps us optimise code in terms of its execution time. It is a systematic way of calculating the time spent in each part of the code. The optimisation phase comes into focus after the development of initial logic. A programmer should first solve the problem and then write the code, after which, it should be analysed and optimised.

If your program includes a loop that runs 1000 times, a minor change in one instruction in the loop can optimise execution time and thus enable faster execution by 1000 times.

16.2 | USING THE `system.time()` FUNCTION

The `system.time()` function can be used to display the time taken by the CPU, wall clock, etc. Instructions can be executed using the same amount of time as that taken by the CPU if 100% of the CPU was allocated to the task. However, this does not happen in reality. Delays occur due to responses from the network or from the CPU being shared by other processes.

The `system.time()` function computes the time required to execute an expression in seconds. It displays

- User time: The time required by the CPU to execute an instruction.
- Elapsed time: The actual "wall clock" time taken to execute the instruction.

Elapsed time may be greater than user time (CPU) when the CPU spends a lot of time waiting.
Elapsed time may be smaller than user time (CPU) when the machine has multiple processors and one task is distributed amongst multiple processors.

In the example given below, lines are read from a website and delays occur due to the Internet speed or server response. In this case, elapsed time is greater than user time as the CPU spends some time waiting for a response from the server. As this does not involve the CPU, user time will be small.

```
system.time(readLines("http://www.jhsph.edu"))
user  system  elapsed
0.13  0.08    8.46
```

16.3 | TIMING LONGER EXPRESSIONS

To calculate the time taken to execute multiple instructions, you need to enclose them in curly brackets and pass them as a single parameter to the `system.time()` function.

```
system.time(
{
n <- 10
 for (i in 1:10)
 {
  print(i*i)
  }
}
)
[1] 1
[1] 4
[1] 9
[1] 16
[1] 25
[1] 36
[1] 49
[1] 64
[1] 81
[1] 100
   user  system elapsed
   0.00    0.00    0.03
```

16.4 | USING THE R PROFILER

The `system.time()` function is used to check the time taken to execute a block of code. This function has a drawback in that it fails if the user does not know where in the code it should be inserted. The starting point depends on the data at execution time. It also displays only the user time, system time and elapsed time.

The R profiler is an alternative for testing the time taken to execute functions or code blocks. We can start the R profiler by using the `Rprof()` function and end it using `Rprof(NULL)`. The summary of the time taken can be displayed using `summaryRprof()`.

The `Rprof()` function keeps track of the function call stack at regular intervals and tabulates how much time is spent inside each function. By default, the profiler samples the function call stack every 0.02 seconds.

If you are using only simple instructions and the code is executed quickly, the profiler is not very useful. However, for complex code, it can help you optimise the program for execution.

The code you wish to profile or analyse in terms of time should be preceded by `Rprof()`. For example, the code given below contains a function `checknumber()` that checks whether a number is positive, negative or zero. The function is executed 100,000 times.

```
Rprof()
checknumber <- function(x) {
if (x > 0) {
result <- "Positive"
}
else if (x < 0) {
result <- "Negative"
}
else {
result <- "Zero"
}
return(result)
}
for(i in 1:100000)
{print(checknumber(i))
 }
Rprof(NULL)
summaryRprof()
```

To turn off the profiler, we use `Rprof(NULL)`. By default, it creates a file named Rprof.out and stores the time statistics in this file. The contents of this file can be displayed using `summaryRprof()`.

You can also specify the file name (say "temp") to store this output.

For example:

```
Rprof("temp")
<Code>
Rprof(NULL)
summaryRprof("temp")
```

16.5 | USING THE `summaryRprof()` FUNCTION

The `summaryRprof()` function tabulates the R profiler output and calculates how much time is spent in which function. We can use two methods for normalising the data:

- `by.total` divides the time spent in each function by the total run time
- `by.self` performs the same task as `by.total` but first subtracts the time spent in functions above the current function in the call stack

Give below is the output of `summaryRprof()` for `by.total`:

```
$by.total
                    total.time   total.pct   self.time   self.pct
"print"             1.38         100.00      0.46        33.33
"print.default"     0.84         60.87       0.84        60.87
"checknumber"       0.08         5.80        0.08        5.80
```

The `checknumber()` function is called from `main()` and is used in the `print()` function as argument; therefore, 100% of the time is spent in the `print()` function. The `print()` function immediately calls another function, `print.default()`. In reality, most of the time of `print()` is spent in `print.default()`.

The `by.self` output is shown below:

```
$by.self
                  self.time    self.pct    total.time   total.pct
"print.default"   0.84         60.87       0.84         60.87
"print"           0.46         33.33       1.38         100.00
"checknumber"     0.08         5.80        0.08         5.80
```

We can see that 33% of the run time is actually spent in `print()`, whereas 60% of the run time is spent in `print.default()` and only 5% of time is taken by the `checknumber()` function. Thus, most of the operation is performed by `print.default()`.

The sampling interval default is .02 seconds and the total time spent is 1.38 seconds.

```
$sample.interval
[1] 0.02
$sampling.time
[1] 1.38
```

Thus, these four parameters – `by.total`, `by.self`, `sample.interval` and `sampling.time` – display the time statistics provided by the R profiler.

EXERCISES

Multiple Choice Questions

1. ________ is a systematic way to examine how much time is spent in different parts of a program.
   a. Profiling b. Monitoring
   c. Logging d. Debugging
2. Choose the correct statement:
   a. The `Rprof()` function starts the profiler in R
   b. The `system.time()` function enables you to test certain functions or code blocks to see if they are taking excessive amounts of time to execute
   c. R must not be compiled with profiler support
   d. The `Rprof()` function tabulates how much time is spent inside each function
3. The _______ function computes the time (in seconds) needed to execute an expression.
   a. `system.timedeb()`
   b. `system.time()`
   c. `system.datetime()`
   d. `system.deb()`
4. The elapsed time may be ________ than the user time if your machine has multiple cores/processors.
   a. Smaller b. Greater
   c. Equal to d. Null
5. _________ time is the time charged to the CPU(s) for the R expression.
   a. Elapsed b. User
   c. Response d. Monitor

Answers

1. a	**2.** b	**3.** b	**4.** a	**5.** a

Programming Questions

1. What is profiling in R?
2. Write a code and calculate the execution time of your code.
3. Use the R profiler in your code and generate the summary.
4. How can you display the user time, system time and elapsed time of any website request and response?

CHAPTER 17

Descriptive Statistics using R

Objectives

At the end of this chapter, you will be able to

- List the built-in statistical functions in R used to measure central value, dispersion and shape
- Explain the functions to compute mean, mode and median
- Explain the functions to compute range, standard deviation, variance, quartiles and coefficient of variation
- Explain how to compute the five-number summary
- Explain how to compute skewness and kurtosis

17.1 | INTRODUCTION TO STATISTICAL ANALYSIS IN R

In the previous chapters, you learned about various functions that help to transform data and organise it in the appropriate format. After organising the data, you can explore it to determine the relationships present or you can perform statistical analysis on it.

Statistical analysis in R is carried out with the help of built-in functions and methods that are available in the R base package library. They usually take R vectors and other arguments as input to produce the necessary output. This analysis comprises the calculation of measures of central value, measures of dispersion or variability and also covers covariance, correlation of data and measures of shape using kurtosis and skewness. In addition, user-defined functions can be specified

For illustrative purposes, the data set `ToothGrowth` has been used in this chapter for many examples. You can view details of this data set by using the `help(ToothGrowth)` command at the R prompt.

```
>head(ToothGrowth)
   len supp dose
1  4.2   VC  0.5
2 11.5   VC  0.5
3  7.3   VC  0.5
4  5.8   VC  0.5
5  6.4   VC  0.5
6 10.0   VC  0.5
```

17.2 | MEASURES OF CENTRAL TENDENCY OR LOCATION

In many situations, we may need one value to represent or describe the whole data. Measuring mean, median and mode helps us obtain a one-value representation of the data.

17.2.1 Data Summarisation

The `summary()` function in R provides details of the measures of central value such as minimum, maximum, quartiles, median and mean for numerical variables. For factors and logical variables, it measures the frequencies.

```
> summary(ToothGrowth)
      len         supp         dose      
 Min.   : 4.20   OJ:30   Min.   :0.500  
 1st Qu.:13.07   VC:30   1st Qu.:0.500  
 Median :19.25           Median :1.000  
 Mean   :18.81           Mean   :1.167  
 3rd Qu.:25.27           3rd Qu.:2.000  
 Max.   :33.90           Max.   :2.000  
```

17.2.2 Mean

Mean is calculated by adding all the items and dividing this total by the number of items. The different mean measurements we can obtain are simple or arithmetic mean (AM) and weighted mean.

If $x_1, x_2, x_3, \ldots, x_n$ are the sample values, the simple mean is defined as

$$\overline{x} = \frac{1}{n}\sum_{i=1}^{n} x_i$$

When each sample value x_i is associated with a weight w_i, for $i = 1, 2, \ldots, n$, then it is defined as

$$\overline{x} = \frac{\sum_{i=1}^{n} w_i x_i}{\sum_{i=1}^{n} w_i}$$

Trimmed mean: If there are extreme values (also called outliers) in a sample, the mean is then greatly influenced by these values. Trimmed mean can be used to offset the effect caused by the extreme values. Trimmed mean is defined as the mean obtained after discarding the values at the high and low extremes.

Sometimes, data is provided in continuous form; that is, as classes, and the frequency for each class is given. Three methods can be used to calculate the mean of such data:

- Direct method
- Assumed mean method
- Step deviation method

Direct method: The following formula is used to obtain mean through the direct method:

$$X = \sum fx / N = \sum fx / \sum f$$

where f is the frequency, X is the value of the variable and N is the sum of frequency or $N = \sum f$.

Assumed mean method: Here, we take a value as the assumed mean and then compute the deviations of the variable from it. We obtain X using the following formula:

$$\bar{X} = A + \frac{\sum fdx}{\sum f} = A + \frac{\sum fdx}{N}$$

where A is the assumed mean, dx is $(X - A)$, f is the frequency $\sum f$ and N is the total number of terms.

Step deviation method: The following formula is used to obtain mean through the step deviation method:

$$X = A + (\sum fdx \ / \ N) * i = A + (\sum fdx \ / \ \sum f) * i$$

where A is the assumed mean, dx is $(X - A)$, i is the class size or class interval, f is the frequency $\sum f$ and N is the total number of terms.

The R function to calculate mean is given below:

```
> mean(a, trim = 0, na.rm = FALSE, ...)
```

where `a` is the input vector of integers and the input data cannot be of character type; `trim` is used to drop some observations from the vector and `na.rm` is a logical value (TRUE indicates removal of NA values from the input vector); this helps deal with missing values.

```
> x <- c(12,7,4.2,18,2,54,-21,-5)          # Create a vector
> result.mean <- mean(x)                   # Find the mean
> print(result.mean)
```

When we execute the above code, the following output is produced:

```
[1] 8.9
```

Geometric mean: This is arithmetic mean in log space. Geometric mean of n observations (none of which are zero) is defined as:

$$\tilde{x} = \left(\prod_{i=1}^{n} x_i \right)^{1/n}$$

where, $n \neq 0$.

However, it is practically not possible to compute it. So we calculate it using the log scale.

Harmonic mean: If all observations are non zero, the reciprocal of the arithmetic mean of the reciprocals of observations is known as harmonic mean.

For ungrouped data

$$\hat{x} = \frac{n}{\sum_{i=1}^{n} \frac{1}{x_i}}$$

For grouped data

$$\hat{x} = \frac{\sum_{i=1}^{n} f_i}{\sum_{i=1}^{n} \left(\frac{f_i}{x_i} \right)}$$

where f_i is the frequency of the *i*th class, with x_i as the centre value of the *i*th class.

A simple inequality exists between the three means and this can be represented as follows:

AM >= GM >= HM

Example 17.1: Write your own function to calculate arithmetic mean

Code:

```
> arith.mean <- function(a)  sum(a)/length(a)
> res<-c(3,3,4,5,5)
> arith.mean(res)
[1] 4
> mean(res)
[1] 4
```

Example 17.2: Write your own function to calculate geometric mean

Ideally, we calculate geometric mean by taking the Nth root of a product of N items. For instance, for two items, we take the square root; for three items, we take the cube root; and so on. On the log scale, multiplying numbers together means we add their logarithms. To take the roots, we divide the logarithms by the root. So, finding `antilog(exp)` of the averages of the logarithms (log) of the data will result in the GM.

Code:

```
> insects <-c(1,10,1000,10)
>geom <-function (x) exp(mean(log(x)))
>geom(insects)
[1] 17.78
```

Example 17.3: Write your own function to calculate harmonic mean

Code:

```
>harmonic <-function (a) 1/mean(1/a)
>harmonic(c(1,2,4,1,6))
[1] 1.714286
```

17.2.3 Median

Median refers to the middle-most value in a data distribution. Here, one-half of the items in the distribution has a value smaller than the median, while the other half has a value larger than the median value. Median is called positional average.

Median of a sample is the middle value when the data are arranged in increasing (or decreasing) order. Symbolically,

$$\hat{x} = \begin{cases} x_{(n+1)}/2 & \text{if } n \text{ is odd} \\ \dfrac{1}{2}\left\{x_{n/2} + x_{\left(\frac{n}{2}+1\right)}\right\} & \text{if } n \text{ is even} \end{cases}$$

Median of grouped data is given by

$$\hat{x} = l + \left\{\frac{\frac{N}{2} - cf}{f} h\right\}$$

where h is the width of the median class and $N = \sum_{i=1}^{n} f_i$, (where f_i is the frequency of the *i*th class and n is the total number of groups), cf is the the cumulative frequency, N is the the total number of samples and l is the lower limit of the median class.

Note: A class is called median class if its cumulative frequency is just greater than $N/2$.

In R, the following function is used to calculate the median:

```
> median(a, na.rm = FALSE)
```

where `a` is the input vector and `na.rm` is the logical value (TRUE indicates removal of NA values from the input vector) that helps to deal with missing values.

```
> x <- c(12,7,3,4.2,18,54,-21,8,-5)     # Create the vector
> medn.result <- median(x)              # Find the median
> print(medn.result)
```

When we execute the above code, the following output is produced:

```
[1] 7

> y <-c(3,5,5,4,4,4,2,5)
> median(y)
[1] 4

> y <-c(3,5,5,4,4,4,2,5,5,5)
> median(y)
   [1] 4.5
```

Example 17.4: Write your own function to calculate median

We can write the function in two ways. The first is simple but does not always give the correct output for all sequences of data. It works correctly only for an odd number of items. The second solution will give the correct result for all inputs.

(1)

```
>arith.median <-function(a){
sort(a)[ceiling(length(a)/2)]}
>y <-c (3,5,5,4,4,4,2)
> arith.median(y)
[1] 4
> y <-c(3,5,5,4,4,4,2,5,5,5)
> median(y)
[1] 4.5
> arith.median(y)    # Gives wrong output
[1] 4
```

(2)

```
>arith.median <-function(a){
odd.even <-length(a) %% 2
if ( odd.even ==0 ) (sort(a)[length(a)/2] +sort(a)[1+length(a)/2])/2
else sort(a)[ceiling(length(a)/2)]}

 > y <-c (3,5,5,4,4,4,2,5,5,5)
> median(y)
[1] 4.5
> arith.median(y)
[1] 4.5
```

17.2.4 Mode

Mode is the most common value that occurs in a set of observations. Mode can be calculated for categorical or character data, whereas mean and median can be calculated only for numeric data. In R, there is no built-in function to compute mode. Hence, the user needs to create the required function.

Select the modal class (it is the class with the highest frequency). Then the mode $\tilde{x}$ is given by

$$\tilde{x} = l + \left(\frac{\Delta_1}{\Delta_1 + \Delta_2}\right)h$$

where h is the class width, Δ_1 is the difference between the frequency of the modal class and the frequency of the class just after the modal class, Δ_2 is the difference between the frequency of the modal class and the class just before the modal class and l is the lower boundary of the modal class.

Note: If each data value occurs only once, then there is no mode!

Example 17.5: Write your own function to calculate mode

Code:

```
>getmode <- function(a) {
   uniqv <- unique(a)
   uniqv[which.max(tabulate(match(a, uniqv)))]
}
> v <- c(2,1,2,3,1,2,3,4,1,5,5,3,2,2)  # Create the vector with numbers
> result <- getmode(v)          # Calculate mode using the user function
> print(result)
>charv <- c("o","it","the","it","it")  # Create the vector with
characters
> result <- getmode(charv) # Calculate mode using the user function
> print(result)
```

When we execute the above code, the following output is produced:

```
[1] 2
[1] "it"
```

17.2.5 Other Statistical Functions

R has some other very simple statistical functions, as listed below:

```
> v <- c(2,1,2,3,1,2,3,4,1,5,5,3,2,3)  # Create the vector with numbers
> sum(v)           # Outputs 37
> diff(v)          # Outputs  -1  1  1 -2  1  1  1 -3  4  0 -2 -1  1
> min(v)           # Outputs 1
> max(v)           # Outputs 5
> range(v)         # Outputs 1 5
```

17.3 | MEASURES OF DISPERSION

The measures of central value discussed above give us only a single value that represents the entire data. Sometimes, it may be necessary to measure variability of data, as two distributions of data may have the same central values but there can be wide disparity in the data distribution. Measures of dispersion help in measuring variation among data items. Dispersion measures the extent of spread of observations in a sample.

The main measures of dispersion, such as range, interquartile range, quartile deviation, mean or average deviation, standard deviation, variance and coefficient of variation, can be calculated with standard functions from the native `stats` package.

17.3.1 Range

Let $X = x_1, x_2, x_1, ...x_n$ be n sample values that are arranged in increasing order.

The range R of these samples is then defined as:

$$R = \max(X) - \min(X) = x_n - x_1 z$$

17.3.2 Standard Deviation

Standard deviation measures the variability of distribution. A small standard deviation means high uniformity of the data series. Standard deviation is defined as the square root of variance, and it is considered as the best measure of variation. Standard deviation is amenable to further algebraic treatment and is less affected by fluctuations of sampling.

Let $X = \{x_1, x_2, x_1, \ldots x_n\}$ be sample values of n samples. Then, variance denoted as σ^2 is defined as:

$$\sigma^2 = \frac{1}{n-1}\sum_{i=1}^{n}(x_i - \bar{x})^2$$

where $\bar{x}$ denotes the mean of the sample.

The standard deviation, σ, of the samples is the square root of the variance σ^2.

```
> v <- c(2,1,2,3,1,2,3,4,1,5,5,3,2,3)    # Create the vector with numbers
   >sd(v)                                # Find standard deviation
```

When we execute the above code, the following output is produced:

```
[1] 1.336306
```

Example 17.6: Write your own function to calculate standard deviation

Code:

```
>dev <-function(a) {
temp <-sum((a-mean(a))^2)/(length(a)-1)
sqrt(temp)}
>dev(v)
[1] 1.336306
```

17.3.3 Variance

Variance defines how data values are dispersed around the mean value. Variance is the square of standard deviation.

```
> v <- c(2,1,2,3,1,2,3,4,1,5,5,3,2,3)    # Create the vector with numbers
   >var(v)                               # Find variance
```

When we execute the above code, the following output is produced:

```
[1] 1.785714
```

Example 17.7: Write your own function to calculate variance

Code:

```
>variance <-function(a) sum((a-mean(a))^2)/(length(a)-1)
>variance(c(13,7,5,12,9,15,6,11,9,7,12))
[1] 10.25455
>var(c(13,7,5,12,9,15,6,11,9,7,12))   # Built-in functionality
[1] 10.25455
```

17.3.4 Quartiles

Range is based on two extreme values and does not account for scatter within the data. Quartiles give some indication of the centre and scatter within data and the shape of the distribution. Quartiles along with deciles and percentiles are the measures of position. R has a `quantile()` function that helps in calculating the quartiles.

The first quartile (denoted by Q_1), second quartile (median) and third quartile (denoted by Q_3) are the 25th percentile, 50th percentile and 75th percentile, respectively. The distance between the third and first quartiles is called the interquartile range (IQR) and is defined as

$$IQR = Q_3 - Q_1$$

In R, we use the function `quantile(a, probs = seq(0, 1, 0.25), na.rm = FALSE,names = TRUE, type = 7, ...)`

where `a` represents the data points, `prob` is the location to be measured, `na.rm` is a logical value (TRUE indicates the removal of NA values from the input vector) and helps deal with missing values, `names` is a logical value (FALSE indicates that there are no attributes to speed up the computation) and `type` represents the type of the quantile algorithm.

Example 17.8: The statistics students of CCOEW have the following scores: 92,89, 86, 88, 84, 83, 80, 94, 90, 81, 79, 79, 81, 85. Determine and interpret the quartiles of these scores.

```
>scores <- c(92,89, 86, 88, 84, 83, 80, 94, 90, 81, 79, 79, 81, 85)
>quantile(scores)

0%     25%    50%    75%    100%
79.0   81.0   84.5   88.75  94.0
```

Interpretation: Half the scores are below 84.5. One-fourth of the scores are below 81, one-fourth of the scores are above 88.75 and the minimum and maximum values are 79.0 and 94.0, respectively.

17.3.5 Coefficient of Variation

A related measure is the coefficient of variation *CV*, which is defined as follows

$$CV = \frac{\sigma}{x} \times 100$$

This gives a ratio measure for spread.

17.3.6 Five-Number Summary

A five-number summary is a very simple way of summarising five descriptive statistics of a continuous univariate data set. This comprises the computation of:

- Minimum
- First quartile
- Median
- Third quartile
- Maximum

Two functions are commonly used to calculate the five-number summary in R: `fivenum()` and `summary()` (also used for mean). The difference between them lies in the lack of universal agreement on how the first and third quartiles should be calculated (their algorithms are different).

17.4 | MEASURES OF SHAPE

The measures of central value and variability do not reveal all the characteristics of a given set of data. Two widely different distributions may have the same mean and standard deviation. Measures of shape help us identify the overall shape of distribution of data. Skewness and kurtosis are used to measure the shape of data. R has a package called `moment` that helps in measuring the shape of data.

17.4.1 Skewness

Dispersion measures the amount of variation in data. It does not deal with the direction of variation. Skewness measures the direction of the variation or variations from symmetry.

Example 17.9: Sandhya spends a few hours studying (excluding weekends). She obtained the following data: 19.09, 19.55, 17.89, 17.73, 25.15, 27.27, 25.24, 21.05, 21.65, 20.92, 22.61, 15.71, 22.04, 22.60 and 24.25. Compute and interpret the skewness.

Code:

```
>time <- c(19.09, 19.55, 17.89, 17.73, 25.15, 27.27, 25.24, 21.05, 21.65,
20.92, 22.61, 15.71, 22.04, 22.60, 24.25)
>install.packages("moments")
>library(moments)
>skewness(time)

[1] -0.01565162
```

The skewness here is –0.01565162. This value implies that the distribution of the data is slightly skewed to the left or is negatively skewed. It is skewed to the left because the computed value is negative, and slightly, because the value is close to zero.

Example 17.10: Write your own function to calculate skewness of data

Code:

```
>mystats <- function(x){
 m <- mean(x)
 n <- length(x)
s <- sd(x)
temp<-sum((x-m)^3/s^3)/n
return (temp)  }
>sapply(mtcars[vars], mystats)

        mpg         hp          wt
skew    0.611       0.726       0.4231

>mystats(time)
[1] -0.01411284
```

17.4.2 Kurtosis

Kurtosis is the degree of peakedness or the sharpness of the curve in frequency distribution or in data items. Skewness measures the degree of symmetry of distribution. It talks about the amount and direction of the skew, whereas kurtosis talks about the height and sharpness of the central peak.

Example 17.11: Sandhya spends a few hours studying (excluding weekends). She obtained the following data: 19.09, 19.55, 17.89, 17.73, 25.15, 27.27, 25.24, 21.05, 21.65, 20.92, 22.61, 15.71, 22.04, 22.60 and 24.25. Compute and interpret the kurtosis.

Code:

```
>time <- c(19.09, 19.55, 17.89, 17.73, 25.15, 27.27, 25.24, 21.05, 21.65,
20.92, 22.61, 15.71, 22.04, 22.60, 24.25)
>install.packages("moments")
>library(moments)
> kurtosis(time)

[1] 2.301051
```

We have obtained 2.301051 as kurtosis, implying that the distribution of the data is platykurtic, since the computed value is less than 3.

The graphical interpretation of the above depicts the distribution of the time elapsed as slightly skewed to the left and platykurtic. Given below is the code to draw its histogram (shown in Fig. 17.1):

```
>library(ggplot2)
>qplot(time, geom = 'histogram', binwidth = 2) + xlab('Time')
```

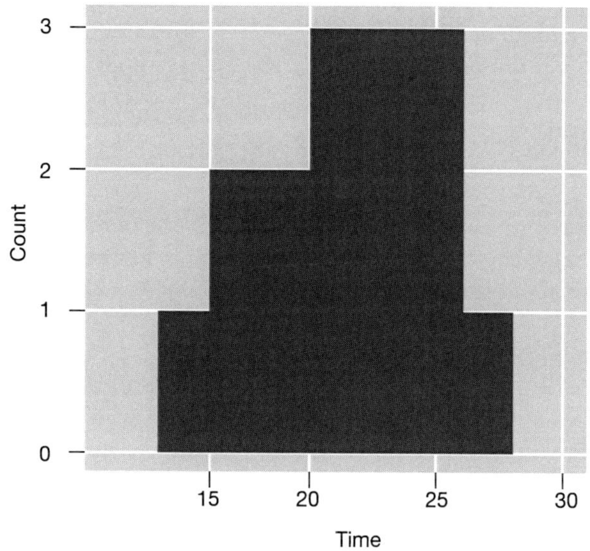

Fig. 17.1: Histogram of time data given in Example 17.11

Example 17.12: Write your own function to calculate kurtosis

Code:

```
> mystats <- function(a){
m <- mean(a)
n <- length(a)
s <- sd(a)
temp <-sum((a-m)^4/s^4)/n
return(temp) }
> sapply(mtcars[vars], mystats)

      mpg          hp          wt
kurtosis -0.373    -0.136      -0.0227

>mystats(time)
[1] 2.004471
```

EXERCISES

Multiple Choice Questions

1. If a single value in data changes, which of the following will always change?
   a. Mean
   b. Median
   c. Mode
   d. All of the above
2. For analysing the central tendency of data, which of these measures are used?
   a. Median and Normal Distribution
   b. Mean, Median and Mode
   c. Mode, Variance and Range
   d. Standard Deviation, Mode and Mean

e. Mean, Range and Normal Distribution

3. If a distribution has a mean of 23, median of 24 and mode of 25.5, it can be said that the distribution is
   a. Nothing can be said
   c. Positive skewed
   b. Asymmetrical
   d. Negatively skewed
4. Which of the following is characteristic of the sum of the deviations about the mean?
   a. It is a range
   b. It is equal to zero
   c. It is also called the total standard deviation
   d. It is always positive
   e. It is always negative
5. The middle value of an ordered observation of numbers is the
   a. Mean b. Median
   c. Mode d. Mid-value
6. Which one of these divides a group of data into four sub-groups
   a. Percentile b. Deciles
   c. Median d. Quartile
7. A survey collected the height of students in a school. Height is ____.
   a. Ordinal variable
   b. Continuous variable
   c. Categorical variable
   d. Quantitative variable
8. What would be the sum of deviations of individual data points from their mean for (5, 10, 20, 5, 20)?
   a. 10 b. 25
   c. 50 d. 0
   e. None of the above
9. The scores of six persons in an IQ test were 92, 89, 86, 88, 84, 83. The median is:
   a. 87 b. 86
   c. 88 d. 92
   e. None of the above
10. Identify which of the following is a measure of dispersion:
    a. Median
    b. Mode
    c. Interquartile range
    d. Mean
11. A small sample of Grade 5 students spends the following hours on study per day: 4, 0, 3, 2, 5, 1, 2, 1, 0. The mean number of hours spent on study per day (rounded to the nearest tenth) is:
    a. 1.7 b. 2.0
    c. 2.5 d. 3.0

Answers

1. a	**2.** b	**3.** d	**4.** b	**5.** b	**6.** d	**7.** b	**8.** d	**9.** a	**10.** c
11. b									

Programming/Concept-based Questions

1. Perform the following operations in R:
   Create a vector named `marks` (6.5,5.0,8.4,7.7,10.2,9.8).
   a. Calculate the mean of the vector
   b. Calculate the median of the vector
   c. Calculate the mode by defining a function
   d. Calculate the standard deviation and variance of the vector
   e. Find the maximum and minimum marks in the given vector
2. Use `summary()` to find all the statistical measures of a vector T `<- c(20,30,40,50,60,70)`.
3. Obtain the first five sorted elements from the vector data `<-(20,30,50,33,11,08,45,78,02)`.

4. Consider the anorexia data set available in the `MASS` package. The data set contains the weights of girls before and after treatment for anorexia. Perform the following operations in R and check if the treatment caused any change in weight:
   a. Load the data and inspect its structure
   b. Generate descriptive statistics on weight after treatment
   c. Generate descriptive statistics on weight before treatment
   d. Create a new variable that contains the difference in weight before and after treatment. Interpret the result.
5. Determine the association between gender and preference for ice cream flavour from the given table:

Gender/Flavour	Chocolate	Vanilla	Strawberry	Total
Male	100	120	60	280
Female	350	200	90	640
Total	450	320	150	920

6. Consider the AirPassengers data set. Find the frequency of AirPassengers, obtain its summary and interpret it.
7. Consider that the marks of students are normally distributed, with a mean value equal to 85 and standard deviation equal to 20. What is the 98th percentile of the distribution of marks of students?
8. The gonorrhoea data set contains data about gonorrhoea infection rates in the US by year, age, ethnicity and gender. Explore how the infection rate changes with age. Do ethnicity and gender affect the infection rates?
9. Find the median and mode of the following data:
   a. X = [15,12,31,12,51,15]
   b. Y = [7,65,9,7,8,55,95]
10. Using the scaling transformation, find the GM of the following data:
    a. X = [5 ,65,27, 48, 9, 89]
    b. Y = [2202, 2503, 3406, 4008, 6301]
11. Suppose the data for analysis includes the age attribute. The age values for the data tuples are (in increasing order) 113, 115, 116, 116, 119, 220, 220, 221, 222, 222, 225, 225, 225, 225, 330, 333,333, 335, 335, 335, 335, 336, 440, 445, 446, 552, 770.
    a. Calculate the mean, median and mode of the data. Comment on the data's modality.
    b. Find the first quartile (Q1) and third quartile (Q3) of the data
    c. Summarise the data using the five-number summary
    d. Visualise the data using box plot
12. A manufacturer wants to determine the inner diameter of a piece of chalk. Ideally, the diameter should be 57 mm. The data is as follows: 72, 57, 53, 58, 569, 57, 56, 50. Calculate the measures of central value and dispersion, and comment on the quality of the chalk produced.

CHAPTER 18 Probability

Objectives

At the end of this chapter, you will be able to

- Define probability and distinguish between probability and statistics
- Define random variables
- Explain probability distribution and discrete and continuous variables
- Describe discrete probability distributions such as binomial, multimodal and Poisson
- Describe continuous probability distributions such as normal, chi-squared, student's t and F test

18.1 | INTRODUCTION TO PROBABILITY

Probability offers a way of dealing with uncertainty and randomness in processes. It helps us make a judgement about future events based on previous event data. It also helps in prediction in an informed manner.

Many statistical methods in data science use probability theory. It can be inferred statistically to predict trends or patterns in data. Hence, probability theory and probabilistic distribution play an important role in computer science.

18.2 | PROBABILITY AND STATISTICS

Probability is the chance that a particular outcome occurs in an experiment (also called an event). It deals with predicting the likelihood of future events. For example, consider an event such as tossing a coin, where the outcome could be heads or tails.

As another example, let us suppose there are five red balls and six white balls. If we randomly select two balls, what is probability that both the balls are red (P1) or of selecting two differently coloured balls (P2)?

If we have no knowledge about the total number of balls of each colour in the above example, then statistics comes into play. Statistics helps us infer population based on random samples. It analyses the frequency of past events.

Statistics can answer the following questions:

S1: A random sample of five balls is selected from a bag and two red and three white balls are picked. What is the total population of red and white balls?

S2: We perform an experiment of random sampling of four balls. We count the number of red balls in each experiment and perform this experiment 10 times; the average of these trials is 3. What is the true number of red balls in the population?

In probability, we are given a model and asked what kind of data we are likely to see. In statistics, we are given data and asked what kind of model is likely to have generated it.

18.3 | RANDOM VARIABLES

A random variable stores the output of a random event. The range of values of a random variable can be fixed, but the exact value will be determined after the occurrence of the event. For example, a random variable can store the side of a flipped coin, as heads (0) or tails (1).

If you throw a dice and wish to store the outcome, it will be a number in the range 1–6. You need to use a random variable because the outcome of throwing a dice is not known. Random variables are used to quantify the outcomes of random occurrences in probability and statistics.

A random variable is different from an algebraic variable. The variable in an algebraic equation is an unknown value that can be calculated. The equation $10 + x = 13$ shows that we can calculate the specific value of x, which is 3. On the other hand, a random variable has a set of values, and any of those values could be the outcome, as seen in the example of the dice above.

18.4 | PROBABILITY DISTRIBUTION

A probability distribution is a list of all of the possible outcomes of a random variable, along with their corresponding probability values. For example, the probability distribution of a six-sided dice roll is shown in Table 18.1.

Table 18.1 Probability distribution of a six-sided dice roll

Outcome of dice roll	1	2	3	4	5	6
Probability	1/6	1/6	1/6	1/6	1/6	1/6

Probability distributions can be discrete or continuous. Discrete probability distribution is defined using discrete variables, while continuous probability distribution is defined using continuous variables.

Discrete vs continuous variables If a variable can take any specified value, then it is called a discrete variable. For example, you throw a dice (the specified values will be 1, 2, 3, 4, 5 or 6) or toss a coin (the specified values will be heads or tails).

If a variable can take a specified range of values and all the values in between (continuous), then it is a continuous variable. For example, measuring height in centimetres, where the values can be 150 cm, 150.5 cm, 150.6 cm, and so on. Generally, real-time values are stored in continuous variables.

18.4.1 Discrete Probability Distribution

If a random variable is a discrete variable, its probability distribution is called discrete probability distribution. The probability is distributed amongst all possible discrete outcomes.

For example, if you throw a dice, the possible outcomes are 1, 2, 3, 4, 5 and 6. A random discrete variable X can store these values. The probability distribution for throwing a dice may be as is shown in Table 18.1.

This relates the output values of a discrete random variable to the probability values.

Binomial probability distribution A binomial random variable contains a number of successes in n repeated trials of an event. Each event trial has two possible outcomes (success or failure).

Binomial probability distribution is the distribution of the probability of a binomial random variable. It allows you to perform n trials, where the outcome of each trial is success or failure and the probability of success of each trial is P. Every trial is independent, which means that the outcome of one trial is not dependent on another.

Suppose we toss a coin in two trials and count the number of heads. The binomial probability distribution with the number of heads and their probability is shown in Table 18.2.

Table 18.2 Binomial probability distribution with the number of heads and their probability

Binomial random variable or number of heads	Probability
0	0.25
1	0.50
2	0.25

Mathematical formula: Suppose n trials of an experiment are performed and the number of successes is counted (x). The probability of success in each trial is P. Then, the binomial probability is:

$$b(x; n, P) = {}^{n}C_{x} * P^{x} * (1 - P)^{n-x}$$

or

$$b(x; n, P) = \{ n! / [x! (n - x)!] \} * P^{x} * (1 - P)^{n-x}$$

Suppose you toss a coin five times. The probability of getting three heads is shown below:

Number of trials (n) = 5
Number of successes (x) = 3
Probability of success (P) in each trial = ½ = 0.5
Applying the formula for binomial distribution

$$b(3; 5, 0.5) = {}^{5}C_{3} * (0.5)^{3} * (0.5)^{2} = 0.625$$

Taking another example, suppose there are 15 multiple choice questions, each question has four possible answers and one of them is correct. A student attempts all the questions. We can find out the probability of (a) his getting exactly five correct answers and (b) his getting four or fewer correct answers.

(a) Number of trials (n) = 15
Number of successes (x) = 5
Probability of success (P) in each trial = 1/4 = 0.25
We can use the `dbinom(x,n,P)` function in R.

```
> dbinom(5, size=15, prob=0.25)
[1] 0.165146
```

(b) To find the probability of four or fewer correct answers, we need to add all the binomial probabilities of x = 0, 1, 2, 3, 4.
In R programming:

```
> dbinom(0, size=15, prob=0.25) +
+ dbinom(1, size=15, prob=0.25) +
+ dbinom(2, size=15, prob=0.25) +
+ dbinom(3, size=15, prob=0.25) +
+ dbinom(4, size=15, prob=0.25)
[1] 0.6864859
```

Probability of success of four or fewer correct answers is 68.6%.

Alternatively, we can use the cumulative probability function for binomial distribution, `pbinom()`.

```
> pbinom(4, size=15, prob=0.25)
[1] 0.6864859
```

Multinomial distribution A multinomial distribution is the probability distribution of n repeated trials, where each trial can have a number of possible outcomes (k). The probability of each outcome is $p_1, p_2, \ldots, p_k$. All trials are independent.

Mathematical formula: Suppose a multinomial experiment consists of n trials and k possible outcomes ($E_1, E_2 \ldots E_k$) and the probabilities of k possible outcomes is $p_1, p_2, \ldots, p_k$. The event E_1 occurs n_1 times, E_2 occurs n_2 times, . . . and E_k occurs n_k times. The multinomial probability P is calculated as:

$$P = [\, n! \,/\, (n_1! * n_2! * \ldots n_k!)\,] * (p_1^{n_1} * p_2^{n_2} * \ldots * p_k^{n_k})$$

where $n = n_1 + n_2 + \ldots + n_k$.

For example, two people play a game of chess and the probability that A would win is 0.30, B would win is 0.50 and that the match would be drawn is 0.20. The players played 10 games. To find out the probability that A would win three games, B would win four games and that three games would be drawn, the following computation can be used.

A wins $n_1 = 3$ games with probability p_1 0.30.

B wins $n_2 = 4$ games with probability p_1 0.50.

Match draw $n_3 = 3$ times with probability 0.20.

$$P = [\, n! \,/\, (n_1! * n_2! * \ldots n_k!)\,] * (p_1^{n_1} * p_2^{n_2} * \ldots * p_k^{n_k})$$
$$P = [\, 10! \,/\, (3! * 4! * 3!)\,] * [\, (0.30)^3 * (0.50)^4 * (0.20)^3 \,] = 0.0567$$

The R code for this is given below:

```
dmultinom(x=c(3,4,3), prob = c(0.3,0.5,0.2))
[1] 0.0567
```

Poisson distribution A Poisson distribution is the probability distribution that finds the probability of events based on average past probability. Poisson probability is defined as

$$P(x; \mu)$$

where x is the actual number of successes and μ is the mean number of successes.

Mathematical formula: The Poisson probability is defined as

$$P(x; \mu) = (e^{-\mu})\ (\mu^x)\ /\ x!$$

where e = 2.71828.

Suppose the average number of cars sold by a company is five per day. We can find out the probability that six cars will be sold tomorrow, as shown below.

$\mu = 5$ (average 5 cars per day)

$x = 6$ (calculate that 6 cars will be sold tomorrow)

e = 2.71828

Applying the Poisson formula

$$P(x; \mu) = (e^{-\mu})\ (\mu^x)\ /\ x!$$
$$P(6; 5) = (2.71828^{-5})\ (5^6)\ /\ 6! = 0.762$$

The probability of selling six cars will be .76 or 76%.
The R code to perform this is given below:

```
> ppois(6, lambda=5)
[1] 0.7621835
```

18.4.2 Continuous Probability Distribution

A continuous random variable takes a continuous range of values. Continuous probability distribution is defined over a continuous random variable. It can be represented using an equation or function.

A function that describes a continuous probability distribution is called a probability density function (PDF). Sometimes referred to as density function, PDF has the following properties:

a. $F(b) = \Pr(X \leq \int_{-\infty}^{x} f(t)dt$

b. $f(x) \geq 0$ for any value of x

c. $\int_{-\infty}^{\infty} f(t)d(t) = 1$

PDF can be represented using graphs that are continuous over a range. The area under the curve of the density function should be in the given range and the x axis should be 1; that is, the sum of all probabilities should be 1.

Continuous uniform distribution PDF takes continuous uniform values over a range. It can be rectangular or constant (saturated) after some values of x, as shown in Fig. 18.1.

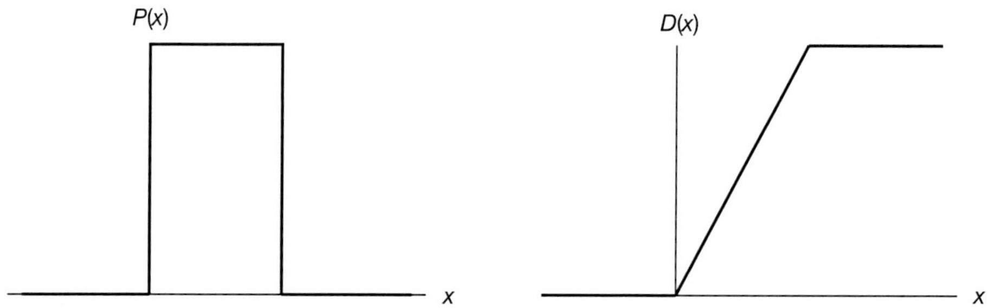

Fig. 18.1: Continuous uniform distribution over a range

The PDF and cumulative distribution function over an interval $[a, b]$ is defined as

$$P(x) = \begin{cases} 0 & \text{for } x < a \\ \dfrac{1}{b-a} & \text{for } a \leq x \leq b \\ 0 & \text{for } x > b \end{cases} \tag{1}$$

$$D(x) = \begin{cases} 0 & \text{for } x < a \\ \dfrac{x-a}{b-a} & \text{for } a \leq x \leq b \\ 1 & \text{for } x > b \end{cases}$$

For example, to generate five numbers between 1 and 5 in R, we apply the generation function `runif()` of the uniform distribution.

```
> runif(5, min=1, max=5)
[1] 4.495818 4.020850 4.210616 1.223877 4.842501
```

Normal distribution This is the continuous probability distribution of a bell-shaped curve. It is also called Gaussian distribution. The bell-shaped curve is also known as a normal curve, as shown in Fig. 18.2. It is used in various instances, such as in grading of marks in student examinations, rainfall studies, measurement of area, manufacturing parts, etc.

A continuous random variable X having a bell-shaped distribution is called a normal random variable. *Mathematical formula*: Normal probability density function is defined as

$$P(x) = \frac{1}{\sigma\sqrt{2\pi}} e^{-(x-\mu)^2/(2\sigma^2)}$$

where X is a continuous random variable $x \in (-\infty, \infty)$; μ is the mean and σ^2 is the variance.
Standard normal distribution: In the above formula, if $\mu = 0$ and $\sigma^2 = 1$, it can be called a standard normal distribution.

$$z \equiv (X - \mu)/\sigma$$

So $dz = dx/\sigma$.

Yield

$$P(x)dx = \frac{1}{\sqrt{2\pi}} e^{-z^2/2} dz.$$

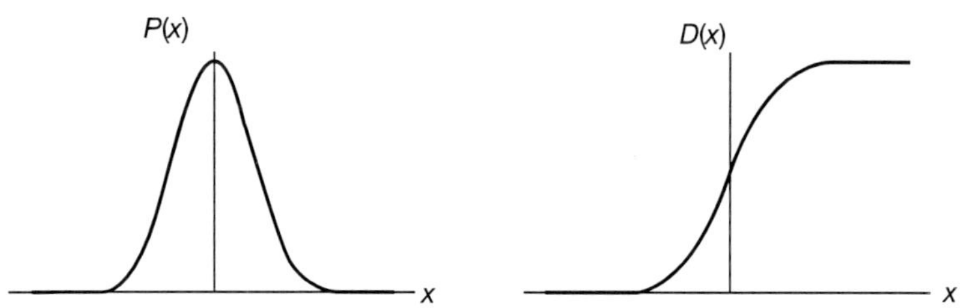

Fig. 18.2: Continuous normal distribution

For example, a student examination system follows normal distribution. In a subject, the mean test score is 78 and standard deviation is 20. To find out what percentage of students score 90% or more, we can apply the function for normal distribution in R as follows:

```
> pnorm(90, mean=78, sd=20, lower.tail=FALSE)
[1] 0.2742531
```

Therefore, 27% of students scored 90% or more.

Exponential distribution Exponential distribution is described for randomly recurring events. If the average time of the recurring event is μ, then exponential distribution calculates the probability of the recurrence of the next event. Its PDF is defined as follows:

$$f(x) = \begin{cases} \frac{1}{\mu} e^{-x/\mu} & \text{when } x \geq 0 \\ 0 & \text{when } x < 0 \end{cases}$$

Figure 18.3 shows a graph with e(x) when μ = 1.

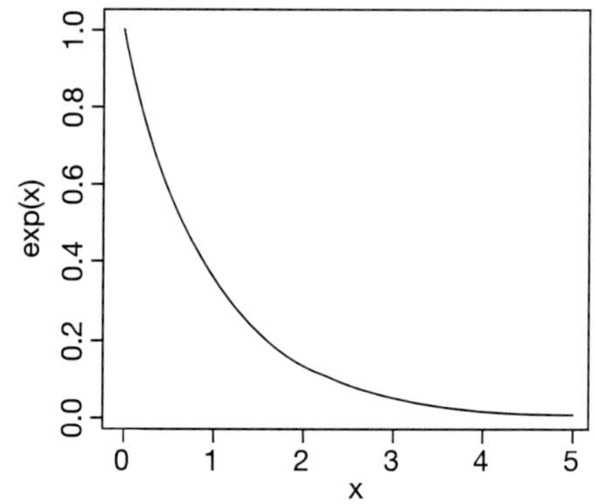

Fig. 18.3: A graph with e(x) when μ = 1

Let us assume that the mean check-out time of a cash counter is 5 minutes. We can find out the probability that a customer check-out will be completed by the cashier in <=3 minutes, as follows:

Check-out rate = 1/5

$X = 3$

The R code is given below:

```
> pexp(3, rate=1/5)
  [1] 0.4511884
```

Chi-squared distribution This is an extension of standard normal distribution, where m independent random variables $X_1, X_2, \ldots, X_m$ are involved. Its degree of freedom is m and variance is $2m$.
Mathematical formula:

$$V = X_1^2 + X_2^2 + \cdots + X_m^2 \sim X_{(m)}^2$$

Chi-squared distribution is shown in Fig. 18.4.

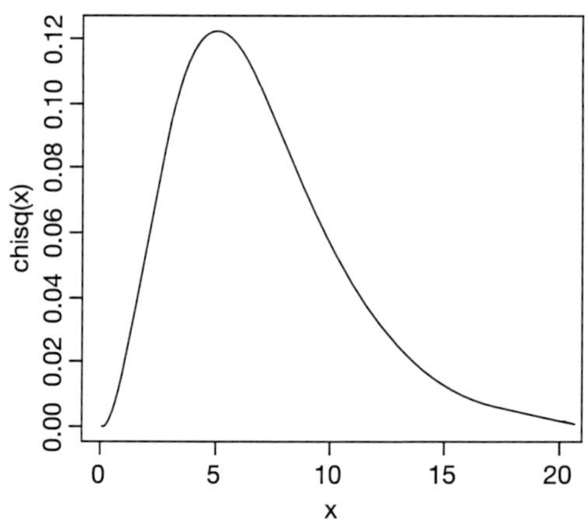

Fig. 18.4: Chi-squared distribution (degrees of freedom = 7)

As an example, what would be the 86th percentile of the chi-squared distribution, if the degree of freedom is 6?

To find out, we can use the `qchisq()` function in R, with the percentile passed as .86.

```
> qchisq(.86, df=6)
  [1] 9.65399
```

Student's t distribution This is a form of continuous probability distribution where the sample size is small and standard deviation of the population is not known. This type of distribution was so named because William Sealy Gosset, who developed it, was better known as Student.
Mathematical formula:

$$t = \frac{z}{\sqrt{V / m}} \sim t_{(m)}$$

where z is the same as in a standard normal distribution, V is the chi-squared distribution and m is the degree of freedom. A student's t distribution is shown in Fig. 18.5.

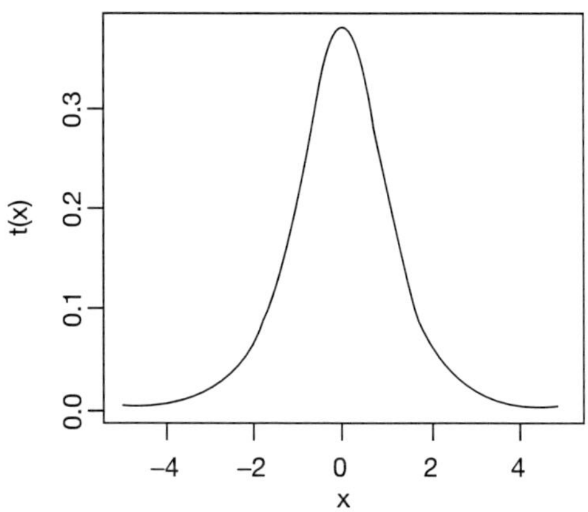

Fig. 18.5: Student's t distribution (degree of freedom = 5)

For example, to find the 12th and 88th percentiles of a student's t distribution with degree of freedom = 7, we can use the R function `qt ()`, and pass .12 as the value for `Z` and .88 for `V`.

```
> qt(c(.12, .88), df=7)
[1] -1.284014  1.284014
```

F distribution The F distribution is defined on two independent random variables having chi-squared distribution.
Mathematical formula:

$$F = \frac{V_1 / m_1}{V_2 / m_2} \sim F_{(m_1, m_2)}$$

where V_1 and V_2 are two independent random variables and m_1 and m_2 represent the degrees of freedom. An F distribution is shown in Fig. 18.6.

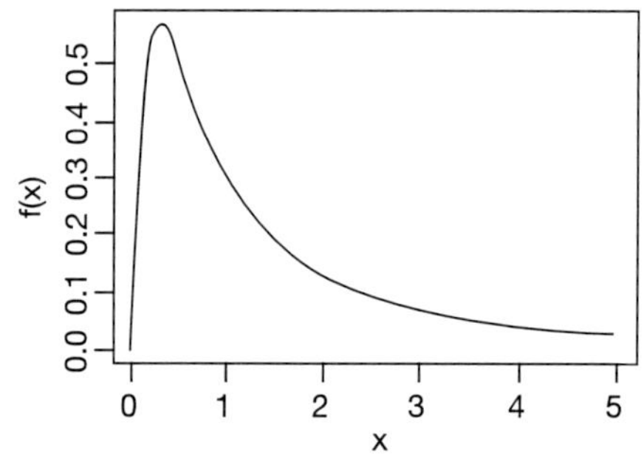

Fig. 18.6: F distribution (degree of freedom = (5,2))

To find out the F distribution of the 88th percentile, with degree of freedom as 7, 3, we can use the `qf()` function in R:

```
> qf(.88, df1=7, df2=3)
[1] 4.559049
```

EXERCISES

Multiple Choice Questions

1. Which of the following standard probability density functions is applicable to discrete random variables?
   a. Gaussian distribution
   b. Poisson distribution
   c. Rayleigh distribution
   d. Exponential distribution
2. What is the area under a conditional cumulative density function?
   a. 0
   b. Infinity
   c. 1
   d. Changes with CDF
3. A table with all possible values of a random variable and its corresponding probabilities is called______.
   a. Probability mass function
   b. Probability density function
   c. Cumulative distribution function
   d. Probability distribution
4. A variable that can assume any value between two given points is called ________.
   a. Continuous random variable
   b. Discrete random variable
   c. Irregular random variable
   d. Uncertain random variable
5. A variable that can contain certain integer values between two given points is called __________.
   a. Continuous random variable
   b. Discrete random variable
   c. Irregular random variable
   d. Uncertain random variable
6. The expected value of a discrete random variable 'x' is given by
   a. P(x) b. $\sum P(x)$
   c. $\sum x\, P(x)$ d. 1
7. Of the following values, which is not possible in probability?
   a. P(x) = 1 b. $\sum x\, P(x) = 3$
   c. P(x) = 0.5 d. P(x) = – 0.5
8. In binomial probability distribution, the dependents of standard deviation must include
   a. Probability of q
   b. Probability of p
   c. Trials
   d. All of the above

Answer

1. b	2. c	3. d	4. a	5. b	6. c	7. d	8. d

Concept-based Questions

1. Give some examples of random variables. Also, specify the range of values and whether they are continuous or discrete.
2. In the following cases, what are the probability distributions likely to be followed? In each case, you should mention the random variable and the parameter(s) influencing the probability distribution function.
   a. In a retail source, how many counters should be open at a given time period
   b. The number of people suffering from cancer in a town
3. In the following cases, what are the probability distributions likely to be followed? In each case, you should mention the random variable and the parameter(s) influencing the probability distribution function.
   a. A missile will hit the enemy's aircraft
   b. A student in the class will secure EX grade
   c. Salary of a person in an enterprise
   d. Accident involving cars in a city
   e. People quit education after (i) primary, (ii) secondary and (iii) higher secondary education
4. How you can calculate the mean and standard deviation of a population if the population follows the following probability distribution functions with respect to an event?
   a. Binomial distribution function
   b. Poisson distribution function
   c. Hypergeometric distribution function
   d. Normal distribution function
   e. Standard normal distribution function

CHAPTER

19 Sampling Distributions

Objectives

At the end of this chapter, you will be able to

- Define sampling distribution
- Explain the Central Limit Theorem
- Describe the chi-squared distribution
- Describe the student's t distribution
- Explain the F distribution

19.1 | INTRODUCTION TO SAMPLING DISTRIBUTIONS

In statistics, very often data from the entire population cannot be collected and used for analysis or training. We need to select samples that would represent the entire population. In some cases, when the population is large, we cannot accommodate all the possible samples. Instead, we use the probability distribution of sample statistics. This depends on the size of the population, the samples and the method of sampling. A sample drawn from a population having a specific probability distribution is called sampling distribution. It is the distribution of the frequency of a range of different outcomes.

The procedure used to draw samples from a population is based on the number of observations in the sample and the number of observations in a population. This also determines variability in sampling distribution. Sample statistics vary from sample to sample, even if all the samples are taken from the same population.

For example, suppose you have selected 10 male students from among all the male students in the age group of 16–20 years in an institute and measured their height. You then calculate the mean height (h_1) of your sample. This mean height of sample S_1 may be higher or lower than the mean height of the entire male student population (h). If you take a second sample S_2 of 10 male students and calculate the mean height (h_2), you may find that

$$h_1 \neq h_2 \neq h$$

If a population with mean μ and variance σ2 exists and a random sample (S_1) of size n is drawn from it, the parameters of the sampling distribution of S_1 are as follows:

Mean $\overline{X} = \mu$

Variance $S^2 = \sigma 2/n$

From $\overline{X}$ and S^2 (mean and variance of the sample), we can make an inference about μ and $\sigma 2$ (the mean and variance of the population).

If this experiment is conducted many times, and many samples of size n are drawn, we can calculate $\overline{X}$ of each sample and also find the mean of all $\overline{X}$ and the difference between $\overline{X}$ and true μ. This process is repeated for S^2 and $\sigma 2$ to give information about variability in sampling distribution statistics.

19.2 | CENTRAL LIMIT THEOREM

According to this theorem, the average of the sample mean and standard deviation of a sample of large size is equal to the population mean and standard deviation. Distribution of sample mean approximates normal distribution as the sample size becomes larger. The sample size should be greater than 30 for the Central Limit Theorem to hold true. Therefore, if a sample of sufficiently large size is drawn, it can represent the entire population correctly.

The Central Limit Theorem is represented using the formula

$$Z = \frac{\overline{X} - \mu}{\sigma / \sqrt{n}}$$

where $\overline{X}$ is the mean of a random sample of size n; μ is the mean of the population and $\sigma 2$ is the variance of the population.

As $n \rightarrow \infty$, the distribution tends to the standard normal distribution.

For example, in an institute, the mean height of male students is 160 cm, with standard deviation of 20 cm. If a sample of 80 male students is drawn, what is the probability that their mean height will be greater than 155 cm?

Here, $\overline{X} = 155$, $\sigma = 20$, $n = 80$ and $\mu = 160$.

Applying the Central Limit Theorem formula

$$(155 - 160)/(20/\sqrt{80}) = -2.23$$

Looking up the z-score in the z-table of standard normal probabilities = 98.71%.

Thus, 98.71% of students will have a mean height greater than 155 cm.

19.3 | SAMPLING DISTRIBUTION OF χ^2

In the previous section, we studied variability in mean values in the Central Limit Theorem and learned that the larger the size of the sample, the more the distribution tends towards standard normal distribution. In a sampling distribution of χ^2, variability needs to be considered. We will now explore the relation between variations in a sampling distribution of size n and population variance $\sigma 2$.

The chi-squared distribution with $v = n - 1$ degrees of freedom is given by

$$X^2 = \frac{(n-1)S^2}{\sigma^2} = \sum_{i=1}^{n} \frac{(X_i - \overline{X})^2}{\sigma^2}$$

To calculate the probability that a random sample produces a chi-squared distribution value greater than χ^2_a, we need to use a graph, as shown in Fig. 19.1.

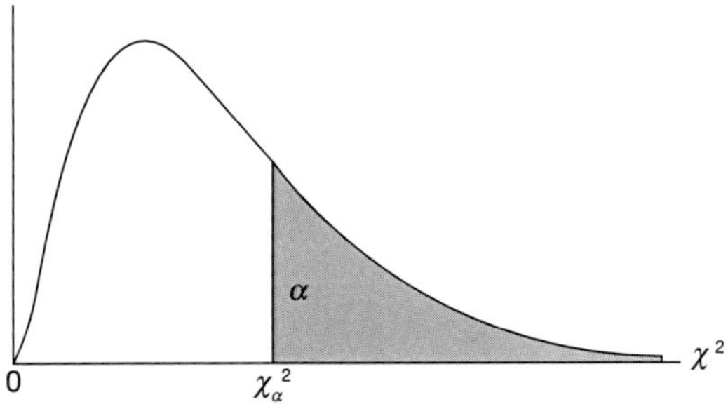

Fig. 19.1: Chi-squared distribution

The probability will be equal to the area under the curve on the right-hand-side of χ^2_a (shaded area).

For example, car batteries are sold with a lifetime guarantee of three years on average. The battery lifetime is normally distributed. The standard deviation is 1 year and the number of batteries is 5. The lifetime of five batteries in years = 1.9, 2.4, 3.0, 3.5 4.2. We want to find the percentage of confidence that the standard deviation of the battery is 1 year.

X = 1.9,2.4,3.0,3.5,4.2, n = 5, σ = 1 (standard deviation of 1 year), $\overline{X}$ = 3.0

$$s^2 = \frac{\sum(x_i - \overline{x})^2}{n-1}$$
$$= 0.815$$

$$\chi^2 = \frac{(n-1)s^2}{\sigma^2}$$
$$= 3.26$$

Checking 3.26 with 4 degrees of freedom in the chi-squared table, we obtain the value 95%.

Therefore, the confidence percentage that the standard deviation of the batteries is 1 year is 95%.

19.4 | STUDENT'S T DISTRIBUTION

This distribution is the same as the normal distribution, which is bell shaped, but with heavier tails and lower peaks. It tends to produce values far from the mean. Student's t distribution is used to estimate the significance of the values. It is used when you want to estimate the mean in a normally distributed population of small size where the standard deviation of the population is not known. It can construct a confidence interval between two mean values of two populations. It is used to study the mean of a population rather that individual members of the population.

If the standard deviation σ is not known, t distribution can be used. Its mathematical formula is

$$T = \frac{\overline{X} - \mu}{S / \sqrt{n}}$$

where $\overline{X}$ is the sample mean, μ is the population mean, S represents the sample standard deviation and N represents the degree of freedom.

As the degree of freedom increases, the t distribution tends towards standard normal distribution. Some sources state that if the value of n > 30, the t distribution is the same as standard normal distribution.

It can be defined in terms of the Z standard normal random variable as

$$T = \frac{Z}{\sqrt{V / v}}$$

where V is the chi-squared random variable and v represents the degree of freedom.

Thus, the t distribution is used to check the means of two samples that are different from each other or to compare means when the standard deviation of the population is not known.

19.5 | F DISTRIBUTION

This type of distribution is related to the $\chi 2$ distribution. It is used to test whether two samples have the same variance. A chi-squared distribution deals with one variable and one degree of freedom, but F distribution deals with multiple variables and multiple degrees of freedom. It is a skewed distribution of probabilities similar to a chi-squared distribution. The ANOVA model utilises the F distribution. It is a method of obtaining the probabilities of a specific set of events.

If U has $\chi 2$ distribution with v_1 degree of freedom and V has $\chi 2$ distribution with v_2 degree of freedom, F distribution is defined as

$$F = \frac{U / v_1}{V / v_2}$$

The F distribution can handle v_1 and v_2 degrees of freedom. It arises when we want to work with a ratio of variance.

If the variance of two samples is S_1 and S_2 and the population variance is $\sigma^2{}_1$ and $\sigma^2{}_2$, the chi-squared distribution with n_1 and n_2 degrees of freedom is defined as

$$\chi_1^2 = \frac{(n_1 - 1)S_1^2}{\sigma_1^2} \text{ and } \chi_2^2 = \frac{(n_2 - 1)S_2^2}{\sigma_2^2}$$

$$F = \frac{S_1^2 / \sigma_1^2}{S_2^2 / \sigma_2^2} = \frac{\sigma_2^2 S_1^2}{\sigma_1^2 S_2^2}$$

An F distribution uses $n_1 - 1$ and $n_2 - 1$ degrees of freedom. The area and percentile of the F distribution can be found in the F table.

EXERCISES

Multiple Choice Questions

1. What does the Central Limit Theorem state?
   a. If the sample size increases, the sampling distribution must approach normal distribution
   b. If the sample size decreases, the sampling distribution must approach normal distribution
   c. If the sample size increases, the sampling distribution must approach an exponential distribution
   d. If the sample size decreases, the sampling distribution must approach an exponential distribution

2. Standard error is always non-negative.
   a. True   b. False
3. Sampling error increases as we increase the sampling size.
   a. True   b. False
4. The difference between the sample value expected and the estimated value of the parameter is called _______.
   a. Bias
   b. Error
   c. Contradiction
   d. Difference
5. In which of the following types of sampling is information collected based on the opinion of an expert?
   a. Quota sampling
   b. Convenience sampling
   c. Purposive sampling
   d. Judgement sampling
6. Sampling error is defined as _______.
   a. Difference between population and parameter
   b. Difference between sample and parameter
   c. Difference between population and sample
   d. Difference between parameter and sample
7. Any population that we want to study is referred to as _______.
   a. Standard population
   b. Final population
   c. Infinite population
   d. Target population
8. Suppose we want to make a voters list for the general elections in 2019, we require _______.
   a. Sampling error   b. Random error
   c. Census   d. Simple error
9. Selection of a football team for FIFA World Cup is called _______ sampling.
   a. Random   b. Systematic
   c. Purposive   d. Cluster

Answers

1. a	2. a	3. b	4. a	5. d	6. c	7. d	8. c	9. c

Programming/Concept-based Questions

1. What are the degrees of freedom in the following cases:
   Case 1: A single number
   Case 2: A list of n numbers
   Case 3: A table of data with m rows and n columns
   Case 4: A data cube with dimension $m \times n \times p$
2. Suppose $\overline{X}$ and S denote the sample mean and standard deviation of a sample. Assume that the population follows normal distribution with population mean μ and standard deviation σ. Write down the expression of z and t values with degree of freedom n.

CHAPTER

20 Correlation and Regression Analysis

Objectives

At the end of this chapter, you will be able to

- Define correlation and covariance
- Explain the correlation coefficient
- Explain regression analysis and its types
- Describe and build simple and multiple regression models in R
- Explain and build the logistic regression model in R

20.1 | INTRODUCTION TO CORRELATION AND REGRESSION ANALYSIS

We may often come across problems involving the determination of relationships among variables; that is, change or movement in one variable causes movement in another variable. For example, there exists a relationship between the number of hours of study and the marks obtained, rainfall and the production of crops. These require measures of the association between variables. The degree of relationship between variables is measured through correlation analysis. Regression analysis helps in estimating the value of a variable, given the value of another variable.

20.2 | CORRELATION ANALYSIS

The association between variables, that is, correlation, can be studied graphically by creating a scatter plot of the variables or by computing the correlation coefficient. Both of these types of analysis are described below.

20.2.1 Measures of Association (Covariance and Correlation)

In statistics, correlation denotes some form of association between two variables. For example, weight is correlated to height. The correlation may be positive, negative or zero (Fig. 20.1).

Positive correlation: If the value of the attribute A increases with an increase in the value of the attribute B, and vice-versa.

Negative correlation: If the value of the attribute A decreases with an increase in the value of the attribute B, and vice-versa.

Zero correlation: When the value of attribute A varies at random with attribute B, and vice-versa.

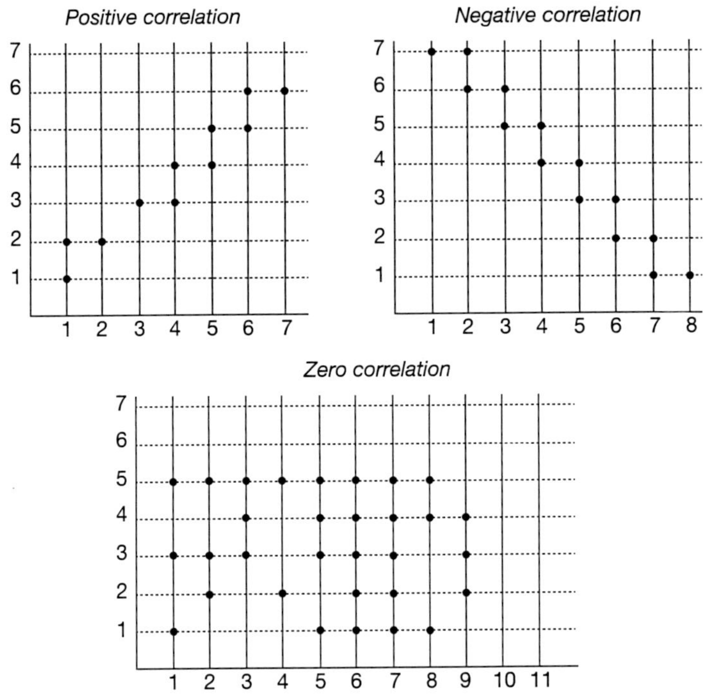

Fig. 20.1: Scatter plot

20.2.2 Correlation Coefficient

The correlation coefficient is used to describe the linear relationship among quantitative variables. It measures the strength and direction of a relationship. The + and – signs indicate the direction of the relationship, and the magnitude indicates the strength of the relationship (ranging from 0 to 1 for a perfect predictable relationship). If the correlation coefficient is close to 1, it would indicate that the variables are highly positively related, and for –1, it indicates that the variables are negatively linearly related. For zero, it would indicate that the variables do not move together – there is a weak linear relationship between the variables.

Karl Pearson's coefficient of correlation is used to find the correlation coefficient between two numerical attributes. This is defined as follows.

Let us consider two attributes X and Y.

The Karl Pearson's coefficient of correlation is denoted by r^* and is defined as

$$r^* = \frac{\sum (X_i - \bar{X})(Y_i - \bar{Y})}{\sigma_X \cdot \sigma_Y}$$

where X_i is the *i*th value of the *X* variable, $\bar{X}$ is the mean of *X*, Y_i is the *i*th value of the *Y* variable, $\bar{Y}$ is the mean of *Y*, *n* is the number of pairs of observations of *X* and *Y*, σ_X is the standard deviation of *X* and σ_Y is the standard deviation of *Y*.

Charles Spearman's coefficient of correlation can be used to find the correlation coefficient between two ordinal attributes. We can assign a rank to the different values of a variable with the ordinal data type. The rank correlation can be defined as

$$r_s = 1 - \frac{6\sum d_i^2}{n(n^2-1)}$$

where d_i is the difference between the ranks of the *i*th pair of two variables and *n* is the number of pairs of observations.

Correlation and covariance describe the degree of a relationship. Correlation is dimensionless, while covariance is not. Its unit is obtained by multiplying the units of the two variables. Dividing the covariance by the product of x and y's standard deviation produces a "scaleless" quantity, known as the correlation coefficient in general.

Covariance is defined in terms of mean as:

$$s_{xy} = \frac{1}{n-1}\sum_{i=1}^{n}(x_i - \bar{x})(y_i - \bar{y})$$

Here, x_i, and y_i are observations, $(\bar{x}, \bar{y})$ represents the mean of observations and *n* is the total number of observations.

Formally, the correlation coefficient is defined by the formula:

$$r_{xy} = \frac{s_{xy}}{s_x s_y}$$

where s_x and s_y are the standard deviations and s_{xy} is the covariance.

20.2.3 Correlation Function in R

R has functions that can be used to produce covariance (`cov()`) and a variety of correlation coefficients (`cor()`) specified in the `method` parameter.

```
>cor(a,use=,method=)
```

where `a` is a matrix or data frame; `use` specifies the handling of missing data (default is "everything"); and `method` specifies the type of correlation (default is "pearson", others can be "spearman", "kendall", "partial", "polychoric", "polyserial", etc.).

```
> states<-state.x77[,1:4]
> cov(states)
```

When we execute this code, the following output is produced:

```
             Population      Income        Illiteracy      Life Exp

Population  19931683.7588   571229.7796   292.8679592     -407.8424612
Income      571229.7796     377573.3061   -163.7020408    280.6631837
Illiteracy  292.8680       -163.7020      0.3715306       -0.4815122
Life Exp    -407.8425       280.6632      -0.4815122      1.8020204

> states<-state.x77[,1:4]
> cor(states, method="spearman")
```

When we execute this code, the following output is produced:

```
            Population    Income      Illiteracy    Life Exp
Population  1.0000000     0.1246098    0.3130496   -0.1040171
Income      0.1246098     1.0000000   -0.3145948    0.3241050
Illiteracy  0.3130496    -0.3145948    1.0000000   -0.5553735
Life Exp   -0.1040171     0.3241050   -0.5553735    1.0000000


>x<-states[,c("Population","Income","Illiteracy")]
>y<-states[,c("Life Exp")]
>cor(x,y)
```

When we execute this code, the following output is produced:

```
              Life Exp
Population -0.06805195
Income      0.34025534
Illiteracy -0.58847793
```

For example, find the correlation and covariance of `len` and `dose` in the data set `ToothGrowth`. Observe if there is any linear relationship between the variables.

Code:

```
>head(ToothGrowth)
   len   supp  dose
1  4.2   VC    0.5
2  11.5  VC    0.5
3  7.3   VC    0.5
4  5.8   VC    0.5
5  6.4   VC    0.5
6  10.0  VC    0.5
> cor(ToothGrowth$len, ToothGrowth$dose)
[1] 0.8026913

> cov(ToothGrowth$len, ToothGrowth$dose)
[1] 3.861299
```

The correlation coefficient of `len` and `dose` is 0.8026913. The variables are positively linearly related. The covariance is 3.86. It indicates a positive linear relationship between the two variables.

20.3 | REGRESSION ANALYSIS

The purpose of regression analysis is to estimate the value of the dependent variable, given the value/values of the independent variable. It is a statistical modelling method used to formulate the mathematical model of the relationship among variables.

Regression analysis models can be classified as linear and non-linear. Linear models in turn can be categorised as simple and multiple, as shown in Fig. 20.2.

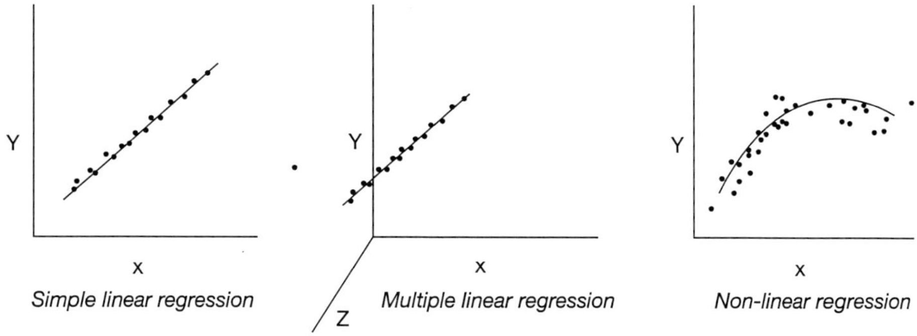

Fig. 20.2: Regression analysis model

20.3.1 Simple Linear Regression

In simple linear regression, we have only two variables: dependent (also called response), usually denoted by Y, and independent (alternatively called regressor), usually denoted by X. The relationship between X and Y is a linear relationship of the form shown in Fig. 20.3.

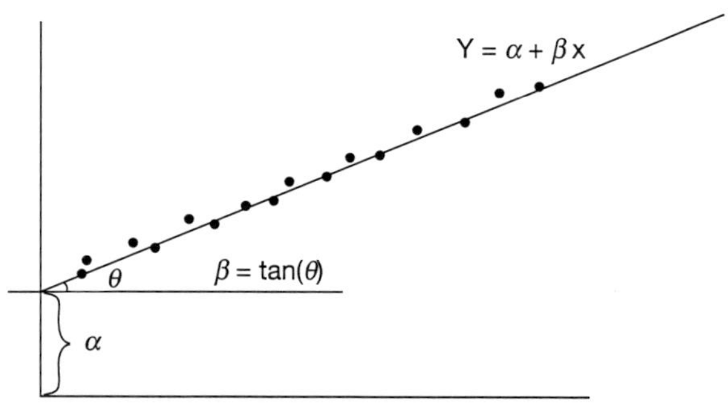

Fig. 20.3: Simple linear regression

There are an infinite number of lines, but the concept of regression analysis deals with finding the best relationship between *Y* and *X* (and hence, the best fitted values) quantifying the strength of that relationship. The task in regression analysis is to estimate the regression coefficients α and β. It uses the method of least squares to find the optimal values.

20.3.2 Multiple Linear Regression

When more than one variable is independent (k-independent variables $x_1, x_2 \ldots\ldots x_k$), the regression can be estimated as a multiple regression model. When this model is linear in coefficients, it is called multiple linear regression model. The multiple linear regression model is given by

$$y_i = \beta_0 + \beta_1 x_1 + \beta_2 x_2 + \beta_k x_k$$

20.3.3 Non-Linear Regression

When the regression equation is expressed in terms of *r*-degree, $r > 1$, then it is called non-linear regression model. When more than one independent variable, $x_1, x_2......x_r$ is present, it is called multiple non-linear regression model (alternatively, polynomial regression model). In general, it takes the form

$$y_i = \beta_0 + \beta_1 x + \beta_2 x^2 + \beta_r x^r$$

20.3.4 Regression in R

R has the `lm()` and `glm()` functions to build a linear regression model, which is used for predicting continuous data.

```
> lm(formula, data)
```

where `data` represents the variable that contains the data set and `formula` describes the model. The formula should be given in a specific format; that is, *varY~varX* in simple linear regression, where *varY* is the dependent or predicted variable and *varX* is the independent or predictor variable.

```
>glm(formula, family=familytype, data=)
```

where `data` is the variable that contains the data set; `formula` describes the model and `family` takes the values "binomial", "gaussian", "gamma", "poisson", "quasi", "quasipoisson", "quasibinomial" and "inverse gaussian" to perform logistic and other regressions/classifications.

To illustrate, assume that we have the height (x) data in inches of 40 adults. We can use the `rnorm()` function to generate a vector of heights with a mean of 80 (roughly the population mean), and a standard deviation of 5 inches. Similarly, weight (y) can be generated using `rnorm()` with a mean of 70 and standard deviation of 6 inches.

```
> x <- sort(rnorm(40, 80, 5))
> y <- sort(rnorm(40, 70, 6))
> x
 [1] 72.29567 72.66903 73.09784 73.50450 73.64954 73.76746 73.86345
74.34988 74.71307
[10] 75.23004 75.41412 76.64838 76.65357 76.91688 76.91959 78.14783
78.24718 78.30815
[19] 78.44426 78.83618 78.97446 79.33560 79.43489 79.51845 79.64263
81.03059 81.25577
[28] 81.33077 81.52023 81.97705 82.34121 82.80985 83.59965 83.68032
84.44598 84.79393
[37] 87.46072 89.04929 89.87698 90.03100

> y
 [1] 58.22440 58.51788 59.53612 62.04827 62.71820 64.31005 64.34964
64.37748 64.89418
[10] 64.99198 65.27528 65.51288 65.82426 65.99872 66.10643 66.64399
67.28812 67.41870
[19] 67.51661 67.74208 68.78102 69.13897 69.49860 69.55153 70.19040
70.30193 70.97490
[28] 72.69387 72.80264 73.30903 73.62901 74.49935 74.68253 75.03388
75.54728 75.85518
[37] 76.09700 77.64013 79.63913 81.26086

>cor(x,y)
[1] 0.9757246
```

The correlation of x and y shows that there is a strong positive linear relation between height and weight. The basic function to build a linear regression model in R is the `lm()` function. Here, y (weight) is the dependent variable and x (height) is the independent variable. The linear regression model is graphically depicted in Fig. 20.4. Predicting the value of weight given the height can be carried out as specified below.

```
>plot(x, y, xlab = "height", ylab = "weight", main = "height and weight")
>abline(lm(y ~ x))
```

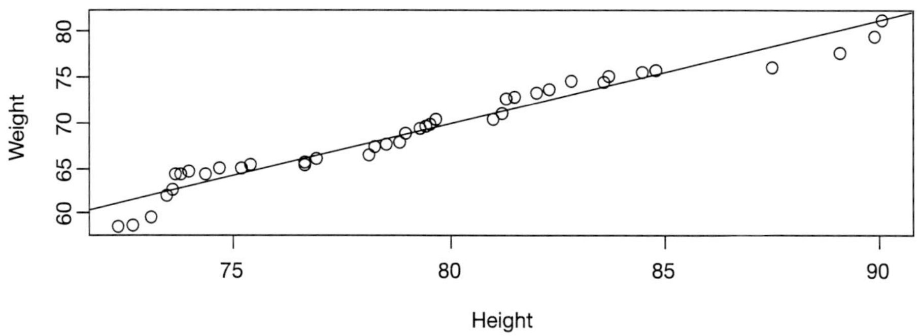

Fig. 20.4: Linear regression model for height and weight variables

```
> m1<-lm(y~x)
> summary(m1)
Call:
lm(formula = y ~ x)

Residuals:
    Min      1Q  Median      3Q     Max
-1.2938 -0.3970  0.2273  0.3721  0.8682

Coefficients:
             Estimate Std. Error t value Pr(>|t|)
(Intercept) -34.91903    1.90760   -18.3   <2e-16 ***
x             1.32064    0.02397    55.1   <2e-16 ***
---
Signif. codes:  0 '***' 0.001 '**' 0.01 '*' 0.05 '.' 0.1 ' ' 1

Residual standard error: 0.5897 on 38 degrees of freedom
Multiple R-squared:  0.9876,    Adjusted R-squared:  0.9873
F-statistic:  3036 on 1 and 38 DF,  p-value: < 2.2e-16
```

Using the `summary()` function for the model, we can obtain information such as the formula called, the error in our model, the values of the coefficients and their significance. We can also access information on the overall performance of the model with the adjusted R-squared (.9876 in our case) that represents the amount of variation in y explained by x; so 98% of the variation in 'weight (y)' can be explain by the variable 'height (x)'.

```
> predict(m1)
 1         2        3        4        5        6        7        8        9
59.43206  60.90593 63.35430 63.56232 63.82316 63.84543 64.27267 64.67051
64.70872
      10        11       12       13       14       15       16       17
18
64.83711  65.13128 65.22970 65.23072 65.32096 67.76135 68.32733 68.58346
68.62780
      19        20       21       22       23       24       25       26
27
68.65912  68.84693 68.97648 69.49723 70.01205 70.03058 70.04389 70.15092
70.15788
      28        29       30       31       32       33       34       35
36
70.92202  71.32928 73.18019 73.85014 74.17816 74.95200 75.25782 75.80803
75.98907
      37        38       39       40
76.60038  76.97475 77.77062 78.68721
```

A regression model can be built for assessing a bank's risk for home-loan customers based on their age, income, expenses, occupation, number of dependents, total credit limit, etc. Here, age, income, expenses, occupation, number of dependents and total credit limit can be used as independent variables for a multiple regression model.

20.3.5 Logistic Regression in R

Linear regression is used to model data when Y is a continuous variable. However, we cannot use it when the output variable is binary categorical. There are many applications where the output is only 0 or 1. Such problems are called binary classification problems. For example, to identify an email as spam or not, review comments about a movie (good or bad), if a credit card transaction is fraudulent or not, whether the given tissue sample is malignant or not, and so on. Logistic regression can be used to model such problems.

Logistic regression takes the log odds of the event $\ln(P/1-P)$, where, P is the probability of the event. The probability value always lies between 0 and 1. It uses the concept of maximum log likelihood to optimise the results.

$$Z_i = \ln\left(\frac{P_i}{1-P_i}\right) = a + \beta_1 x_1 + \cdots + \beta_n x_n$$

Taking the exponent on both sides of the equation gives:

$$P_i = E(y=1 \mid x_i) = \frac{e^z}{1+e^z} = \frac{e^{a+\beta_i x_i}}{1+e^{a+\beta_i x_i}}$$

Logistic regression can be built using the `glm()` function, with the `family` argument set to "binomial".

Implementation in R

Step 1: Build the logistic regression model.

```
>logMod <- glm(Y ~ X1 + X2, family="binomial", data = trainingData)
```

Step 2: Predict Y.

```
>predY <- predict(logMod, testData, type="response")
```

Sample code using the breast cancer data set:

```
>install.packages("mlbench")
>data(BreastCancer, package="mlbench")
>bc <- BreastCancer[complete.cases(BreastCancer), ]  # Create copy

>head(bc)
 Id Cl.thickness Cell.size Cell.shape Marg.adhesion Epith.c.size Bare.
nuclei
1 1000025  5         1          1             1            2           1
2 1002945  5         4          4             5            7          10
3 1015425  3         1          1             1            2           2
4 1016277  6         8          8             1            3           4
5 1017023  4         1          1             3            2           1
6 1017122  8        10         10             8            7          10
  Bl.cromatin Normal.nucleoli Mitoses     Class
1           3               1       1    benign
2           3               2       1    benign
3           3               1       1    benign
4           3               7       1    benign
5           3               1       1    benign
6           9               7       1 malignant
```

We need to divide the data into the train and test sets. You can use the `caret` library and its functions to split the data set.

```
# trainDataIndex <- createDataPartition(bc$Class, p=0.7, list = F)  # 70%
training data

>trainData <- bc[100, ]
>testData <- bc[-100, ]
>logitmod <- glm(Class ~ Cl.thickness + Cell.size + Cell.shape, family =
"binomial", data=bc)
>summary(logitmod)
>pred <- predict(logitmod, newdata = testData, type = "response")
>y_pred_num <- ifelse(pred > 0.5, 1, 0)
>y_pred <- factor(y_pred_num, levels=c(0, 1))
>y_act <- testData$Class
```

The output of some actual and predicted values is as follows:

```
[1] benign    benign    benign    benign    benign    malignant benign
benign
  [9] benign    benign    benign    benign    malignant benign
malignant malignant
 [17] benign    benign    malignant benign    malignant malignant benign
benign

 [57] malignant malignant malignant benign    malignant malignant benign
malignant
Levels: benign malignant

> y_pred
  1   2   3   4   5   6   7   8   9  10  11  12  13  14  15  16  17  18
19  20  21
  0   0   0   1   0   1   0   0   0   0   0   0   1   0   1   1   0   0
1   0   1
 22  23  25  26  27  28  29  30  31  32  33  34  35  36  37  38  39  40
42  43  44
  1   0   0   0   0   0   0   0   0   0   1   0   0   0   1   0   0   1
1   1   1
 45  46  47  48  49  50  51  52  53  54  55  56  57  58  59  60  61  62
63  64  65
  1   0   1   0   0   1   1   1   1   1   1   1   1   1   0   1   1   0
1   0   0
 66  67  68  69  70  71  72  73  74  75  76  77  78  79  80  81  82  83
84  85
  1   0   1   1   0   0   1   0   1   1   0   0   0   0   0   0   0   0
0   1
Levels: 0 1
```

EXERCISES

Multiple Choice Questions

1. Logistic regression algorithm is:
   a. Supervised machine learning
   b. Unsupervised machine learning
2. Logistic regression is mainly used for:
   a. Regression b. Classification
3. Which of the following methods is used to best-fit the data in logistic regression?
   a. Least Square Error
   b. Maximum Likelihood
   c. Entropy
   d. None of the above
4. Logistic regression algorithm can be used for the three-class classification problem.
   a. True b. False
5. Which of the following methods do we use to find the best fit line for data in linear regression?
   a. Least Square Error
   b. Entropy
   c. Logarithmic Loss
   d. None of the above
6. Suppose the Pearson correlation between V1 and V2 is zero. Is it correct to conclude that V1 and V2 do not have any relation between them?
   a. True b. False

7. Which of the following statements is true about outliers in linear regression?
   a. Linear regression is sensitive to outliers
   b. Linear regression is not sensitive to outliers
   c. Cannot say
   d. All of the above are true
8. How many coefficients do you need to estimate in a simple linear regression model?
   a. 1 b. 2
   c. 3 d. 4
9. If we change the input variable by 1 unit in a simple linear regression model, by how much will the output variable change?
   a. By 0
   b. By 1
   c. Only by intercept
   d. By its slope
10. The function used for linear regression in R is ___:
    a. `lm(formula, data)`
    b. `lr(formula, data)`
    c. `lrm(formula, data)`
    d. `regression.linear(formula, data)`
11. In the syntax of linear model `lm(formula,data,..)`, `data` refers to
    a. Matrix b. Vector
    c. Array d. List

Answers

1. a	**2.** b	**3.** b	**4.** a	**5.** a	**6.** b	**7.** a	**8.** b	**9.** d	**10.** a
11. b									

Concept-based/Programming Questions

1.

Country/ State/City	Alc. consumption	Death rate from cirrhosis
AP	42.7	46.1
HP	51.2	23.6
Italy	21.3	23.7
Australia	21.4	17
UK	33.8	2.3
USA	4.9	14.2
Canada	5.3	7.4
London	7.2	13.0
Sweden	6.6	1 7.2
Japan	5.8	22.6
Netherland	5.7	3.7
Pakistan	5.6	5.6
Delhi	4.2	3.4
Ireland	3.1	5.4

a. Can you draw conclusions about the association of two variables without performing any calculations but only using a scatter diagram? Draw a scatter diagram.
b. Calculate Pearson's correlation coefficient for the above sample data.

2. The power of an engine (y) is a function of temperature (x) in °F. Consider the following data.

x	y	x	y
4300	1760	4010	1665
4650	1652	3810	1550
3200	1485	4500	1700
3150	1390	3008	1270
4950	1820		

Fit a simple linear regression to the data and plot the line through the data.

3. Build a logistic regression model to detect spam email. Use the built-in data set emails.csv or build the appropriate data for the model.
4. Build a logistic regression model to detect credit card fraud. Use the built-in data set creditcard.csv or build the appropriate data for the model.
5. Build a logistic regression model to detect breast cancer. Use the built-in data set BreastCancer for the model.
6. Determine the association between gender and preference for ice cream flavour from the given table:

Gender/Flavour	Chocolate	Vanilla	Strawberry	Total
Male	100	120	60	280
Female	350	200	90	640
Total	450	320	150	920

CHAPTER

21 Statistical Inference

Objectives

At the end of this chapter, you will be able to

- Explain statistical inference and its two main approaches
- Describe one- and two-tailed tests
- Define the null and alternative hypotheses
- Define the types of errors
- Explain how to implement t-tests in R
- Explain how to implement the chi-squared test in R

21.1 | INTRODUCTION TO STATISTICAL INFERENCE

One of the objectives of performing statistical analysis is to make some judgment about the population or sample. Inferential statistics deals with the techniques used to help analysts make some judgment about the state of a population or sample. It deals with uncertainty in decision-making and uses the concept of probability.

Two main methods are used in inferential statistics: hypothesis testing and estimation. Based on these two methods, the basic approaches are as follows:

Approach 1: Hypothesis testing: Here, tests are conducted based on a hypothesis. In this approach, we make some assumption that one or more parameters have some specific value(s) or relationship(s). Sample statistics is used to make decisions about the assumed parameters. The result of sample statistics is the probability that the decision is incorrect.

Approach 2: Confidence interval measurement: This approach deals with estimating one (or more) parameter(s) using sample statistics. Estimation is in the form of interval measurement and the result takes the form of level of confidence.

21.2 | HYPOTHESIS TESTING

A hypothesis is a statement or assumption about the relationship between variables. It can be defined in many ways:

"A hypothesis is an educated prediction that can be tested" (study.com).

"A hypothesis is a proposed explanation for a phenomenon" (Wikipedia).

"A hypothesis is used to define the relationship between two variables" (Oxford English Dictionary).

Example 21.1: Avogadro's Hypothesis (1811) – "The volume of a gas is directly proportional to the number of molecules of the gas."

Statistical hypothesis: This is stated in terms of population parameters, such as mean and variance. The validity of the hypothesis is tested from sample data using some test of the hypothesis. The result of the test of hypothesis enables us to agree (or disagree) with the statistical hypothesis.

Example 21.2: "To determine whether the wages of men and women are equal." "A product in the market is of standard quality." "Whether a particular medicine is effective in curing a disease."

There are two types of hypothesis: null (H_0) and alternative (H_a). The hypothesis to be tested is considered as the null hypothesis, while the alternative hypothesis is assumed to be true when the null hypothesis is proved to be false.

Example 21.3: One hypothesis might claim that "Men and women are equally intelligent", while the alternative might claim that "Women are more intelligent than men."

Example 21.4: The Ministry of Human Resource Development (MHRD) of the Government of India has started an initiative to improve the country's human resources and set up 23 IITs in the country. To measure the engineering aptitude of graduates, MHRD conducts the GATE examination carrying a total mark of 1000 every year. Data about a sample of 300 students who took the GATE examination in 2018 was collected and the mean score was observed to be 220.

In this context, statistical hypothesis testing is carried out to determine the mean mark of all the GATE-2018 examinees.

Here, the two hypotheses are:

$H_0: \mu = 220$

$H_a: \mu < 220$

Note: It is customary to have an equal to sign in the null hypothesis.

For the alternative hypothesis, many options are available: $H_a: \mu<220$ or $H_a: \mu>220$ or $H_a: \mu$!= 220.

21.2.1 One-tailed Test

In a one-tailed test, the alternative hypothesis states that the population parameter lies entirely above or below (left- and right-tailed test) a specified value.

21.2.2 Two-tailed Test

In this test, the alternative hypothesis states that the parameter can lie on both sides of the value specified.

In Fig. 21.1, the black regions differentiate the one-tailed and two-tailed tests. The alternative hypotheses formed for the one-tailed and two-tailed tests are different, as shown in Fig. 21.2.

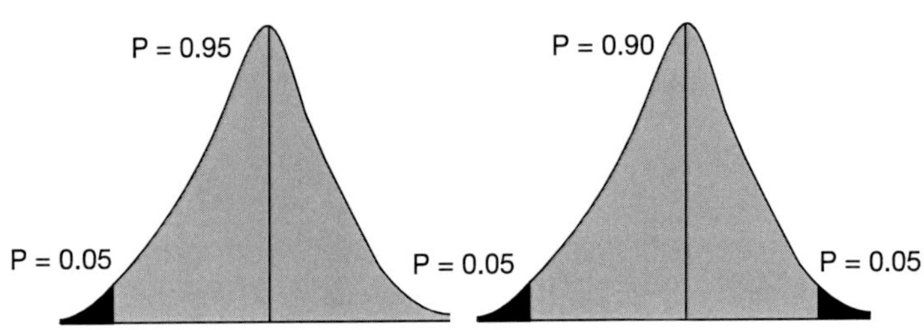

Fig. 21.1: One-tailed vs two-tailed test

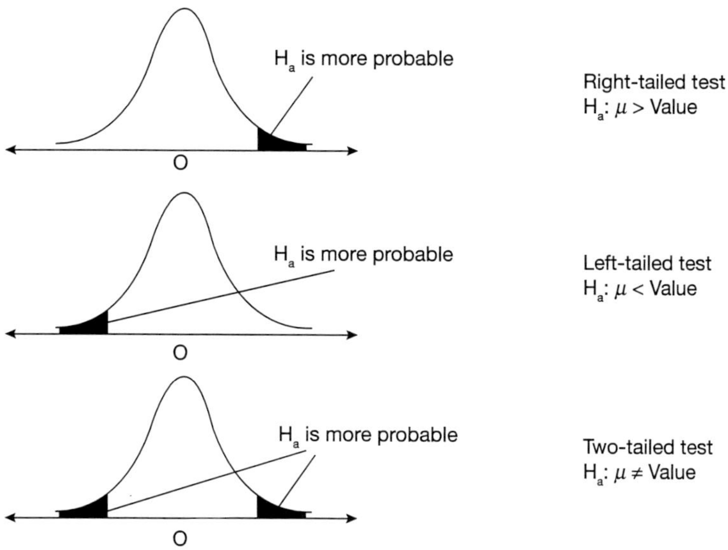

Fig. 21.2: Alternative hypothesis for one-tailed and two-tailed tests

For hypothesis testing, we follow the five steps given below:

1. Form the null and alternative hypotheses, and the acceptable level of hypothesis.
2. Determine appropriate sample-based test statistics and the rejection region.
3. From the sample data, calculate the test statistics.
4. Make a decision to accept or reject the null hypothesis.
5. Interpret the result in a language suitable for practitioners.

The standard procedure is to assume that the hypothesis is true (just as we presume innocence until guilt is proven). We accept H_0 if the test statistics fall within the area of acceptance, and we reject it otherwise. The procedure is based on probability theory; that is, there is a chance that we can make errors.

21.2.3 Types of Errors

Two types of errors can occur in hypothesis testing (Fig. 21.3).

Type I: A type I error occurs when we incorrectly reject (we reject the null hypothesis when it is actually true).

Type II: A type II error occurs when we incorrectly fail to reject (we accept the null hypothesis when it is actually not true).

	Observation	
Decision	H_0 is true	H_0 is false
H_0 is accepted	Decision is correct	Type II error
H_0 is rejected	Type I error	Decision is correct

Fig. 21.3: Types of errors

21.2.4 Using the t-test

A t-test is used for only two samples of inferential statistics. It determines if the mean of two populations differs significantly. It can be used for hypothesis testing of the mean of one sample, two independent samples and two dependent samples. The formulae used for t-test statistics are given below:

For one-sample–based t-statistics

$$t = \frac{\overline{X} - \mu}{S_x / \sqrt{n}} \quad df = n - 1$$

where x is the sample mean, μ represents the proposed population mean, S_x is the standard deviation of the sample, n is the number of samples and df is the degree of freedom.

For two-independent-samples–based t-statistics

$$t = \frac{m_A - m_B}{\sqrt{\frac{s^2}{n_A} + \frac{s^2}{n_B}}}$$

where m_A and m_B are the mean of two different samples, n_A and n_B are the sample sizes and S is an estimator of the common variance of two samples, such as:

$$S^2 = \frac{\sum (x - m_A)^2 + \sum (x - m_B)^2}{n_A + n_B - 2}$$

Here, the degree of freedom is $n_A + n_B - 2$.

For two-dependent (paired)-samples–based t-statistics

The paired t-test is also treated as the test for two dependent samples. This test is normally applied when we deal with before/after treatment sample data or when we want to compare two variants in A?B testing. The mean of the given sample data is computed twice. The paired t-test statistics formula is as follows:

$$t = \frac{m}{s / \sqrt{n}}$$

where m is the mean of the sample, μ is the population mean, s is the standard deviation of the sample and n is sample size. Degree of freedom in this test is $n - 1$.

In t-tests, we use the same logic as in the testing of hypothesis theory in the earlier section. We compare the calculated t-statistics with the t-critical value to determine acceptance or rejection of the null hypothesis.

21.2.5 The t-test in R

R has the `t.test()` function that is used to perform the t-test.

```
t.test(v1, v2 = NULL, alternative = c( "two-ided", "less", "greater"), mu
= 0, paired=FALSE, var.equal = FALSE, conf.level=0.95)
```

where `v1` is the vector used to compute the one-sample t-test, `v2` is the second vector used to compute the two-sample t-test, μ is the mean of the population, `var.equal` is a logical value (default 'FALSE') used to specify if the variance of the two vectors are equal or not, `paired` is a logical value (default 'FALSE') used to specify whether or not you want a paired t-test (TRUE = yes) and `conf.level` specifies the confidence level.

Example 21.5: A bulb manufacturing company claims that their bulb life averages 31 hours. You randomly select 8 bulbs from a local vendor and test their average life under similar conditions. You obtain the following average life of bulbs (in hours):

30 28 32 26 33 25 28 30

Is the actual average life of a bulb 31 hours or does it deviate from this mean life (α = .05 or significance level is 95%)?

Solution: Data indicates testing of the mean against the value 31.00, with a one- or two-tailed t-test of the mean.

H_0: μ=31.00

$$t = \frac{\bar{X} - \mu}{S_X / \sqrt{n}} \quad df = n - 1$$

Compute the test statistics: Compute the mean and standard deviation of the given sample and compute the t-statistics.

$$t = \frac{29.00 - 31.00}{2.775 / \sqrt{8}} = -2.04$$

Hypothesis testing: The degree of freedom (*df*) is equal to n – 1, which is 8 – 1 = 7. A two-tailed test can be performed on this sample data, with α = .05. The absolute value of the calculated t-statistics is 2.04 and the given critical table value of t-statistics is 2.365. Therefore, we can accept the null hypothesis, which indicates that the average life of a bulb does not differ significantly from the population mean. In fact, we can conclude that the average bulb life of the sample did not differ significantly from 31.00.

T-test results:

```
>mpg <-c(30,28,32,26,33,25,28,30)
>t.test(mpg, mu=31, conf.level=0.95, paired = FALSE)
```

Output:

```
One Sample t-test
data:  mpg
t = -2.0367, df = 7, p-value = 0.08111
alternative hypothesis: true mean is not equal to 31
95 percent confidence interval:
 26.67799 31.32201
sample estimates:
mean of x
       29
```

Example 21.6: Let us consider the `ToothGrowth` data set to study different tests. It consists of the length of the teeth of guinea pigs when given different supplements (OJ and VC) at different dosages (0.5, 1, 2).

```
data("ToothGrowth")           # Loads the dataset
head(ToothGrowth)             # Prints first five rows of dataset
```

Output:

```
len   supp dose
  4.2   VC  0.5
 11.5  VC  0.5
  7.3   VC  0.5
  5.8   VC  0.5
  6.4   VC  0.5
10.0  VC  0.5
```

Let us apply the one-sample t-test to determine if the use of any supplement has any effect on tooth growth. Let us consider that the average tooth length is 16 cm; hence μ = 16. The null hypothesis states that the supplements have no effect on tooth growth.

Formula:

$$t = \frac{\bar{X} - \mu}{\frac{S}{\sqrt{n}}}$$

Implementation in R:

```
# Built-in function
>t.test(ToothGrowth$len , mu=16)
```

Output:

```
t_calc=2.8489
```

Here, `t_calc > t` and hence the null hypothesis is rejected. Therefore, supplements do have an effect on tooth growth.

Example 21.7: For a random sample of 10 persons trained under training1, the increase in performance in a period was: 10, 6, 16, 17, 13, 12, 8, 14, 15, 9. For another sample of 12 persons trained under training2, the increase in performance in the same period was: 7, 13, 22, 15, 12, 14, 18, 8, 21, 23, 10, 17. Test whether training1 and training2 differ significantly as regards their effect on increase on performance.

Code:

```
dietA <-c(10,6,16,17,13,12,8,14,15,9)
dietB <- c(7,13,22,15,12,14,18,8,21,23,10,17)
t.test(dietA, dietB, alternative="greater", conf.level = 0.95, paired =
FALSE)
```

Output:

```
data:  dietA and dietB
t = 1.5571, df = 19.355, p-value = 0.06783
alternative hypothesis: true difference in means is greater than 0
95 percent confidence interval:
 -0.3283719        Inf
sample estimates:
mean of x mean of y
       15        12
```

The result shows that the t-statistic is equal to 1.55, which is less than the given table value of 2.09 at *df* = 20; so the null hypothesis is accepted. There is strong evidence that training 1 and training2 do not differ significantly as regards their effect on increase in performance.

Example 21.8: A study was performed to test whether the sales of a company improved after an advertisement campaign. Company sales are recorded before and after the campaign. Before the advertisement, the campaign sales was recorded as: 16, 20, 21, 22, 23, 22, 27, 25, 27, 28 and after the campaign, the sales recorded was: 19, 22, 24, 24, 25, 25, 26, 26, 28, 32. We can use a paired t-test to check whether sales improved significantly after the advertisement campaign.

Code:

```
>beforesale <- c(16,20,21,22,23,22,27,25,27,28)
>aftersale <- c(19,22,24,24,25,25,26,26,28,32)
>t.test(aftersale, beforesale, alternative="greater", conf.level=0.95,
paired = TRUE)
```

Output:

```
data:  aftersale and beforesale
t = 4.4721, df = 9, p-value = 0.0007749
alternative hypothesis: true difference in means is greater than 0
95 percent confidence interval:
 1.180207      Inf
sample estimates:
mean of the differences  2
```

The result shows that the t-statistic is equal to 4.47, which is greater than the table value for *df* = 9; so the null hypothesis is rejected. There is strong evidence for an increase in sales after the advertisement campaign.

Example 21.9: A two-sample t-test is used to determine whether two samples are from the same population. To check if different supplements have different effects on the growth of teeth, we define our null hypothesis as follows: 'There is no difference in tooth growth in cases where OJ or VC is used'. So we can say that both these cases are from the same population, and hence, the above hypothesis could be tested using the t-test.

Implementation in R:

```
split.supp <- split(ToothGrowth$len, ToothGrowth$supp)       # Splits the
len column according to the supp column

# Built-in function
t_cal=t.test(split.supp$OJ, split.supp$VC)$statistic
# Performs t-test on given samples
# Statistic is the t value calculated which comes out to be 1.9153

df = length(split.supp$OJ)+length(split.supp$VC)-2
# Degree of freedom

 t=abs(qt(0.05/2,df))
# The first argument specifies the significance level as 5%
# t=2.0017

if (t_obs < t_calc){
  print("Null hypothesis accepted")
}else{
  print("Null hypothesis rejected")}
```

As `t_calc < t`, the null hypothesis is accepted. Hence, different supplements do not have different effects on tooth growth.

21.2.6 Chi-squared Test

Chi-squared ($\chi 2$) is another important test used in hypothesis testing, mostly for categorical variables. It is a non-parametric test, and the data used is random, mutually exclusive and drawn from a large sample. In the chi-squared ($\chi 2$) test, we measure expectation and compare it with the actual observed data.

There are two main types of chi-squared tests: the test of independence and the goodness-of-fit test. Test of independence deals with questions about relationships, such as "Is there a relationship between intelligence and income?", while goodness-of-fit tests if the given sample data is appropriate for the given distribution.

The formula for the chi-squared test of independence is given below:

$$\chi_c^2 = \sum \frac{(O_i - E_i)^2}{E_i}$$

where O is the observed frequency and E is the expected frequency.

We follow the same logic as in testing of hypothesis. We compare the calculated chi-square value with the chi square-critical value to determine acceptance or rejection of the null hypothesis.

Example 21.10: In an anti-malarial campaign in certain a locality, quinine was administrated to 812 persons out of a total population of 3248. The number of cases of fever is shown below:

Treatment	Fever	No fever	Total
Quinine	20	792	812
No Quinine	220	2216	2436
Total	240	3008	3248

Is the quinine useful in preventing malaria?

Solution:

Treatment	Fever		(O – E)²/E	No fever		(O – E)²/E	Total
	Observed frequency (O)	Expected frequency(E)		Observed frequency (O)	Expected frequency (E)		
Quinine	20	(812*240)/ 3248 = 60	1600/60=26.67	792	(812*3008)/ 3248 = 752	1600/752 =2.128	812
No Quinine	220	(2436*240)/ 3248 = 180	1600/180=8.89	2216	(2436*3008)/ 3248= 2256	1600/2256 =.709	2436
Total	240			3008			3248

Chi-squared ($\chi 2$) statistics = 26.67 + 8.89 + 2.128 + .709 = 38.39.

The calculated chi-square ($\chi 2$) value is greater than the table value of 3.84 at df = 1; so the null hypothesis is rejected, which indicates that quinine is useful in preventing malaria.

21.2.7 Chi-squared ($\chi 2$) Test in R

The above data is analysed using a chi-squared test. A data frame of two vectors of `fever` and `nofever` is created, which contains data for quinine and no quinine.

```
>fever <-c(20,220)
>nofever <- c(792,2216)
>df <- data.frame(fever,nofever)
>print(df)
>chisq.test(df)
```

Output:

```
    fever  nofever
1   20     792
2   220    2216
> chisq.test(df)
       Pearson's Chi-squared test with Yates' continuity correction
data:  df
X-squared = 37.439, df = 1, p-value = 9.434e-10
```

EXERCISES

Multiple Choice Questions

1. A statement about a population developed for the purpose of testing is called:
a. Hypothesis
b. Hypothesis testing
c. Test statistics
d. Level of significance

2. A statement about the value of a population parameter is called alternative hypothesis.
a. False b. True

3. A quantitative statement about a population is called statistical hypothesis.
a. True b. False

4. The alternative hypothesis is also called research hypothesis.
a. True b. False

5. In a criminal trial, a type II error will occur when:
a. A guilty person is set free
b. An innocent person is sent to jail
c. A guilty person is sent to jail
d. No decision is made about whether to send a person to jail or to set him free

6. A type I error occurs when we:
a. Reject a true null hypothesis
b. Accept a true null hypothesis
c. Fail to make a decision regarding whether to reject a hypothesis or not

Answers

1. a	**2.** a	**3.** a	**4.** a	**5.** a	**6.** a

Programming/Concept-based Questions

1. About 1000 college students are graded according to their IQ level and economic condition. Use the chi-squared test to find out whether there is any association between economic condition and the level of IQ.

	High	Medium	Low
Rich	160	300	140
Poor	140	100	160

CHAPTER

22 Analysis of Variance

Objectives

At the end of this chapter, you will be able to

- Explain the purpose of ANOVA
- Describe the types of ANOVA
- Implement ANOVA in R

22.1 | INTRODUCTION TO ANALYSIS OF VARIANCE

Analysis of variance is used to determine if two or more samples are from the same population. It helps in the design of experiments as well. It is a way of finding out if the experiment results are significant or not.

For example, a study claims that using activities in class enhances concentration and helps children absorb more information. A teacher needs some proof about whether the activities actually work or not. So, the teacher decided to implement it on randomly selected students from different classes. Three different groups of five randomly selected children from three different classrooms were taken and each was provided with three different environments to study in.

Class 1 children were exposed to activities in every teaching lesson.

Class 2 children were exposed to activities in some teaching lessons.

Class 3 children were exposed to no activity during teaching lessons.

A test was conducted after one month for all three groups to check the students' academic performance, and their test scores were collected. It was noticed that activities were useful as the observation data revealed that the mean score of class 1 students was greater than that of the other two groups.

This may be true, but it may also have occurred because the samples taken from Group A were from the best students and this eventually resulted in good test scores for Group A students (as students were selected at random). So this leads to questions about how we can decide if their performance was different because of different situations, and not by chance. Also, we need to know how these three samples were different from each other.

Other examples: Doctors want to determine which therapy is better for psychiatric patients – counselling, feedback or medication. Testing the performance of different colleges or a manufacturing process, and so on.

22.2 | IMPLEMENTING ANALYSIS OF VARIANCE

Analysis of variance (ANOVA) is a statistical technique that is used to check if the means of two or more groups are significantly different from each other. It is derived from the partitioning of total variability into its component parts.

It is similar in application to techniques such as t-test, z-test and $\chi 2$ test in that it is used to compare means and the relative variance between them.

The t-test is used to infer the mean of a single population or to compare two populations, but it is not useful for comparing the mean of more than two populations. ANOVA can be used for more than two populations.

For example, consider the two sets of data shown below:

Set 1			**Set 2**		
Sample 1	**Sample 2**	**Sample 3**	**Sample 1**	**Sample 2**	**Sample 3**
5.7	9.4	14.2	3.0	5.0	11.0
5.9	9.8	14.4	4.0	7.0	13.0
6.0	10.0	15.0	6.0	10.0	16.0
6.1	10.2	15.6	8.0	13.0	17.0
6.3	10.6	15.8	9.0	15.0	18.0
$\bar{y} = 6.0$	$\bar{y} = 10.0$	$\bar{y} = 15.0$	$\bar{y} = 6.0$	$\bar{y} = 10.0$	$\bar{y} = 15.0$

When we examine the mean for the two sets of three samples, we notice that they look similar as the means are the same in both sets. This indicates that there is no significant difference in the two sets. However, if we look at the box plots of both the data sets, we can see that they are quite different. The Set1 observations are more closely bunched compared to Set2 data. We also know that the sample mean from a population with small variance will be less variable. This indicates that for Set1, variance among the observations within the individual samples is small. This is strong evidence to support the view that the two sets are different.

To analyse these kinds of situations, analysis of variance is used. It helps us make inferences about the differences among means. Some terminology with respect to ANOVA is explained below:

Factor: A characteristic under consideration.

Level (also called treatment): A value of the factor.

22.3 | VARIANTS OF ANOVA

Based on the number of independent and dependent variables considered for the study, we can define the different variants of ANOVA:

- One-way ANOVA: Deals with only one independent variable (factor).
- Two-way ANOVA: Deals with two independent variables or factors.
- Three-way ANOVA: Deals with three independent variables or factors.
- Multivariate ANOVA: It is used to test the significance of the effect of more independent variables.

The steps for computing ANOVA are as follows:

1. Create the null hypothesis.
2. Calculate the mean for each of the groups.
3. Calculate the overall combined mean of the groups.
4. Calculate the sum of deviation of each member's score from the group mean, that is, variation within samples.
5. Calculate the deviation of each group mean from the overall mean, that is, variation between samples.
6. Find the F statistic, which is the ratio of 'between sample' variation to 'within sample' variation, or vice-versa.
7. Make the decision using the F-test statistical results.

22.3.1 One-way ANOVA

In the one-way ANOVA, we can study the effect of the level of a single factor. This type of ANOVA makes certain assumptions. The null hypothesis to be tested is that the two means are equal, using F distribution. This method can be used only for one independent variable and two levels.

We can summarise the results of an ANOVA test in a table. A one-factor analysis takes the form shown in Table 22.1.

Table 22.1 One-way ANOVA

Source of variation	Sum of squares (SS)	Degree of freedom (df)	Mean squared	F-ratio
Between	SS(B)	k-1	SS(B) ----------- k-1	MS(B) -------------- MS(W)
Within	SS(W)	N-k	SS(W) ----------- N-k	.
Total	SS(W) + SS(B)	N-1	.	.

For example, we may want to study the lifetime of electric light bulbs of three different brands under controlled conditions. Assuming all lifetimes are normally distributed with common variance, test the hypothesis that there is no difference between the three brands with respect to mean lifetime, given the significance level.

22.3.2 Two-way ANOVA

Two-way ANOVA is an extension of one-way ANOVA, where two factors can be taken into account.

It works with two independent variables. For example, you may want to study the quality of clothes washed with different types of detergent and quantities of water. You may also want to study if there is a relation between income and gender for anxiety levels in interviews.

22.4 | ANOVA IN R

Let us use ANOVA to check if different dosages have different effects on tooth growth.

The null hypothesis states that "There is no difference in tooth growth with respect to different dosages". The F-score is calculated as the variance between samples divided by variance within samples, and the null hypothesis will be accepted if the calculated F-score is less than the given F value.

$$F = msc / mse$$

where msc = ssc/v1; ssc = sum of squares between samples and v1 = c – 1; mse = sse/v2; sse = sum of squares within samples and v2 = n – c.

Implementation in R:

```
>aov(len ~ dose,ToothGrowth)
 aov(formula = len ~ dose, data = ToothGrowth)
```

Output:

```
dose      Residuals
Sum of Squares  2224.304  1227.905
Deg. of Freedom        1           58

Residual standard error: 4.601171
Estimated effects may be unbalanced

# F-score can then be calculated by extracting
required values from the result
# msc = 2224.304/1 = 2224.304
# mse = 1227.905/58 = 21.1707
# f = 2224.304/21.1707 = 105.06
# F value is sufficiently large and hence the
null hypothesis will be rejected
```

EXERCISES

Multiple Choice Questions

1. Analysis of variance is a statistical way of testing a hypothesis about the ________ of several populations.
   a. Standard deviation
   b. Variance
   c. Mean
   d. None of the above
2. Which of the following distributions does the ANOVA test use?
   a. Z b. Chi-squared
   c. t d. F
3. The t-test and ANOVA are used for sample mean testing, but the ANOVA can be used for more than two populations.

a. True b. False

4. In a one-way ANOVA, if the computed F value is less than the critical F value, what decision is made regarding the null hypothesis?
   a. Accept H_0 as there is no evidence of a difference in mean
   b. Reject H_0 because there is no evidence for a difference in mean

Answers

1. c	2. d	3. a	4. a

Programming/Concept-based Questions

1. The following data represents the number of units of production with different number of workers and different types of machines – A, B, C and D. Test for the mean productivity of the different machines and workers.

	Machine A	Machine B	Machine C	Machine D
Worker 1	44	38	47	36
Worker 2	46	40	52	43
Worker 3	34	36	44	32
Worker 4	43	38	46	33
Worker 5	38	42	49	39

2. To study the performance of the detergents Arial, Surf Excel and Rin and three different water temperatures – cold, warm and hot – the following 'whiteness' readings were obtained:

Water temperature	Detergent Arial	Detergent Surf Excel	Detergent Rin
Cold water	75	55	76
Warm water	94	25	86
Hot water	45	64	85

   Perform a two-way analysis of variance using 5% level of significance (given that the F-value at 5% is 6.94).

3. Perform ANOVA on variables of built-in data sets.

CHAPTER

23 Machine Learning Algorithms in R

Objectives

At the end of this chapter, you will be able to

- Define machine learning (ML), supervised ML, unsupervised ML and reinforcement learning
- Describe the naive Bayes classifier and its implementation in R
- Describe the decision tree classifier and its implementation in R
- Describe the k-Nearest Neighbour method and its implementation in R
- Describe clustering techniques, in particular, K-means, in R
- Explain association rule mining and its implementation in R

23.1 | INTRODUCTION TO MACHINE LEARNING ALGORITHMS

Machine learning (ML) is the study and development of computer programs that can learn progressively from themselves to improve their performance of a particular task. Using machine learning algorithms, we can make machines behave like humans in different situations/environments.

Many machine learning algorithms such as linear regression, logistic regression, decision tree, support vector machine (SVM), k-nearest neighbor (kNN), naive Bayes and random forest are applied to almost any data problem.

Machine learning algorithms are categorised as follows:

- **Supervised learning:** In this type of learning, the algorithm is provided with labelled sample inputs (training data), where the labels indicate the desired output. It can be further categorised as classification (output is categorical) and regression (output is numerical). Regression, decision tree, random forest, kNN and logistic regression are examples of supervised learning.
- **Unsupervised learning**: Here, we do not have any label inputs. This type of algorithm focuses on detecting the structure of unlabelled input data. Clustering is an example of unsupervised learning, where data is grouped in different categories. Apriori algorithm and K-means are examples of unsupervised learning.
- **Reinforcement learning**: In this type of algorithm, the machine trains itself using trial and error. The machine learns continuously from past experiences using feedback about its own actions in the form of positive or negative rewards and captures the best knowledge from it. For example, the Markov decision process.

23.2 | NAIVE BAYES CLASSIFIER

The naive Bayes classifier is based on the Bayes Theorem. It is a supervised learning algorithm that uses the conditional probability formula as its base:

$$P(A \mid B) = P(A) * P(B \mid A) / P(B)$$

In a supervised learning–based classification algorithm, there are some features/data values along with the target class. We use this as training data to learn the algorithm. This learning model is used to predict the class of a given unknown observation. In naive Bayes, we calculate the probability of each class for a given unknown observation and we assign the observation to the class that gives the highest probability value. This assumes that predictor variables are independent of each other. In naive Bayes, $P(A \mid B)$ is called the posterior probability, $P(B \mid A)$ is the likelihood and $P(A)$ and $P(B)$ are prior probabilities of proposition and evidence, respectively.

Naive Bayes states that:

Posterior probability = (Likelihood of event).(Prior Probability of Proposition)/ Prior Probability of Evidence

To demonstrate the naive Bayes classifier for predicting values using different data sets, we will use `diabetes` data and the `naivebayes` library.

```
> naiveBayes(x1, y1, ...)                          ## Default  method
> naiveBayes(formula1, data1, ..., subset1, na.action = na.pass)
```

where `x1` is a numeric matrix/data frame of categorical and/or numeric values or independent variables; `Y1` is a class vector or dependent variable; `formula1` is a formula of the form class ~ `x1` + `x2` + ...; and `data1` is a data frame of predictors.

Other parameters deal with handling missing values or data preprocessing.

We need to install and load the `naïveBayes` library as follows:

```
>install.packages("naivebayes")
>install.packages("e1071")
>library(e1071)
```

In this example, we want to use the `diabetes` data set, which can be downloaded from the UCI repository:

```
>data<- read.csv("/Users/sandhy/Desktop/pima-indians-diabetes.csv")
> str(data)  # Displays the structure of data set, variables it contains,
its type, values, etc.
```

This data set contains eight independent variables: `Pregnancies`, `Glucose`, `BloodPressure`, `SkinThickness`, `Insulin`, `BMI`, `Age` and `DiabetesPedigreeFunction`, and one dependent variable, `Outcome`. The `Outcome` variable is our target and contains value 0/1 (0 indicates no diabetes, 1 indicates diabetes). This data set has 768 objects of nine variables.

```
# Model building
>Naive_Bayes_Model=naiveBayes(Outcome ~., data=data)
> Naive_Bayes_Model

# Displays the naive Bayes classifier parameters

A-priori probabilities:
Y
    False      True
0.6510417 0.3489583

Conditional probabilities:
       Pregnancies
Y           [,1]     [,2]
  False 3.298000 3.017185
  True  4.865672 3.741239

       Glucose
Y           [,1]     [,2]
  False 109.9800 26.14120
  True  141.2575 31.93962

       BloodPressure
Y           [,1]     [,2]
  False 68.18400 18.06308
  True  70.82463 21.49181

       SkinThickness
Y           [,1]     [,2]
  False 19.66400 14.88995
  True  22.16418 17.67971

       Insulin
Y           [,1]      [,2]
  False  68.7920  98.86529
  True  100.3358 138.68912

       BMI
Y           [,1]     [,2]
  False 30.30420 7.689855
  True  35.14254 7.262967

       DiabetesPedigreeFunction
Y           [,1]      [,2]
  False 0.429734 0.2990853
  True  0.550500 0.3723545

       Age
Y           [,1]     [,2]
  False 31.19000 11.66765
  True  37.06716 10.96825

# Prediction on the dataset
> NB_Predictions=predict(Naive_Bayes_Model,data)
> table(NB_Predictions,data$Outcome)

NB_Predictions False True
         False   421  104
         True     79  164
```

The accuracy of this model is about 76%, as calculated using the confusion matrix (discussed in the decision tree classifier case study below).

23.3 | DECISION TREE CLASSIFIER

Decision tree is a type of supervised learning algorithm that can be used for categorical or continuous data and where the data is continuously split according to a certain parameter. The parameters are determined based on information gain. The leaves of the tree are the decisions or final outcomes. The decision nodes are where the data is split on the basis of a parameter. An example of a decision tree for the `Titanic` data set is shown in Fig. 23.1, where the survival of passengers is displayed as a classification problem.

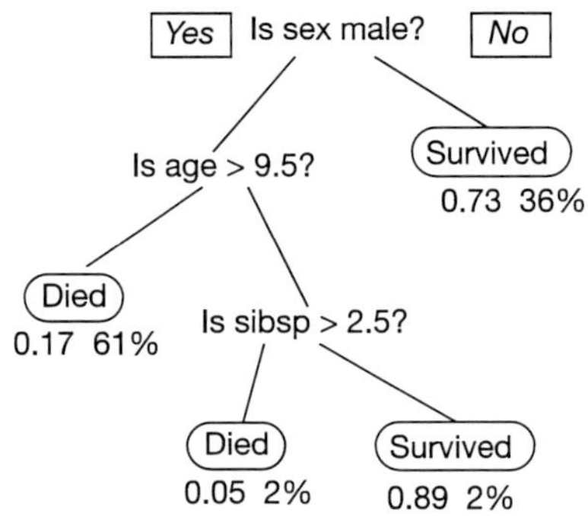

Fig. 23.1: Decision tree for `Titanic` data set (Source: Wikipedia; Stephen Milborrow)

Each leaf node represents the probability of survival and the percentage of passengers in that category. For instance, the very first node on the right-hand-side indicates that the probability of female survival is 0.73% and females comprise 36% of the total observation data.

Here is another example to illustrate the use of decision trees, in this case for the prediction of the birth weight of infants. The data set `birthwt` is part of the `MASS` library. We need to load the `MASS` and `rpart` libraries for this problem.

```
>library(MASS)
>library(rpart)
>head(birthwt)      # Displays the first six records of the data set
>str(birthwt)# Displays the structure of the birthwt data set
```

It has columns such as `low`, `age`, `lwt`, `race`, `smoke`, `ptl`, `ht`, `uti`, `ftv` and `bwt`. These indicate whether the birth weight is <2.5 kg (1 indicates weight <2.5 kg, 0 indicates weight >2.5 kg), the age of the mother (in years), the weight of the mother, the race of the mother, the smoking status of the mother, number of instances of premature labour of the mother, hypertension, presence of uterine irritability, physicians visited and birth weight.

The distribution of infant weight can be visualised using a histogram (Fig. 23.2):

```
>hist(birthwt$bwt)
```

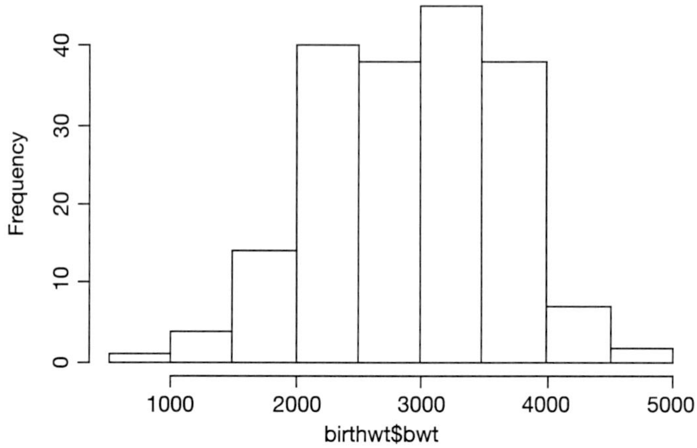

Fig. 23.2: Histogram of distribution of infant birth weight

From the histogram, we can see that most of the infants weigh between 2 and 4 kg.

```
>table(birthwt$low)          # Number of infants born with low weight
  0   1
130  59
```

If we just guess the most common occurrence, that is, weight >2.5 kg, the accuracy of this model would be 130/(130 + 59) = 68.78%. Here, the weight of 130 infants is more than 2.5 kg, while 59 infants weigh less than 2.5 kg. Let us try to build a prediction model or decision tree model for this data.

First, we must convert all the categorical variables to factors, as all the variables are numeric.

```
>cols <- c('low', 'race', 'smoke', 'ht', 'ui')
>birthwt[cols] <- lapply(birthwt[cols], as.factor)
```

Next, we need to split the data set into the training and testing sets.

```
>set.seed(2)
>train <- sample(1:nrow(birthwt), 0.80 * nrow(birthwt))
```

To build the model using a decision tree, we can use the `rpart()` function, whose syntax is as follows:

```
>rpart(formula, data=, method='')
```

where `formula` indicates the function for prediction; `data` represents the data specified; and `method` could be 'class' (for a classification tree for categorical data) or 'anova' (for a regression tree for contiguous data).

```
>bTree <- rpart(low ~ . - bwt, data = birthwt[train, ], method = 'class')
# Build the model
```

Exclude `bwt` from the model as it is our dependent variable for the purposes of classification. We must specify `method` = 'class' for the classification task. We can then visualise the tree shown in Fig. 23.3 and associate it with proper text for appropriate interpretation.

```
>plot(bTree)
>text(bTree, pretty = 0)
```

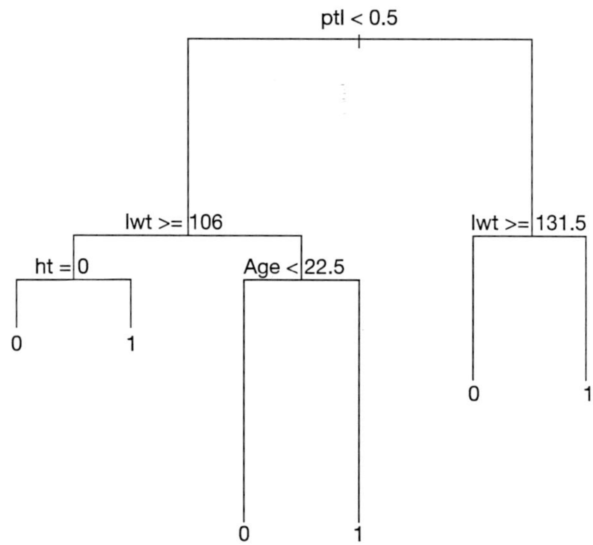

Fig. 23.3: Partial decision tree for `birthwt` data set

A part of the tree is displayed in Fig. 23.3. The leaf nodes are classes of low birth weight.

Interpretation of this part of the tree: If the mother has had less than one premature labour previously, and her weight at the last menstrual period was greater or equal to 48 kg (106 pounds in Fig. 23.3), and her age is greater than 22.5, then the infant is likely to be born with low weight.

The other nodes are interpreted in a similar manner.

Model performance on the test set.

```
>bPred <- predict(bTree, birthwt[-train, ], type = 'class')
>table(bPred, birthwt[-train, ]$low)
bPred  0  1
       0 25  6
 3  4
```

Hence, the accuracy is (25 + 4) / (25 + 4 + 6 + 3) = 76.31%. Here, the accuracy is measured using the formula:

$$\text{Accuracy} = \frac{TP + TN}{TP + TN + FB + FN}$$

where *TN*, *FN*, *TP* and *FP* are as shown in Fig. 23.4.

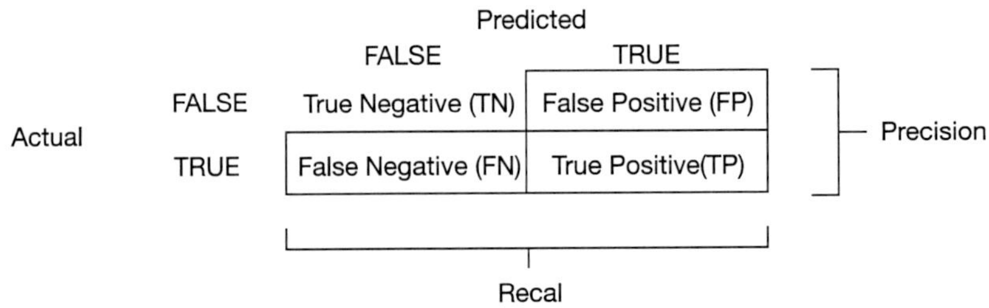

Fig. 23.4: Confusion matrix

23.4 | THE K-NEAREST NEIGHBOUR METHOD

The k-Nearest Neighbour (kNN) method is a supervised form of the classification algorithm. It takes labelled training cases as input and classifies new cases based on similarities that can be measured using many different methods such as Euclidean, Manhattan distance, and so on. For a new instance, the classification is carried out by searching the entire training set and identifying the k most similar cases (called neighbours of the new case). The new instance will be assigned to the most probable class of these k neighbours. The k value is usually considered as an odd value, which helps in summarising the class of the new data.

Here, we demonstrate kNN using the `knn()` function of the `package` class for modelling the `iris` data set. The syntax of the `knn()` function is as follows:

```
>knn(trainset, testset, cl, kneighbours = 1, l = 0, prob = FALSE, use.all
= TRUE)
```

where `trainset` is the data frame or matrix of the training data, `testset` is the data frame or matrix of the test data – a single test data is specified as a row vector, `cl` is the factor of true classifications of the training set, `kneighbours` represents the number of neighbours to be considered for classification and l is the minimum vote for a definite decision (otherwise doubt), `prob` is a logical value (TRUE indicates that the proportion of the votes for the winning class are returned as attribute `prob`) and `use.all` is a logical value used to handle ties in decision making.

This example uses the `iris` data set and attempts to classify it. For this, the `FNN` package needs to be installed and the `class` library should be included. We can view the structure of the data set using the `str(iris)` function, which will display its column names and types.

```
>install.packages("FNN")
>library(class)

# To generate a random_sample value which has 90% of data set values
>  random_sample <- sample(1:nrow(iris), 0.9 * nrow(iris))

# iris_norml contains 1 to 4 columns from iris data set (90% of samples of
iris data set) as training samples
> iris_norml <- as.data.frame(iris[,c(1,2,3,4)])
> iris_train <- iris_norml[random_sample,]

# iris_test contains remaining 10% samples as test samples
> iris_test <- iris_norml[-random_sample,]
```

```
# iris_target_category contains the target class of training samples.
Target class is in 5th column of training data samples
> iris_target_category <- iris[random_sample,5]

# iris_test_category contains the target class of training samples. Test
class is in 5th column of test data samples

> iris_test_category <- iris[-random_sample,5]

# Build knn model
> knnmodel <- knn(iris_train,iris_test,cl=iris_target_category,k=13)

# Calculate the accuracy of model for test data samples
> tabpred <- table(knnmodel,iris_test_category)
> accuracy <- function(d){sum(diag(d)/(sum(rowSums(d)))) * 100}
> accuracy(tabpred)

[1] 96.66667
```

The accuracy of this model is 96.66%. We can normalise columns 1 to 4 as they are the predictor variables. The kNN method works on numeric as well as categorical variables.

23.5 | CLUSTERING TECHNIQUES: K-MEANS CLUSTERING

Clustering (unsupervised machine learning algorithm) is the task of grouping objects with similar characteristics in the same category. It tries to find patterns in data. As it is a form of unsupervised learning, there are no outcomes that we can predict and the input data is also not labelled. Input data needs to be labelled using some similarity measure, that is, by calculating the distance between data points.

An example of clustering is in categorising clients based on the type of products they purchase, frequency of purchase, brand of their purchase product, and so on. There are many methods of clustering, such as K-means, density-based and hierarchical/divisive. Here, we discuss the simplest clustering method, which is K-means implementation in R.

K-means clustering in R This method clusters input data in different groups based on some similarity. The number of clusters in which we want our data to be grouped is specified. Initially, each observation is randomly assigned to a cluster, and the centroid of each cluster is calculated. Then, the algorithm iterates through the following steps:

1. Calculate the distance of each data point with the calculated cluster centroid and reassign the data point to the closest cluster.
2. Calculate the new centroid of the cluster.

These two steps are repeated till there are no further changes in the cluster; that is, the within-cluster variation cannot be reduced any further.

The `kmeans()` function is used for clustering using k-means in R. The syntax of this function is as follows:

```
> kmeans(x1, k, iter.max = 10, nstart=1,.....)
```

where `x1` represents the matrix or data frame containing the numeric values, `k` represents the number of clusters, `iter.max` specifies the maximum number of iterations and `nstart` represents how many random sets should be chosen.

For example, we are interested in the price and sales of an item. We can see that if price is high, the sales is low, and vice-versa. Hence, the data can be classified within two categories. So, if we apply k-means for two clusters, we obtain the following results:

```
> price <- c(10,20,30,102,105,119)
> sale <- c(5,6,4,1,2,1)
> df <-data.frame(price,sale)
> df
  price sale
1    10    5
2    20    6
3    30    4
4   102    1
5   105    2
6   119    1
> knnmodel <- kmeans(df,2,nstart=25)
> knnmodel
```

K-means clustering with two clusters of sizes 3 and 3.
Cluster:

```
     price       sale
1 108.6667  1.333333
2  20.0000  5.000000
```

Clustering vector:

```
[1] 2 2 2 1 1 1
```

Within-cluster sum of squares by cluster:

```
[1] 165.3333 202.0000
 (between_SS / total_SS =  97.0 %)
```

Available components:

```
[1] "cluster"      "centers"      "totss"       "withinss"     "tot.
withinss"
[6] "betweenss"    "size"         "iter"        "ifault"
```

23.6 | ASSOCIATION RULE MINING

Association is a spatial or temporal relation between things, attributes, occurrences, etc. To understand the concept of association, let us take an example, where we examine four things, namely, "boy", "girl", "chocolate" and "cigarette". Several associations from one (or more) element(s) to the other(s) can be interpreted. For example, 'girl prefers chocolate' or 'in college canteens, there is high sales of cigarette and chocolate, if both boys and girls are present'. In this example, a few simple things are associated through simple relations. Associations can be complicated, with a relatively large collection of things.

Market basket analysis This is a concept of analysis of the supermarket. When a person goes to a supermarket, he buys various items. Market basket analysis determines the relationship or patterns based on the user's buying transactions. In other words, it analyses a customer's buying habits by finding associations between the different items that he places in his shopping basket; hence the name. These identified association rules can help the owner of the supermarket design and implement marketing strategies as it helps her gain insight into matters such as "which items are most frequently purchased by customers". It also helps in inventory management, sales promotion strategies, supply chain management, etc.

Association rule mining derives all logical dependencies among different attributes, given a set of entities. It is used to find the association between variables. It is controlled by the support, lift and confidence parameters. These parameters help to generate and filter the association rules.

- Support is an indication of how frequently the item set appears in the data set.
- Confidence is an indication of how often the rule has been found to be true.
- Lift is a measure of the importance of a rule.

Association rule mining in R In R, we use the `arules` and `arulesViz` packages to implement association rule mining.

These can be installed on the system using the following commands:

```
> install.packages("arules")
> install.packages("arulesViz")
```

These packages are bundled with the `AdultUCI` data set, which is used in this example.

```
> data("Groceries")
> inspect(head(Groceries, 2))
```

The first two transactions, `{citrus fruit, semi-finished bread, margarine, ready soups}` and `{tropical fruit, yogurt, coffee}`, will be displayed.

For generating rules, the `apriori()` method can be used.

```
>grocery_associationrules <- apriori(Groceries, parameter = list(support =
0.01, confidence = 0.5))
Apriori
```

Parameter specification:

```
confidence minval smax arem  aval originalSupport maxtime support minlen
maxlen target   ext
       0.5    0.1    1 none FALSE            TRUE       5    0.01      1
10  rules FALSE
```

Algorithmic control:

```
filter tree heap memopt load sort verbose
    0.1 TRUE TRUE  FALSE TRUE    2    TRUE

Absolute minimum support count: 98

set item appearances ...[0 item(s)] done [0.00s].
set transactions ...[169 item(s), 9835 transaction(s)] done [0.01s].
sorting and recoding items ... [88 item(s)] done [0.00s].
creating transaction tree ... done [0.01s].
checking subsets of size 1 2 3 4 done [0.00s].
writing ... [15 rule(s)] done [0.00s].
creating S4 object  ... done [0.00s].
```

The Apriori algorithm generates 15 rules with the given constraints.

The output parameters are as follows:

- minval is the minimum and smax is the maximum support value that an item set should satisfy to be a part of a rule.
- arem is an additional rule evaluation parameter. It helps in defining constraints to the rules.
- aval is a logical value that indicates whether arem should be returned.
- originalSupport is a logical value. FALSE indicates that only the LHS items should be used for the calculation of support.
- maxtime indicates the maximum amount of time that can be used to check for subsets.
- minlen indicates the minimum number of items in the rule.
- maxlen represents the maximum number of items present in the rule.

The top three rules sorted by confidence can be displayed as follows:

```
>inspect(head(sort(grocery_associationrules, by = "confidence"), 3))
lhs                                     rhs                  support
confidence lift     count
[1] {citrus fruit,root vegetables}    => {other vegetables} 0.01037112
0.5862069  3.029608 102
[2] {tropical fruit,root vegetables} => {other vegetables} 0.01230300
0.5845411  3.020999 121
[3] {curd,yogurt}                     => {whole milk}       0.01006609
0.5823529  2.279125  99
```

In many cases, we want to limit the number of rules generated. This can be achieved as follows:

```
>wholemilk_rules <- apriori(data=Groceries, parameter=list
(supp=0.001,conf = 0.08), appearance = list (rhs="whole milk"))
```

This will display and generate various parameters, values and rules that lead to buying "whole milk". If we inspect the rules generated by this method, it will reflect the products bought before buying "whole milk".

EXERCISES

Multiple Choice Questions

1. Which clustering algorithm terminates when the mean value of the current iteration is the same as the computed mean value of the previous iteration?
   a. K-means clustering
   b. Conceptual clustering
   c. Hierarchical clustering
   d. K-medoids clustering
2. Which of the following about k-means clustering is true?
   a. Attribute values must be non-numeric
   b. Attribute values may be of any type
   c. Attributes must be numeric
3. Which of the following are interestingness measures for association rules?
   a. Precision b. Lift
   c. Support d. Confidence
4. Which of the following is a widely used and effective machine learning algorithm based on the idea of bagging?
   a. Decision tree b. Regression
   c. Classification d. Random forest
5. Which of the following is a disadvantage of decision trees?
   a. Factor analysis
   b. Decision trees are robust to outliers

c. Decision trees are prone to be overfit
d. None of the above

6. The kNN algorithm can be used for both classification and regression.
a. True b. False

7. Which of the following distance measures can be used in kNN if the variables are categorical?
a. Hamming distance
b. Euclidean distance
c. Manhattan distance

Answers

1. a	**2.** c	**3.** b	**4.** d	**5.** c	**6.** a	**7.** a

Programming/Concept-based Questions

1. Consider a transactional database where 1, 2, 3, 4, 5, 6, 7, 8 are items. The ID of item t_1: 1, 2, 3, 6; t_2 : 1, 2, 3, 4, 5; t_3: 1, 2, 3, 8; t_4: 1, 3, 7; t_5: 1, 2, 4, 6, 8. Find all frequent item sets if support is 80%. Write the R code to perform this.
2. Develop a profile for credit card customers likely to carry an average monthly balance of more than $1000.00.
3. Do meaningful attribute relationships exist in a database containing information about credit card customers?

CHAPTER

24 Text Mining in R: Sentiment Analysis

Objectives

At the end of this chapter, you will be able to

- Define text mining
- Explain text preprocessing in R
- Explain how to implement sentiment analysis in R
- Describe the N-grams model

24.1 | INTRODUCTION TO TEXT MINING

Natural language is different from programming language as the semantics or meaning of text is associated with context, tone and other factors pertaining to a statement. Text mining is a term that denotes a set of algorithms that help computers understand the 'meaning' of text. Sentiment analysis of text and text classification are common applications of text mining.

24.2 | TEXT PREPROCESSING

The very first step in analysing text is preprocessing. This refers to the processes we need to perform on the text to make it suitable for analysis or mining. Text often contains punctuation, uneven whitespaces and stop words (characters or words that do not convey meaningful information relating to the sentiment of the text; for example, "the", "is", etc). We can deal with such characters and words differently based on the application in hand. This eventually leads to more efficient text mining, with the more important words.

For example, let us try to visualise emails. We begin by first obtaining the data and then performing preprocessing on it. The relevant data set can be downloaded from Kaggle. The steps in text analysis are as follows:

1. Read the data from the .txt/CSV file. Let it be stored in the `emailRaw` variable. Then implement the preprocessing steps.
2. Preprocess the data to clean it for further text mining by performing the following steps:
   (a) Change all the text to lowercase so that words such as "read" or "Read" are considered the same for analysis.
   (b) Remove numbers, stop words such as "is", "an", "the", "of", "to", punctuations such as "!", "?", ",", ":" and eliminate the extra spaces between words.
   (c) Stem the text. Stemming is the process of reducing the derived words to their root form. For example, changing "bats" and "bat's", to "bat". Some words that have the same semantic

R PROGRAMMING

FOR BEGINNERS

To Our Beloved
Father, the late Sh. B.D. Bhagat
and
Mother, Smt. Kaushalya Bhagat

meaning but different verb tenses such as "go", "goes", "going" or "do", "does", "doing" can also be dealt with using stemming techniques.

R has a package called tm that helps perform all of the above steps. To manage documents in tm, we can create a corpus. A corpus is nothing but a collection of text documents.

```
# Import library, create corpus
library("tm")
data <- Corpus(VectorSource(emailRaw))
```

This will create a corpus of emails in the variable data. We can now apply stemming techniques to perform cleaning of data, as specified above. The tm_map() function can be applied to all "data" elements to perform stemming operations.

```
# Change all "data" text to lower case
>data <- tm_map(data, content_transformer(tolower))
# To remove numbers and common English stop words, punctuation,
whitespaces
>data <- tm_map(data, removeNumbers)
>data <- tm_map(data, removeWords, stopwords("english"))
>data <- tm_map(data, removePunctuation)
>data <- tm_map(data, stripWhitespace)
```

For text stemming, we can use one more library, known as SnowballC, which is useful for converting words to their root form. We can also use this to remove additional stop words.

```
>library("SnowballC")
>data <- tm_map(data, stemDocument)
>data <- tm_map(data, removeWords, c("mailcom", "stategov")
```

3. Next, create a document term matrix in which every row is a document vector and the columns are the terms of the corpus. This matrix will be sparse as every document may not contain every term. The value in each cell of this matrix represents the frequency of the term.

   The tm package contains functions that can be used to create the term document matrix. With the help of this matrix, we can build a word cloud of the most frequently occurring words.

```
datatm <- TermDocumentMatrix(data)
>my <- as.matrix(datatm)
>vy <- sort(rowSums(my),decreasing=TRUE)
>dy <- data.frame(word = names(vy),freq=vy)
>head(dy, 10)

# Generate the WordCloud
>library("wordcloud")
>library("RColorBrewer")
>par(bg="grey30")
>png(file="WordClouddisplay.png",width=1100,height=710, bg="grey30")
>wordcloud(dy$word, dy$freq, col=terrain.colors(length(dy$word),
alpha=0.9), random.order=FALSE, rot.per=0.4 )
>title(main = "Mostly  Used words in the Emails", font.main = 1, col.
main = "cornsilk3", cex.main = 1.5)
>dev.off()
```

24.3 | SENTIMENT ANALYSIS

Sentiment analysis is a technique used to determine whether a piece of text is positive, negative or neutral. R has a package called `syuzhet`, which is widely used for sentiment analysis. It uses the NRC (National Research Council) Emotion lexicon, which has two sentiments: negative and positive, and their associations with eight emotions (joy, fear, anger, disgust, anticipation, sadness, surprise and trust).

```
# Get the data in a frame called 'Emails' and install the library
'syuzhet'
>library('syuzhet')
```

The `get_nrc_sentiment()` function of the package `syuzhet` returns the emotions of the sentences of a text file. The return type is a data frame, where the rows represent a sentence of the specified file and the columns specify the emotion type along with the sentiment value – negative or positive.

```
>sd<-get_nrc_sentiment(Emails$RawText)
emtd<-data.frame(t(sd))
>emtd_newdata <- data.frame(rowSums(emtd[2:7945]))
# This will perform column sums across rows.
# Perform some cleaning and transformation of data
>names(emtd_newdata)[1] <- "count"
>emtd_newdata <- cbind("sentiment" = rownames(emtd_newdata), emtd_newdata)
>rownames(emtd_newdata) <- NULL
>emtd_newdata2<-emtd_newdata[1:8,]
```

A bar graph can be plotted using `ggplot2` to represent emotions and their frequency of occurrence in text, as shown in Fig. 24.1.

```
>library("ggplot2")
>qplot(sentiment, data=emtd_newdata2, weight=count,
geom="bar",fill=sentiment)+ggtitle("Email sentiments")
```

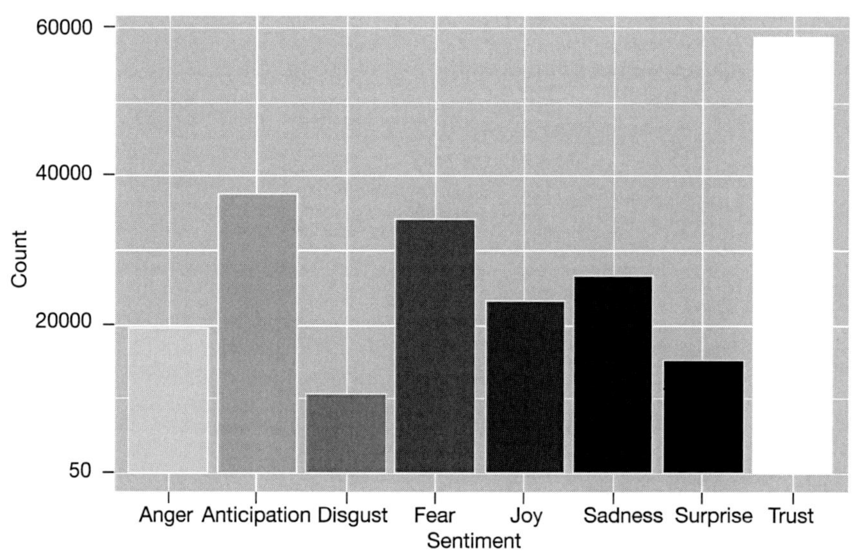

Fig. 24.1: Bar graph of emotions

24.4 | N-GRAMS

An N-gram is nothing but a sequence of N words, a frequently and commonly used term in natural language processing. Auto-captioning, that is, assigning captions automatically, is a common application of N-grams. Auto-captioning uses a feature that helps predict the word that comes after a given sequence.

For example,

Please hand over your ...

In this sequence, the probability that the next word would be "assignment" or "test" is higher than that for the words "coffee" or "school". The N-grams model helps in assigning probabilities to words that frequently co-occur. It uses the occurrence of the previous N – 1 words. If N is 2, it is a bigram model; that is, prediction of the next word takes place only on the basis of the history of the previous word. Similarly, if N is 3, that is, a trigram model, prediction of the next word is on the basis of the history of the previous two words.

The R library `quanteda` can be used to compute trigrams to find the commonly occurring sequences of three words.

```
# Get data of emails  in "emails" and install the packages
>library(tm)
>library(RSQLite)
>library(quanteda)
```

The R package `quanteda's` function `collocations()` can be used to obtain the most frequently used three words in the given data. Here, we use the earlier email data.

```
>collocations(emails, size = 2:3)
>print(removeFeatures(collocations(emails, size = 2:3),
stopwords("english")))
```

EXERCISES

Multiple Choice Questions

1. Find the number of bigrams in the given sentence:
"Rprogramming language is a nice source to understand Machine Learning"
a. 0 b. 5
c. 9 d. 10
2. Identify the trigrams generated from the following sentence after preprocessing the text, that is, removal of stop words and punctuation and reducing of spaces to a single space.
"#Rprogramming language is a nice source to understand @machine_learning."
a. 3 b. 6
c. 5 d. 4
3. Sentiment analysis is a new research area whose domain is:
a. Emotion detection
b. Affect analysis
c. Opinion spam detection

Answers

1. c	**2.** c	**3.** b

Programming/Concept-based Questions

1. What is text mining? Implement the steps involved in text mining with the help a built-in data set.
2. Implement a few features of the engineering techniques used in text mining.
3. Predict interest level using text mining techniques available in R for two sigma rental listing problems on Kaggle.

Index

G

H

I

J

K

L

M